THE MIDDLE ENGLISH
LIFE OF CHRIST

MEDIEVAL CHURCH STUDIES

Previously published volumes in this series are listed at the back of the book.

VOLUME 30

THE MIDDLE ENGLISH LIFE OF CHRIST

Academic Discourse, Translation, and Vernacular Theology

by

Ian Johnson

BREPOLS

British Library Cataloguing in Publication Data

A catalogue record for this book is available from the British Library.

© 2013, Brepols Publishers n.v., Turnhout, Belgium

D/2013/0095/80
ISBN: 978-2-503-54748-0
Printed in the E.U. on acid-free paper

Contents

ACKNOWLEDGEMENTS

Inasmuch as this book, which has its origins in doctoral research, has taken some time to appear there are quite a few people I am very happy to thank for their generosity, academic advice, and encouragement.

I owe so much to the late Malcolm Parkes — a charismatic tutor who got me started as a medievalist and was always there with his own entertaining brand of robustly generous expert support and a wittily critical eye. I also thank John Burrow for generous and constructive comment, and for being so helpful and encouraging while this book was being written.

I thank especially Alastair Minnis, an inspirational mentor and my original PhD supervisor on the topic of Latin literary theory's *translatio* into the vernacular. I acknowledge here a sustained debt of gratitude not only for the unique expertise and insight from which I have benefited so much over so many years, but also for Alastair's endless personal support and patient kindness.

I have been fortunate in being able to benefit from the scholarly expertise, advice, and encouragement of Vincent Gillespie, John Thompson, Jeremy Smith, and Michael Sargent. I would also like to thank for their help or advice at various stages in the production of this book Kevin Alban, Michael Alexander, Jeanette Beer, Margaret Connolly, Rita Copeland, Peter Davidson, Roger Ellis, Kantik Ghosh, Tony Hunt, the late George Jack, Tim Machan, Simon Mitchell, Derek Pearsall, Alessandra Petrina, Denis Renevey, Neil Rhodes, Nick Roe, Susan Sellers, Clive Sneddon, and Myra Stokes. I would also like to acknowledge the practical assistance of the late Patricia Richardson, Sylvia Halley, and the late Dorothy Black. I am also grateful to James Hogg for access to his unpublished typescript introduction to *Speculum devotorum*.

For financial support I am grateful to the University of Bristol for its Hugh Conway Doctoral Research Scholarship, and the British Academy for a PhD studentship. I am also grateful to the British Academy Humanities Research Board for a research leave award during the preparation of this research. Though this book was ongoing before the Queen's University Belfast-University of St Andrews research project, *Geographies of Orthodoxy*, was conceived, I would nevertheless like to thank the Arts and Humanities Research Council for funding a project that taught me much and inevitably and beneficially influenced this monograph. I am therefore happy to acknowledge the *Geographies* project team: John Thompson, David Falls, Stephen Kelly, Ryan Perry, and Allan Westphall.

I am grateful to colleagues at Brepols for their hard work, expertise and helpfulness in seeing this through the press — Simon Forde, Guy Carney, Katharine Handel, Lynda Lamb, Erin Dailey, and Martine Maguire-Weltecke. More personally, I would like to acknowledge for her assistance early on my grandmother, Kay Johnson, and, for their unshakeable support and loyalty, my parents and brothers. And then there is the biggest debt of all — to my wife, Sarah (yes, it is actually finished!), to whom this book is dedicated.

Chapter 1

Introduction: Medieval *Translatio* and Modern Controversy

Medieval Translation, Academic Literary Theory, and Middle English Lives of Christ

This book is obliged to be about several things at once. The initial research from which it has developed was originally concerned with charting the vernacularization of medieval academic literary theory in late medieval English literary culture. In dealing with the transmission of Latin literary theory and ideology into the vernacular it had to come to terms with the role of the translator and the nature of Middle English translation, for translators naturally turned to scholastic literary theory to describe what they were doing and to inform their practice. Then, in alighting on Middle English translations of the life of Christ as prime repositories of academic literary thought and ideology in the vernacular, it was required to take some account of this fascinating, undervalued, and culturally central literary genre. At the same time, this study has had to accommodate the sharpened modern interest in the medieval vernacular, in 'vernacularity' and its cultural/textual politics. And nowhere in medieval English studies has the issue of the vernacular had more of an energizing and transformative impact than in the field of so-called 'vernacular theology', a field in which Middle English lives of Christ (which a decade and a half ago were blithely ignored) are proving increasingly central and problematic. Vernacular literary theory; translation and translators; Middle English lives of Christ; vernacular and vernacularity; vernacular theology: this book moves variously around these five overlapping and shifting areas. When one area is being discussed, the other four are often there or thereabouts.

First of all, however, an assertion: there *was* such a thing as medieval literary theory. Until the mid-1980s, the notion of an identifiable, let alone substantial, tradition of medieval literary theory was unthinkable, especially with regard to vernacular literary culture. Since then, however, there have been several significant attempts to recover Latin academic traditions of literary theory and to assess their significance for such secular English canonical poets as Chaucer and Gower, most notably by Alastair Minnis, Rita Copeland, and Christopher Baswell.[1] In 1999 the first anthology of theoretical writings in Middle English, *The Idea of the Vernacular*, appeared — a useful volume, albeit patchy in coverage and insular in scope.[2] And only as recently as 2005 was the first reasonably comprehensive history of medieval literary theory in Latin and the European vernaculars published.[3]

Much remains to be done. And one key question remains inadequately addressed. How much did the Latin tradition of academic literary theory and commentary on *auctores* inform the most important part of *mainstream* late medieval English literature, that is, religious texts made in the vernacular?[4]

---

[1] See Minnis, *Medieval Theory of Authorship*; Copeland, *Rhetoric, Hermeneutics, and Translation in the Middle Ages*; Baswell, *Virgil in Medieval England*.

[2] Wogan-Browne and others, *The Idea of the Vernacular*.

[3] *The Cambridge History of Literary Criticism*, ed. by H. B. Nisbet and Claude Rawson, 9 vols (Cambridge: Cambridge University Press, 1989–2012), II: *The Middle Ages*, ed. by Alastair J. Minnis and Ian Johnson (2005).

[4] By the term 'vernacular', I am happy to go with the range of terms and concepts cited by Minnis, *Translations of Authority in Medieval English Literature*, amongst which, for example, '[p]ublic, popular, common, manifest' (p. 1), are terms of particular usefulness because they go beyond the merely linguistic. Indeed, as Minnis concludes, 'the term "vernacular" is far too potent to be strait-jacketed within the narrow sphere of language transfer. Rather it can, and I believe should, be recognized as encompassing a vast array of acts of cultural transmission and negotiation, deviation and/or synthesis, confrontation and/or reconciliation. "Native to a given community" which may, or may not, be confined within national boundaries; lacking standardization or at least comprising non-standard versions of words and deeds which *are* standardized; constituted by practices or "forms used locally or characteristic of non-dominant groups or classes", though susceptible to appropriation, authorization, and exploitation by dominant groups or classes: those are a few of the elements of meaning which such terms as *vulgo, vulgum, vulgariter, vulgaritas*, and *vulgatus* carried in the later Middle Ages' (p. 16). Comparable terms and notions of vernacularity are also discussed in the preface to Watson and Somerset, *The Vulgar Tongue*, which attends to notions of 'popular', 'provincial', 'rustic', 'common tongue', 'vulgar', 'social underclass', and 'natural'. For Watson and Somerset, the vernacular 'can encode [...] the prestige of authenticity or integrity conferred upon the subaltern or popular through their very marginalization, or the more assertive prestige that comes through the displacement

Although the secular poetic fiction of Chaucer and Gower has already had a measure of attention,[5] remarkably scant attention has been paid to the commanding heights of orthodox textual culture, from which issued ecclesiastically-sanctioned English versions of biblical materials, devotional treatises, hagiography, works of spiritual instruction and sermonizing (most of which were vernacular adaptations of Latin (and, to a lesser extent, French) materials). What of the impact of learned literary theory here? Any adequate understanding of medieval English literary culture in an age when most literature was translation of one kind or another cannot escape the question of the influence of such theory on the legions of devotional translators and on the circumstances, transactions, and ideology of mainstream literary culture in its negotiations of *auctoritas*. Therefore, with special regard to the place of translation and translators in the ideological landscape of vernacular textuality, this book investigates a sovereignly authoritative tradition and genre holding sway at the epicentre of culture in late medieval England — the Middle English life of Christ. Some twenty-four of them survive in a plethora of manuscripts and early printed books: they are a remarkably rich and still largely untapped resource for understanding medieval translation, the vernacularization of learned literary theory and attitudes, and the vibrancy of mainstream later medieval devotional textual culture.[6]

of the husk of the old by the vigorous growth of the new. Typically, indeed, the term is apologetic and assertive at the same time: for "vernacular" nearly always connotes a language situation in which something important is at stake for the user' (p. x). The observation of a tension between apology and assertion is well made, as it is frequently expressed in translators' prefaces and revealed more indirectly in their practices. An intriguing corollary to this tension, to be found in the same volume, is Larry Scanlon's idea of the 'incompleteness' of the vernacular, which he sees as its driving force and identifying feature: 'the real problem with current assumptions about the vernacular has to do not with the question of its subversiveness, but its putative self-sufficiency. In contrast to the current ideal, I argue that incompletion is the sign of the vernacular, an incompleteness it embraces and proclaims. Moreover, vernacular subversion depends on this incompleteness, for it precisely the vernacular's self-proclaimed incompleteness that gives it the syncretic power to appropriate and redefine other traditions, whether dominant or not' (Scanlon, 'Poets Laureate and the Language of Slaves', pp. 222–23). Though one can see Scanlon's point, that by dint of going beyond itself into previously non-vernacular territory a vernacular textual/cultural act is likely to be one that is aware of the limitations or the vernacular and/or one that is aware of its incompleteness, one might also say that any textual/cultural act, in being an action of *mouvance*, desire, and change, has incompleteness anyway as a necessary condition of its being and operation.

[5] Most notably in Minnis, *Medieval Theory of Authorship*, ch. 5, pp. 160–210.

[6] For a general account of Middle English lives of Christ, see Salter, *Nicholas Love's 'Myrrour of the Blessed Lyf of Jesu Christ'*, pp. 73–118.

Most medieval English literature, then, is a translation of one kind or another.[7] In the later Middle Ages an increasing interest in the process of translation itself is found, as witnessed by debates and writings on the subject. Often these involve Scripture: this is, after all, the age of the Wycliffite Bible.[8] It is also a time of the rising status and use of the vernacular. Literary translation could attract undoubted prestige: Geoffrey Chaucer was praised by the French poet Eustache Deschamps, not so much as a poet, but as the 'great translator'.[9] Translation was a way, perhaps *the way*, of literary life. In England, Latin, French, and English were different but overlapping languages in a culture where translating, oral and written, never ceased in a huge range of social and documentary transactions of varying degrees of formality and informality.[10] The literature of France, which provided models for the English, had a strong tradition of translation, the more notable exponents being Jean de Meun, Nicole d'Oresme, Jean de Vignay, Laurent de Premierfait, Pierre Bersuire, and the translator of the *Ovide Moralisé*, among others.[11] There were also many French biblical translations, a number of which were available in England from the late 1200s.[12] French translators, particularly those of authoritative works, often described their activities in accordance with terminology and attitudes originating in the academic appraisals of the texts of the *auctores* as studied in the medieval schools and universities. These terms and attitudes constitute a palpable body of theory, a tradition, observable in texts. Fully blown traditions of officially sponsored academic translation deriving from commentary and displaying theoretical terms

---

[7] See Johnson, 'Prologue and Practice: Middle English lives of Christ', p. 69. See also my dissertation: Johnson, 'The Late-Medieval Theory and Practice of Translation', p. 1. This is reinforced in the editorial introduction to Ellis, *To 1550*, p. 3. This chapter draws passim on 'Prologue and Practice', pp. 69–75.

[8] For an up-to-date account of the Wycliffite Bible, including consideration of it as a translation, see Dove, *The First English Bible*.

[9] Deschamps's famous remark, with an English translation, is to be found in Brewer, *Chaucer: The Critical Heritage*, I, pp. 40–41.

[10] See Burrow, 'The Languages of Medieval England'. See also the major study of the mutuality of French and English medieval languages and literary culture, Butterfield, *The Familiar Enemy*.

[11] For an account of such learned French translation, see Minnis, 'Absent Glosses: The Trouble with Middle English Hermeneutics', pp. 19–21.

[12] As pointed out by Dove, *The First English Bible*, p. 83. For studies of the medieval French Bible, see Sneddon, 'The "Bible du XIIIᵉ siècle"'; and Sneddon, 'On the Creation of the Old French Bible'.

and attitudes are well attested not only in medieval France but also in Italy and Spain.[13] Such a tradition of translation and the accompanying cultivation of 'vernacular hermeneutics' are markedly less visible in England, though there are honourable exceptions. Alastair Minnis has recently attributed England's 'missing glosses' to the climate of nervousness and (self-)censorship that arose in the period of Lollard controversy and anti-Wycliffite repression:[14] it is telling that the greatest textual monument to academic translation and hermeneutics in late medieval English is the Wycliffite Bible (to which must be added the allied vernacular outpourings of dissenting exegetes and learned polemicists). Even though there may have been more inhibition and less official encouragement of vernacular hermeneutics in England than in France, Italy, and Spain it would still be true to say that the business of rendering authority in the native tongue in England bore, in the self-descriptions and behaviours of texts, the marks of the same academic sensibility. It was this tradition that informed the way texts were made, understood, and appraised. Undoubtedly, the presence of such theory is of particular moment in texts which were culturally central, numerous, and which formally mutated in order to spread their influence and authority: texts like vernacular *vitae Christi*.

The Middle English lives of Christ are immensely varied in the ways in which they treat the holiest of lives and in the types of audiences that they appear to have catered for. How could they have been anything less? Nothing else in the Middle Ages was more important to the individual and to society than the need to be saved through understanding and believing in Christ and His life. The very scheme of human history, from the Creation and Fall to the Redemption and Last Judgement, was Christocentric. Christ's life was the model for all human conduct and self-understanding. Christ, as omniscient, omnipotent, and as human and God, as living and transcendent eucharistic sacrament, as the summation and *sententia* of all Scripture, and as the unendingly addressable, accessible, loving, and affective template of empathetic humanity, was the basis, means, and end of human identity, ethics, happiness, self-understanding, and all meaningfulness in life and beyond. Christ's life and especially His Passion were thus the all-pervading premise, obligation, and empowerment of all human life. It would be no exaggeration to say that Christ's life was humanity's universal and personal, infinitely adaptable, metanarrative. As Thomas Bestul puts it:

---

[13] Minnis, 'Absent Glosses: The Trouble with Middle English Hermeneutics', pp. 18–23.

[14] Minnis, 'Absent Glosses: The Trouble with Middle English Hermeneutics', pp. 24–37.

The story of Christ's Passion, of course, has high and continuous significance for the Christian society of the Middle Ages. It is a 'master narrative' in the theological and religious sense, in that for Christians, it describes the central act of human history, the redemption of mankind, in relation to which every other event in human history is referred and acquires meaning. The Passion story is also a 'master narrative' as that phrase is used by the French historians of the Annales school, in that it is a narrative that organizes perceptions and gives meaning to a society over an extended period of time.[15]

The life of Christ was the apotheosis not only of Scripture itself, it also informed and authorized the discourses, practices, and cultural tropes that shaped medieval religious culture. From the cycle of liturgy to sermons, prayers, and hymns; and from meditations and narratives to texts focusing on the power of the Holy Name: these all served to instruct the faithful and to stir their devotion.[16] A multiplicity of catechetical texts and practices took Passion devotion as their focus:[17] clearly, they gained spiritual energy from the *vita Christi*. Then there were the pervasive and myriad forms of visual imagery confected from Christ's life, as found liberally in painting, the plastic arts and in texts — key images such as those of the Annunciation, the Crucified and suffering Christ, the Deposition, the Man of Sorrows, and the *imago pietatis*. Such representations might include eucharistic or apocalyptic themes. Christ's life also generated highly important devotional traditions such as that of *compassio Mariae*, which served to heighten and structure the engagement of the human imagination with the Gospel events. Likewise, the tradition of the *arma Christi* — in which the tools of Christ's torment and death were visually arranged as a set of devotional mnemonics — was used for stirring affective response and refreshing the imagining of holy narrative.[18] For those who were not able to go to Jerusalem to re-live the key events of the Passion and the Stations of the Cross, it was possible, by reading, hearing, or copying a textual description of the 'pilgrims' Jerusalem' to negotiate a spiritual peregrination via an ordered repertory of devout imagination instead.[19]

[15] Bestul, *Texts of the Passion*, p. 24.

[16] For a guide to the variety of cultural manifestations of Christ's life and Passion in medieval culture, see the essays in MacDonald and others, *The Broken Body*. For a fascinating essay on the cult of the Holy Name in England, see Lutton, '"Love this Name that is IHC"'.

[17] Bast, 'Strategies of Communication: Late-Medieval Catechisms and the Passion Tradition'.

[18] Areford, 'The Passion Measured: A Late-Medieval Diagram of the Body of Christ'.

[19] Miedema, 'Following in the Footsteps of Christ: Pilgrimage and Passion Devotion'. See also the recent study by Rudy, *Virtual Pilgrimages in the Convent*.

Nowhere in Christian culture was the life of Christ more highly valued and put to use as a structuring principle for Christian conduct and a focus of devotion than amongst the Franciscans and those whom they influenced. This mendicant order was responsible for the most important imaginative versions of the life of Christ, such as the Pseudo-Bonaventuran *Meditationes vitae Christi* and the (genuinely Bonaventuran) *Lignum vitae*.[20] Denise Despres observes of the former that the metaphor of Christ's life 'makes historical and spiritual connections between events, creating a design corresponding to the meditator's own life'.[21] This was, in fact, a central feature of the tradition of thinking on the life of Christ and 'conforming' one's own life thereto. Despres accordingly notes of Margery Kempe's at-times confusingly ordered narrative, which falls into the same tradition, that 'the events of Christ's life on which the liturgy is based [...] are the patterns that come to give meaning to and provide a context for Margery's spiritual growth'.[22] The *vita Christi* is therefore her master narrative/metanarrative: the same is true of all lives of Christ — hence the sentiments expressed in the *prefacyon* to the fifteenth-century Carthusian meditative life of Christ, the *Speculum devotorum*:

> & therfore hoso wole [*whoso would*] deuoutly & dylygently beholde oure lordys lyuynge & werkys & folow aftyr be hys powere as he byddyth hymself seyinge thus: He þat seruyth me, lete hym folow me, & where I am there schal my seruaunt be; hosoeuyr do so [*whosoever does so*] he schal fynde in thys lyf grace, & aftyr thys lyf ioye [*joy*] wythoute ende, & be wyth hym as he behetyth [*promises*], the whyche worschype ys aboue alle the worschype that a chosyn soule maye haue, for what maye god ȝeue [*give*] bettyr to a chosyn soule thanne hymself, & to be wyth hym ther he ys?[23]

It is a measure of the superabundant *sententia* of the master narrative that it translated so readily to such a variety of literary forms. For example, the thirteenth-century *Passion of Our Lord* poem in Oxford, Jesus College, MS 29 appropriates the style of the *chanson de geste*.[24] The *Pepysian Gospel Harmony*

---

[20] John de Caulibus, *Meditaciones vitae Christi*, ed. by Stallings-Taney; also *Opera omnia sancti Bonaventurae*, ed. by Peltier, vol. XII (1868), pp. 67–84 for *Lignum vitae* and 509–630 for the *Meditationes vitae Christi*.

[21] Despres, *Ghostly Sights*, p. 46.

[22] Despres, *Ghostly Sights*, p. 78.

[23] *Speculum devotorum*, ed. by Hogg, p. 8. See also Patterson, '*Myrror to Devout People* (*Speculum Devotorum*)'. Professor Patterson is currently preparing a critical edition of this work for the Early English Text Society.

[24] *An Old English Miscellany*, ed. by Morris, pp. 37–57.

(*c.* 1400?) was probably a book of private devotion and is divided into sections suitable for daily use.[25] The late fourteenth-century *Stanzaic Life of Christ* is a compendium of Christological knowledge that moralizes, expounds, and divides themes after the manner of the sermon in order to elucidate and teach the life of Jesus for its mixed audience of clerks and unlearned laity.[26] Licensed and approved by Archbishop Thomas Arundel for the universal edification of the faithful, Nicholas Love's *Mirror of the Blessed Life of Jesus Christ*, written before 1410, is didactic, meditative, and draws on homiletic materials for religious and lay audiences — from Carthusian lay brothers to a whole nation of *simple soules*.[27] The fourteenth-century translation of John of Howden's (Hoveden's) *Philomena* is almost not a life of Christ in that it is rather fractured into lyrical reflections.[28]

Clearly, Middle English lives of Christ differed amongst themselves, but as instances of a culturally central, authoritative, and prestigious genre, they had one paramount function in common, that of instruction in the vernacular on the all-important words and works of Christ. A second important function, featuring more and more prominently during the Middle Ages, was that of stirring the soul affectively towards the love of God by a sympathetic rendering of Christ's life and particularly His Passion.[29] The very number and diversity of the Middle English lives can be seen as a measure of the perceived or actual demand for them by their various audiences. Variety within this genre is also indicative of the diverse spiritual and educational capabilities and needs (in the opinions of the clerical translators) of the intended audience and readership. The different versions are to be regarded as truly complementary. Holy Writ, no part of which was more necessary than the Gospels, could be and had to be expounded in different ways to different people with different rationales, or as the most important Middle English life of Christ, following the famous dictum

---

[25] *Pepysian Gospel Harmony*, ed. by Goates.

[26] *A Stanzaic Life of Christ*, ed. by Foster.

[27] Nicholas Love, *Mirror*, ed. by Sargent. The Latin memorandum of Arundel's ceremonial approval of the work, which accompanied several manuscripts of the *Mirror*, is printed on p. 7 of this edition. For the pre-Arundelian history of this work, see Doyle, 'Reflections on some Manuscripts of Nicholas Love's *Myrrour*'; and for a discussion of this general area and in particular the issue of whether the work was initially intended as a text for lay brothers within the Charterhouse, see Falls, 'Love's *Mirror* before Arundel', pp. 40–45.

[28] See Salter, *Nicholas Love's 'Myrrour of the Blessed Lyf of Jesu Christ'*, pp. 114–16.

[29] See generally MacDonald and others, *The Broken Body*; also Bestul, *Texts of the Passion*, pp. 34–68.

of Gregory the Great, neatly put it: 'holi writte may be expownet & vndur-stande in diuerse maneres, & to diuerse purposes'.[30] Each Middle English life of Christ was a variation of the treatment of the one supremely important life and its teachings. All Christians needed to know and believe it. However, different Christians were deemed capable of knowing and believing according to their limitations, duties, needs, and situations in life. A translator would have in mind whether his audience were learned or 'simple', lay or enclosed religious, male or female, readers or hearers. Such complementary variety was rooted in a common conception of what was right for any given audience. Furthermore, each codicological manifestation and each performative situation of any given life of Christ contributed to constructing (as well as to affecting) its reader-ship or audience. Conversely, the circumstances of a work's readers and hearers contributed to the variegated import and significance of the text each time it was uttered in reading or hearing. Many manuscripts containing lives of Christ show complex and shifting histories of readership, audience, transmission, and patronage. They also reveal a variety of affiliations to textual and social net-works in which not only questions of family, class, and gender arise but also issues of orthodoxy and heterodoxy.[31]

This, then, was the protean nature of this supreme biblical/parabiblical lit-erary form, and it has a telling counterpart in a truism of medieval academic literary thought: the idea that the Bible itself had a multiple mode of commu-nicating truth to accord to the varying capacities and situations in life of any audience; or as Alexander of Hales put it in his *Summa universae theologiae*:

> The understanding may be slow, it may be quick, or it may be moderately quick. So, the truth must be taught in different ways and in a different form to the slow, quick, and moderately quick understanding, so that what the slow intellect does not understand in one form it understands in another. Besides, the simple-minded young must be instructed in a different way from those who are fully adult. As the Apostle says in 1 Cor. 3: 1–2: 'I have given you milk to drink, not food, as you are little children in [your knowledge of] Christ. For you were not yet able for food, nor are you able now'. For this reason a mode which takes many forms is necessary.[32]

---

[30] Nicholas Love, *Mirror*, ed. by Sargent, p. 11.

[31] For information on manuscripts and texts of a key tradition in this area, see the website of the joint Queen's University Belfast-St Andrews research project into Pseudo-Bonaventuran lives of Christ, funded by the UK's Arts and Humanities Research Council, *Geographies of Orthodoxy: Mapping the English Pseudo-Bonaventuran Lives of Christ, c. 1350–1550* <http://www.qub.ac.uk/geographies-of-orthodoxy/>.

[32] Minnis and Scott, *Medieval Literary Theory and Criticism*, p. 219. The pedagogic bibli-

Likewise, Bonaventure in his *Breviloquium* links the Bible's manifold meaning (and its multiformity) with audience-diversity:

> This manifold meaning of Scripture is appropriate to the hearer. [...] And, because the recipients of this teaching do not belong to any one class (*genus*) of people, but come from all classes — for all who are to be saved must know something of this teaching — Scripture has a manifold meaning so that it may win over every mind, reach above the level of every mind, rise above every mind, and illuminate and fire with its many rays of light every mind which diligently searches for it.[33]

Henry of Gent, in his *Summa quaestionum ordinarium*, agreed: 'each may take it in according to his capacity'.[34] Because of this superabundance of form and meaning, makers of lives of Christ, by selecting their expositions accordingly, could produce texts with designs on single or composite audiences, or which reworked the Bible and accompanying sources so as to be capable of being read at different levels according to varying individual capacities by clerks and laity. There was therefore no one right way to make a life of Christ. Rather, the imperative was to make a well-targeted multiplicity of them.

It was not simply a matter of biblical textuality being regarded as protean on a merely discursive level of earthly signs; more profoundly, there was in the Middle Ages a common belief in a transcendent, even sacramental, presence of Christ in such works. This, as David Lawton, writing recently on biblical translation, eloquently attests, is most assuredly so in the customary identification of Christ, Scripture, and His eucharistic presence: this was a matter of the divinely immanent and real far in excess of the dull sublunary mechanics of human signs and signification:

> The Bible is originary. [...] but there is a rift between the biblical and the textual. The biblical belongs to ecclesial practice and therefore to its privileged community of practitioners (and interpreters), the clergy. It is not a book that can simply be opened and checked, but a key sign of sacred history subsisting in Christ's own sacrificial body. Just as that body may be multiplied and copied in the Host, simulacra that retain the identity of the original, so the Bible may be dispersed and renewed through a field of new texts that tell all or some of its story.[35]

---

cal metaphors of milk and solid food were put to work widely in medieval English devotional literature: lives of Christ were no exception (see Nicholas Love, *Mirror*, ed. by Sargent, p. 10).

[33] Minnis and Scott, *Medieval Literary Theory and Criticism*, p. 234.

[34] Minnis and Scott, *Medieval Literary Theory and Criticism*, p. 255.

[35] Lawton, 'The Bible', p. 196.

It was the clerks who tapped, judged, and controlled this holy discourse. It was the clerks who occasioned access to divine presence for the laity. By the early to mid-fourteenth century, however, some of the more cultivated and economically comfortable upper and middle-class laity were showing a recognisably *clergiale* spiritual ambition, inspired by the discipline of the cloister and attracted to the devotional sensibilities of the religious and their practices. At the epicentre of this perfectly non-heterodox lay desire was a yearning to practise *imitatio Christi* in the spirit of what Nicole Rice has recently termed *imitatio clerici*.[36] It was not that these layfolk wished to strike out on their own and dispense with the pastoral guidance of the clergy; this was a matter of 'lay-clerical cooperation rather than a threat to ecclesiastical hierarchy'.[37] Accordingly, fourteenth-century works of spiritual guidance, such as the *Fervor amoris* and *The Abbey of the Holy Ghost*, translated usable aspects of monastic discipline from the cloister to the lay sphere; and texts like *Life of Soul*, *Book to a Mother*, and Walter Hilton's *Epistle on Mixed Life* set about a new task:

> the construction of the inscribed lay reader as a textual interpreter who moves toward an individual understanding of the Bible, in conversation rather than in competition with the priestly advisor. Techniques of reading, writing, and emendation become implicated in lay addressees' reform in the image of Christ, and the Bible is treated as a source to be consumed in the movement toward a simultaneous *imitatio clerici* and *imitatio Christi*. The emphasis these guides place on Christ as identical with scripture, and on unmediated contact with 'holy writ', align [*sic*] them with Wyclif and the later Lollard Bible translators.[38]

These texts were written in the times of relative ideological latitude before Arundel's Constitutions of 1407/09 clamped down on vernacular theologizing. Their devotional adventurousness was not, however, denied entirely to the devout 'after Arundel', because manuscripts of such works were still being copied and circulated in the 1400s — albeit that they were frequently put to more 'conservative' use than they were in earlier, easier days.[39]

The burgeoning fourteenth-century tradition of spiritual guidance and ambition was comfortably adept at Englishing Latin and French sources for new circumstances of use and readership. Its texts rendered, or endeavoured to render, the technical terminology and concepts of cloister and spiritual treatise

---

[36] Rice, *Lay Piety and Religious Discipline in Middle English Literature*, pp. xiii, 50–54.

[37] Rice, *Lay Piety and Religious Discipline in Middle English Literature*, p. xi.

[38] Rice, *Lay Piety and Religious Discipline in Middle English Literature*, p. xiii.

[39] Rice, *Lay Piety and Religious Discipline in Middle English Literature*, p. 136.

in the best manner of medieval academic expository translation and pedagogy, selectively adapting the textual authorities on which they drew. Their translators exploited a repertoire of roles and procedures available from a scholarly tradition of commentary, compilation, and preaching.[40] This may have been an academic tradition but it had a highly practical bent, and was readily put into use by numerous translators, including those of lives of Christ, who did not and could not avoid common medieval literary-theoretical concerns and habits intrinsic to scriptural exegesis and the treatment of authoritative texts. In putting lives of Christ into the vernacular, translators therefore turned to literary terminology and attitudes at once available, appropriable, prestigious, and authoritative, which were to be found in the educational system, in commentaries, lives used as sources, and also the broad tradition of *vitae Christi* itself. In such locations they found the wherewithal to help them translate properly and to justify their activity.

It would be wrong, however, to claim that such texts should only be expounded by the modern critic using medieval literary theory alone. This would be reductive. However, an examination of Middle English lives of Christ indubitably reveals the frequent presence of postures and terminology quite clearly of an academic origin. It can, moreover, be demonstrated that in many important respects translators use such theory, and the vernacular idioms and tropes of thought and expression it begat, creatively, sometimes to the point of self-consciousness or even display. This theoretical tradition offers the modern critic singular interpretative purchase. It is historically and theoretically appropriate to the texts in which it functions, and as such has an advantage over modern critical terms and norms. Modern critical practice might deem some medieval translators' renderings erroneous in their treatment of the Gospels. However, an awareness of medieval hermeneutic tradition shows that the translators deliberately expounded the significance and the teachings of the text according to the priorities of their culture. There is much more to this kind of medieval translating than *just translating*, especially when it comes to dealing, however immediately or remotely, with the Gospels.

The Literary Genre of Translations of the Life of Christ

Before we discuss how Middle English lives of Christ were translated and how important medieval literary theory was for them, it would a good idea to sketch in brief what the genre looked like, what its vernacular repertoire was, and how

---

[40] The classic survey of scholastic literary theory is Minnis, *Medieval Theory of Authorship*.

it developed. It is not necessary extensively to survey the history of the *vita Christi*; that has been done adequately elsewhere.[41] Suffice it to say that the genre developed fruitfully within the context of Latin culture from the earliest times. The tradition begins with Tatian's *Diatessaron*, written in Greek *c*. 170 AD, which strongly influenced Victor of Capua's sixth-century Latin harmony.[42] Both these works contained no extra-biblical material, for they were concerned with the harmonizing of the four Gospel accounts only. Likewise, St Augustine, in his seminally important treatise, *De consensu evangelistarum*, compared, contrasted, and reconciled the four Gospels.[43]

The life of Christ underlay the liturgy and shaped the Church year. The evolving practice of reading from the Canonical Gospels, and preaching on them, gave impetus and authority to the production and use of further *vitae Christi*. As we move further into the medieval period the harmonized Gospels appear in different guises in a growing variety of places — for example, as simple, relatively unadulterated harmonies like the *Unum ex quattuor* of Clement of Llanthony, or compounded with historical exposition, as in Peter Comestor's *Historia scholastica*, which incorporates much didactic and legendary material, and which was important as a source for further reworkings of the life of Jesus.[44] St Bernard and the Franciscans who came after him were at the forefront of a movement in the thirteenth and fourteenth centuries to present Christ as an object of affective devotion and meditation: works like St Bonaventure's *Lignum vitae* and the Pseudo-Bonaventuran *Meditationes vitae Christi* are at the centre of this tradition. One of the most extensively mined sources for rewriting the life of Christ was the famous *Legenda aurea* of

---

[41] See Salter, *Nicholas Love's 'Myrrour of the Blessed Lyf of Jesu Christ'*, pp. 55–118; and the unpublished draft typescript introduction to the *Speculum devotorum*, ed. by Hogg, pp. cxxiv–cxxxvi. I am grateful for access to this, as I draw on both passim. See also Bestul, *Texts of the Passion*, Chapter 2, pp. 26–68.

[42] Tatian's work is extant not in the original but in an Arabic translation, published in *Tatiani Evangeliorum Harmonia Arabice*, ed. and trans. by Ciasca (cited by Salter, *Nicholas Love's 'Myrrour of the Blessed Lyf of Jesu Christ'*, p. 57). For Victor of Capua, *Amonii Alexandrini*, see *Patrologia latina*, LXVIII (1847), cols 251–358.

[43] See Augustine, *De consensu evangelistarum*, in *Patrologia latina*, XXXIV (1841), cols 1041–1230.

[44] For some MSS of the former work, see Salter, *Nicholas Love's 'Myrrour of the Blessed Lyf of Jesu Christ'*, p. 60. For Peter Comestor, *Historia scholastica*, see *Patrologia latina*, CXCVIII (1847), cols 1049–1722.

Jacobus a Voragine, Archbishop of Genoa.[45] The fourteenth-century *Speculum humanae salvationis* was a typological life, drawing key parallels between the Old and New Testaments.[46] The culmination of the medieval Latin literary tradition of the *vita Christi*, however, was the universal all-encompassing life of Christ compiled, probably in the 1350s, by Ludolphus the Carthusian, which incorporated nigh-all previous approaches to the life of Christ — biblical narrative and legend, didactic comment, moralization, theologizing, mysticism, and meditation.[47]

The medieval English lives of Christ, including those texts dealing only with the Passion, mirror not only the central features of the larger Latin tradition but are also eloquent about the needs of their intended audiences. Elizabeth Salter's division of them into six groups, still valid, categorizes them according to their subject-matter and general approach: those consisting of more or less only biblical material; those consisting of biblical narrative and didactic commentary at intervals; those paraphrasing the Gospels and drawing on homily and legend (this being a large group); those like the previous group but significantly different in also being reflective or meditative (another large group); those consisting of lyrical reflection in which the narrative is almost lost sight of; and, finally, one life incorporating a universality of approaches, the English rendering of Ludolphus.[48]

The literary strategies adopted by the translators of the Middle English lives of Christ had one over-riding purpose in common: to communicate without corruption the *sententia* (the teaching/significance) originating in and latent in the Gospels and demanding to be expounded. It was a positive duty, not just a literary task, to spread Christian teaching on the life of Jesus for the benefit of others, with obedience to Holy Church and to orthodox teaching. The ethical preceded the literary. In rendering the part of the Bible which was the ultimate in *auctoritas*, the most dangerous, most powerful, and the most necessary, the translators had two 'Golden Rules'; firstly, the principle of security through *auctoritas*, or as the compiler of the fifteenth-century English life of

---

[45] See Jacobus a Voragine, *Legenda Aurea*, ed. by Graesse.

[46] *Speculum humanae salvationis*, ed. by Lutz and Perdrizet. See also *Speculum humanae salvationis: A Reproduction*, ed. by James.

[47] Ludolph of Saxony, *Vita Jesu Christi*, ed. by Bolard, Rigollot, and Carnandet; cited by Salter, *Nicholas Love's 'Myrrour of the Blessed Lyf of Jesu Christ'*, p. 63. For a study of this work, see Conway, *The 'Vita Christi' of Ludolphus of Saxony*.

[48] Salter, *Nicholas Love's 'Myrrour of the Blessed Lyf of Jesu Christ'*, pp. 73–118.

Christ, *Speculum devotorum*, puts it, 'þe grounde of the boke folowynge ys þe gospel & þe doctorys goynge thervpon'.[49] In other words we have something like an anxiety of influence writ upside-down, that is *an anxiety of not being properly influenced*, an anxiety of authority. This is complemented by the second 'Golden Rule', the principle of security through a good and morally pure intention, or as the writer of the *Speculum devotorum* again aptly puts it, 'hoso cunne not escuse the werke lete hym escuse the entent'.[50] One must never forget the potency and primacy of this Golden Rule of conscience, all the more forceful when exercised by one in holy orders.

Nor must we overlook the dominant conception of translation in the later medieval period, when it was seen as being akin to commentary or exposition. In *the* great dictionary of the age, the *Catholicon* of Joannes Januensis, it is stated that 'translation is the exposition of meaning/teaching through/by another language' ('translatio est expositio sentensie per aliam linguam').[51] Translation, then, elucidates the *sententia*, that is the deeper meaning, the teaching, the significance, the *profundior intelligentia* of the text, not just its surface meaning. The target language was the means of this exegetical opening-up. *Expositio sententie* was carried out in English renderings not only in the elaboration and extrapolation of the literal sense but also in the incorporation of commentary-materials and any discussion of the *sententia*.[52]

Joannes Januensis's definition, much broader than the modern understanding of translation, fits the enormous diversity of types of medieval translations. Tim Machan notes that Chaucer was, in medieval terms, a translator in respect of widely differing works. Medieval translation, he observes, encompassed everything from *Troilus* (in whose case it is impossible to describe its source-treat-

---

[49] *Speculum devotorum*, ed. by Hogg, p. 9.

[50] *Speculum devotorum*, ed. by Hogg, p. 5.

[51] Joannes Januensis, *Catholicon*, s.v. *glossa* (unfol.). For the importance in medieval times of the *Catholicon*, see Orme, *English Schools in the Middle Ages*, p. 93.

[52] For examples drawn from the medieval academic tradition of translating Boethius, which was in method and practice parallel to that of biblical/parabiblical rendering, see Johnson, 'Walton's Sapient Orpheus', for discussion and examination of the relationship between the roles of commentator and translator and for a demonstration of John Walton at work rendering an *expositio sententie* of Boethius. In order to elucidate the *sentence* of his *auctor* Walton draws on glosses from Nicholas Trevet's massively influential commentary on *De consolatione philosophiae*, sometimes incorporating Trevet's glosses in his English text rather than translating the literal sense of Boethius. See also Minnis, '"Glosynge is a glorious thing": Chaucer at Work on the *Boece*'; and Parkes, 'Punctuation, or Pause and Effect', esp. p. 131.

ment in terms of syntax and lexicon) to the first version of the Wycliffite Bible, a literal gloss, and Trevisa's rendering of *De proprietatibus rerum*, 'which is a close translation but decidedly acceptable English at the same time'.[53] Though all are indeed different, all of them come together as vernacular expositions of the *sententia*, the deeper meaning of the original. In that this diversity is both historical fact and ideologically grounded, it is best to recognize both and proceed accordingly. So, when Machan rightly comments that Chaucer, in his incorporation of commentary-tradition into his rendering of Boethius, provides 'evidence not for Chaucer's *translation* of the *Consolatio* [...] but for his *interpretation* of it',[54] he is showing us why the word for 'translator' was *interpres*. Translation and interpretation went hand-in-hand.

The broad range of types of translations has implications for the different ways in which we should assess them, whether they are, at one end of the spectrum, loose adaptations drawing on a mixture of sources of varying authority or, at the other end, literalistic gloss-translations exclusively rendered from one single text. It is, of course, valid and valuable to take due account of the traditional close-linguistic aspects of translation, for example doubleting, or the resolution of problematic Latin constructions and idioms, or shifts in word-classes and clause-types. This approach, buttressed by theoretical linguistics and philology, has been privileged by the modern conception/notion of translation as primarily an interlingual transfer of information, which is a long way indeed from the medieval definition as articulated in the *Catholicon*. Translation needs to be seen by the modern scholar in terms of the making of a whole vernacular cultural artefact for intended audiences, something which necessarily entails adaptation and re-orientation of the matter and manner of the original, not just conservation of the literal sense or the naked word; for even if the literal sense were fully reproduced, the conditions of the work's reception, circulation, and audience in vernacular culture would (and did) militate against formal equivalence.

In the making of the new translational artefact, sometimes materials from beyond the original are added; it is an integral part of some translations of the life of Christ that non-evangelical material describing the birth in maternalistic detail be included, as with the *Speculum devotorum*.[55] It may also be integral to

---

[53] Machan, *Techniques of Translation: Chaucer's Boece*, p. 9.

[54] Machan, *Techniques of Translation: Chaucer's Boece*, p. 103. See also in general Johnson, 'Walton's Sapient Orpheus'.

[55] See Johnson, '*Auctricitas*? Holy Women and their Middle English Texts', pp. 179–81.

the act of translation that anti-Lollard polemic and a treatise on the Eucharist be interpolated into the work (as with Love's *Mirror*, as discussed in Chapter 3 of this book) as a political and theological filter through which an orthodox understanding of the subject-matter must (in the eyes of its sponsors) be refracted to avoid error. Such 'additions' are not just extraneous; they are part and parcel of medieval translation, the purposeful and inevitable conditioning and moving of one text (or more) into another culture (and its subcultures) for other audiences.

Choice of style (or genre) in the vernacular recasting of material also needs to be taken into account, because genre, which conventionalizes human life, experience, ideology, and subjectivity, is a mode of communicating particular aspects of the source to a particular audience. Whatever its generic affiliations, however, each individual life of Christ always had the same invariant core of narrative material and was intended to be in varying ways didactic, edifying, and stirring of devotion. *Expositio sententie* could be rendered variously through the inflections of genre: for example moralizingly, through the thematic divisions of material familiar to sermons, as in the *Stanzaic Life of Christ*; exegetically, through typological allegory, as in the *Mirour of Mans Saluacioun*; affectively and dramatically, through imaginative meditation, as in Love's *Mirror* and the *Speculum devotorum*; lyrically, in rhapsodic bursts of emotionally charged verses, as in the translation of John of Howden (Hoveden),[56] or even subversively, by appropriating and undermining the genre of the *chanson de geste* in order to valorize the genre of vernacular *vitae Christi* and to debunk and replace secular heroes with Christ, as in the thirteenth-century poem in Oxford, Jesus College, MS 29.

Literary Authority as Problem and Solution

Choice of genre or style was, without doubt, motivated by the translator's need to select *which parts* of the authoritative superabundance of meaning of the Gospels and commentary tradition to render for *which audience* with *what intended impact*. The literary authority that this genre drew on and articulated put our translators in a powerful as well as a burdensome cultural position. Not only the literary forms but also the literary roles (often of an academic

---

[56] See *A Stanzaic Life of Christ*, ed. by Foster; also *The Mirour of Mans Saluacioun[e]*, ed. by Henry, and *Miroure of Mans Saluacionne*, ed. by Huth; and for the English rendering of Hoveden, see *Meditations on the Life and Passion of Christ*, ed. by D'Evelyn.

origin) adopted by the *fides interpretes*/translators of the Middle English lives of Christ had one over-riding purpose in common. This was, in line with that first Golden Rule identified above, to communicate effectively, without corruption, writings of authority. A work of authority (in Latin 'auctoritas') was a work of truth and wisdom by an appropriately trustworthy, wise, known author (in Latin 'auctor'). A work possessing *auctoritas* was one to be read, believed, and obeyed. The ultimate in *auctoritas* was, naturally enough, the Bible, and its authority lay not just in being an all-encompassing meta-source, but in the ways in which it could be called on throughout medieval culture to justify the choices made by makers of non-biblical works.[57] The Bible's human authors were divinely inspired by the ultimate author of all things, God. The Bible was the truest book, and its teaching demanded to be broadcast and implemented. Thus it was not merely desirable, but a positive duty, to spread Christian teaching on the life of Christ for the benefit of readers and hearers. To write a life of Christ was an activity not to be understood in narrowly literary terms. It was a duty to be performed with a pure and humble intention for the benefit of others, and with obedience to Holy Church and orthodox doctrine.

We must not under-rate the awesome responsibilities with which these translators had to contend. They had to provide a worthy version of the most holy life. This life was derived from the four equally authoritative but distinct Gospels. These separate accounts constituted the holiest part of the most sacred text of all. Without corruption, our translators had to adapt this life for their intended audiences in a vernacular often thought or portrayed to be too crude and unworthy to do justice to the lofty Latin sources and their loftier-still matter. Latin, the language of the Vulgate Bible and the Church, was the 'natural' language of sanctity, authority, learning, and literary sophistication. It was the language of literacy in general. The overwhelming majority of books made and read in England were in Latin. On the other hand, medieval academics were often pretty relaxed when it actually came to moving conceptual substances from the accidents of one language to another. Translators, nevertheless, for all that they were bolstered by a long-standing ecclesiastical directive to disseminate holy texts and teaching in the mother tongue to lay and religious alike, must have felt that, in one sense, they were pulling somewhat against cultural gravity. On the other hand, since Lateran IV in 1215 (which was subsequently buttressed in England by Pecham's syllabus) there had been an ecclesiastical imperative to vernacularize the rudiments of the faith and to preach the Gospels so that the laity would understand and apply them. The translators'

---

[57] Minnis, *Medieval Theory of Authorship*, pp. 10–12.

problem (and duty) was to render into English lives of Christ authentically embodying their authoritative sources and following the educational and political directives of the Church. Scholastic literary attitudes and literary precedents offered them help with choice of 'correct' procedures. It offered them definitions of their roles. It gave them licence, guide, and concrete examples. This was how and why scholastic literary theory was put into practice in the vernacular. Considering, then, the number and importance of Middle English lives of Christ, and the ways in which they and other Middle English translations of authoritative works drew on learned terms, concepts, and precedents, it would not be inaccurate to speak of an academic literary sensibility as integral to medieval English literary culture.

Though the medieval Latin terms may appear rather alien today, the concepts and categories they represent are familiar enough to us: intentionality, form, structure, value/utility, the life of the author, and sources/subject matter — these are all identified in the academic tradition. This same Latin academic tradition also came up with a usable repertoire of responsible literary roles that writers could (and/or had to) take on, adapt, or claim to follow. The distinctive roles of compiler, commentator, and preacher were the three main exemplars of productive conduct adopted by translators in licensing, defining, performing, and advertising their work.

The impact of such academic terms, roles, and ideology on makers of lives of Christ will be treated in subsequent chapters, particularly Chapter 2, 'Medieval Literary Theoretical Discourse and Translation of Authority in Middle English Lives Of Christ'. This chapter shows how theory goes native and 'middlebrow' as translators adapt learned terms and also the clerkly/clerical literary roles of commentator, compiler, and preacher. This chapter, however, will not claim that academic paradigms are the lone providers of terms for translation and translators. As Nicholas Watson has recently observed, translators' prefaces also use language from outside the idiom of the scholastic prologue:

> translations are true, false, strange, clear, dark, light, common, plain; translators are rude, simple, busy or lewd, while *translate* and its synonyms [...] retain many of their extra-literary associations with transferring, converting, lifting, or going.[58]

Such terms are not, however, 'extra-literary' in any vital sense, for in their common and particular usage they are literary conventions themselves; nor need they be thought of as being at odds with learned terms and ideology.

---

[58] Watson, 'Theories of Translation', p. 75.

We have seen that the *Catholicon* defined translation as a form of exposition: no surprise, then, that medieval translators adopted and adapted the role of commentator in what they said about translating and in what they actually did with their materials. The role of translator-as-commentator was important, but that of preacher had more urgency and authority. As a special sort of commentator, the preacher, through his office of preaching (*officium predicatoris*), upraised by grace through his ordained and licensed status, rendered biblical teaching and the rudiments of the faith to his flock as an instrument of the divine authority which moved, validated, and obligated his conduct — hence the celebrated late fourteenth-century translator John Trevisa's declaration in his famous *Dialogue between a Lord and a Clerk* that 'prechyng is verrey [...] translacion',[59] an equation which Chapter 2 investigates and contextualizes across a range of works, not least in the celebrated formula of the Carthusians, whose enclosed members met a statutory obligation to preach *manibus*, 'with their hands', that is, by making books for the faithful. This order produced some of the most fascinating lives of Christ in Middle English, such as Nicholas Love's famous *Mirror* and the little known but deeply intriguing *Speculum devotorum*.

It is thus the general brief of Chapter 2 to explore the striking interplay between the avowals of theory-driven translators' prologues and the details of their behaviour in their complex renegotiating of Gospels, commentaries, and vernacular antecedents. Here the overlapping yet distinct roles of commentator, compiler, and preacher influence the details of translating, from word-for-word glossing and the elucidation of the intended literal sense of the original, through to extended expositions of teaching and significance, and the insertion of material from commentary tradition. How far, consequently, is a conception of translation as competition against, or displacement of, Latin texts and culture challenged or supported by these readings? How far do such lives of Christ individually, collectively, and comparatively invite ways of reading that assume intertextuality and functional diversity? Chapter 2 thinks about such questions at the same time as discussing a varied selection of Middle English lives of Christ that are of interest in their own right.

---

[59] Waldron, 'Trevisa's Original Prefaces on Translation', p. 293.

Agonistic Translation, Vernacular Theology, and the Modern Devaluing of the Life of Christ

Before proceeding any further, however, we must raise the vexing question of why until so recently there has been such relatively scant attention paid to the Middle English lives of Christ in their own right (let alone with regard to their apparent theoretical dimension).[60] It should not sound so bold as it does here to claim that the genre embodied a true 'sovereign textuality' in late medieval English culture: the life of Christ, derived from the Gospels, was (as indicated earlier) without exaggeration a set metatext for human existence. Yet this genuinely sovereign literary genre has barely been considered in its own right, though a few of its particular manifestations have received some attention. Not even those interested in medieval literary theory for theory's sake have mined too many of its possibilities. This is all the more surprising, since one would reasonably expect vernacular refractions of theory to be at their most consequential here — both in terms of what writers *said* and, in an Age of Translation where most texts derived from other texts, what they actually *did* with their sources. Here, then, is a major opportunity for investigation of crucial ways in which Latin theory (and learned culture) impacted on vernacular textuality. But it has barely been taken up.

---

[60] The classic study of the tradition remains Salter, *Nicholas Love's 'Myrrour of the Blessed Lyf of Jesu Christ'* (Elizabeth Salter's reworking for *Analecta Cartusiana* of her 1950s thesis on Love). More recent published work on aspects of literary culture with a bearing on the Middle English life of Christ includes, most notably, Aers and Staley, *The Powers of the Holy*; Aers, *Sanctifying Signs*; Beckwith, *Christ's Body*; Duffy, *The Stripping of the Altars*; Ghosh, *The Wycliffite Heresy*; Oguro, Beadle, and Sargent, *Nicholas Love at Waseda*; Simpson, *Reform and Cultural Revolution: 1350–1547*; Sargent, 'Versions of the Life of Christ: Nicholas Love's *Mirror* and Related Works', and Sargent, 'Nicholas Love's *Mirror of the Blessed Life of Jesus Christ* and the Politics of Vernacular Translation', pp. 205–21. See also the introduction to Nicholas Love, *Mirror*, ed. by Sargent, and Watson, 'Censorship and Cultural Change in Late-Medieval England', and Watson, 'Conceptions of the Word'. See too Johnson, 'Prologue and Practice: Middle English lives of Christ', and Johnson, 'Vernacular Valorizing: Functions and Fashionings of Literary Theory'; also Karnes, 'Nicholas Love and Medieval Meditations on Christ', and Karnes, *Imagination, Meditation, and Cognition in the Middle Ages*, esp. pp. 207–25. Much useful information on lives and Passions of Christ is contained in Morey, *Book and Verse: A Guide to Middle English Biblical Literature*, esp. pp. 203–343. Very recently, there has been a considerable surge in research and publications in the area in connexion with the major 2009 Oxford conference on the aftermath of Arundel (for the volume of essays arising from this, see Gillespie and Ghosh, *After Arundel*) and the *Geographies of Orthodoxy* research project, <http://www.qub.ac.uk/geographies-of-orthodoxy/>. See also Johnson and Westphall, *The Pseudo-Bonaventuran Lives of Christ*, and Kelly and Perry, '*Diuerse Imaginaciouns of Cristes Life*'.

This failure can be attributed to two powerfully influential developments in Medieval Studies, which began in the early to mid-1990s and continue to bias our understanding of the relationships between Latin and vernacular. They are beguilingly attractive in their focus on the alleged contests and ruptures between Latin and vernacular cultures/texts/ideologies. But such attractiveness is superficial, I contend, because the binarism which underpins these 'modern orthodoxies' is, all too often, unsupported by evidence, reductive, and misconceived. Consequently, our understanding of literary works, textual processes, and culture has been impoverished.[61]

The first of these 'orthodoxies' envisions medieval translation as a matter of Latin-vernacular competition and displacement, with the concomitant that literary theorizing in the vernacular is per se oppositional to, different from, or independent of, a clerical and Latinate overculture.[62] Lives of Christ, in being in general harmony with Latin culture and structures of clerical authority, have been deemed too obedient or safe to attract their share of interest in vernacular glamour. The second orthodoxy (which has obvious connections with the first) holds that in late medieval England there was a distinctive 'vernacular theology', which vied with, opposed, and transcended an oppressively latinate Church and its theology. Both these orthodoxies, however, tend to overlook the ways in which Latin and English religious literary texts were routinely in harmony with each other in a mainstream mutual culture which, for all its preoccupations with *auctoritas*, was nevertheless capable of affording significant licence and flexibility to writers and their work. Inquiry into the Middle English lives of Christ, as we shall see repeatedly throughout this book, yields eloquent and culturally momentous examples of Latin-vernacular compatibility and thereby challenges both modern orthodoxies.

With regard to the first modern orthodoxy: it seems fruitful for modern scholars interested in medieval translation and its role in cultural history to use oppositional or binaristic concepts and terms like 'contest', 'appropriation', 'agonism', 'rupture', 'supplanting', 'displacement', 'dominance', 'dependence', and 'supplementarity'.[63] This is often accompanied by an understandable reliance on

---

[61] The following discussion revises some materials from Johnson, 'The Non-Dissenting Vernacular and the Middle English Life of Christ', pp. 223–28, and from Johnson, 'Vernacular Theology/Theological Vernacular', pp. 74–78.

[62] This is most notably the case in Wogan-Browne and others, *The Idea of the Vernacular*, for example, on p. 313, and in the editorial essay by Evans and others, 'The Notion of Vernacular Theory', pp. 321–22, 327, 329–30.

[63] The most influential example of this approach is in the extremely important study by

the general idea that, as the Middle Ages 'progress', the vernacular, an auton-omous (if rather oppressed) cultural category, determinedly expropriates the *auctoritas* of Latin according to its own distinctively 'vernacular' agenda. This agenda is palpably definable against that of learned, often-clerical, inevitably masculine latin(ate) culture. The inherent binarism of this 'Latin v. Vernacular' approach insists on the 'conflicted' nature of discourses and linguistic cultures. This has led to an overlooking of the intertextual and ideological complementa-rity and the shareable complexities to be found in the translational transactions of Latin and vernacular texts and traditions. It has also perhaps contributed to a diversion of scholarly and critical attention from the varied intravernacular contexts of translation.

One of the most important (and oft-accepted) understandings of how Latin and vernacular works relate, for example, sees medieval exegesis and translation as both having an agenda and effect of displacement of the source text, or, as Rita Copeland puts it:

> Medieval vernacular translation of the classical *auctores* [...] takes over the function of commentary on the *auctores*, and in so doing replicates the characteristic move of academic exegesis, that of displacing the very text it proposes to serve. Like com-mentary, translation tends to represent itself as 'service' to an authoritative source; but also like commentary, translation actually displaces the originary force of its models.[64]

Granted, all explanatory vocabulary, concepts, and imagery used by modern academe to describe complex cultural transactions have their advantages and drawbacks. This is because they are necessarily metaphorical, and, because metaphors represent their objects as something they are not, they are therefore intrinsically insufficient, incomplete, and sometimes prone to mislead. There are therefore particular difficulties as well as benefits in applying the notion of displacement to medieval translation. A translation of a classical work may, for example, valorize that work and its *auctor* as much as displace them. Moreover, if a text is rendered for an audience who cannot understand the source, it may by no means be easy to discern where and how the alleged phenomenon of dis-placement would necessarily occur. Furthermore, the translating of a work does not per se prevent an original from continuing to exert authority. Let us take one particularly illustrious translator of a European classic, Gavin Douglas.

Copeland, *Rhetoric, Hermeneutics, and Translation in the Middle Ages*, and the statement on p. 223.

[64] Copeland, *Rhetoric, Hermeneutics, and Translation in the Middle Ages*, p. 4.

He would doubtless have loved to have been feted as the Scottish Virgil. His translation sought to do justice to the *sententia* and the eloquence of the original with the clear purpose of becoming the Scots *Aeneid*; but it always was and always will be rooted in the authority, value, fame, and irreplaceability of the original, as Douglas's own designation, 'wlgar Virgill', indicates.[65] Douglas may well have been exemplary as an exegete in utilizing text and commentary (which Priscilla Bawcutt has shown he uses plenteously and intelligently).[66] Yet for all the Scottish translator's exegetical labours with the original, Virgil is, in Douglas's eyes, resolutely undisplaceable. Douglas declares himself to be bound to Virgil's enduringly present text, regardless of whatever he might inflict on the *Aeneid* in his rendering: 'Hys wark remanys, my schame I may nocht hyde' ('His work remains — I may not hide my shame').[67] Would that more modern scholars heeded this message about the relations between original and translation, between source culture and target culture.

The lesson that Douglas offers himself and us is that sources do not necessarily go away or get dislodged or demoted by dint of being rendered in the native tongue. Neither, for that matter, do commentaries, translations, and other treatments of related materials — all of which witness to the fact that translators had to make choices.[68] An understanding of the repertoires of medieval translators, who were routinely at home on both sides of linguistic borders and familiar with the cross-cultural yet shared practices of Latin and vernacular, will be hindered or distorted by too great an emphasis on perceived agendas of the separateness of, and mutual antagonism between, Latin and vernacular language and culture. A concern to see textual systems as stories of dominance, control or supplementarity, therefore, can only take us so far. Indeed, Rita Copeland's milestone study contains illuminating and advanced discussion of Douglas's work and of many others — discussion which goes well beyond relatively straightforward considerations of translational displacement.[69]

---

[65] Gavin Douglas, *Virgil's 'Aeneid' Translated into Scottish Verse*, ed. by Coldwell, vol. IV, Book XIII, *Exclamation*, l. 37. For further discussion of Douglas from this angle see Johnson, 'Placing Walton's Boethius', pp. 236–28, and Johnson, 'Hellish Complexity in Henryson's *Orpheus*', pp. 412–13.

[66] Bawcutt, *Gavin Douglas*, pp. 92–127.

[67] Gavin Douglas, *Virgil's 'Aeneid' Translated into Scottish Verse*, ed. by Coldwell, Prologue to Book I, l. 302. Modern English translation mine.

[68] For discussion of Middle English translators' choices, see Ellis, 'The Choices of the Translator in the Late Middle English Period'.

[69] See Copeland, *Rhetoric, Hermeneutics, and Translation in the Middle Ages*, pp. 228–29.

Chapter 2 also has implications for another position, proceeding from the same assumption that Latin and the vernacular are at odds, which deems the vernacular to have had an agenda of evading 'colonial' Latinity.[70] This merits sceptical scrutiny. The related claim that vernacular literary-theoretical terms are stripped of previous 'Latinate' affiliations is also challenged with evidence of continuity from Latin to English despite the new and different circumstances inevitably addressed by Middle English translations.[71] Likewise, an approach to Middle English translation, literary theory, and vernacularity 'which is less concerned with translation as pragmatic or creative practice than a site where cultural relations of dominance and subservience might be played out' will not be the dominant interpretative method in this book: these lives of Christ respond to a more varied and flexible approach.[72] Whichever terms, medieval or modern, are used to aid our understanding of medieval translation, it is not just a matter of grasping how translations were actually written; it is perhaps more significant to try to glimpse some of the contingencies of their intended production and the possibilities entertained by their makers for their particular reception: this is one thing that this book will try, in some interesting cases, to address to a significant extent. In attempting to understand which textual choices were, were not, or could have been made, we might find ourselves better placed to imagine a cultural repertoire of what else might have been. The sanction of tactual *and potential* texts and their protean utterances therefore underpins and lends meaning and significance to the medieval translations left to us — particularly lives of Christ.

This book, in taking some account of lives of Christ and of aspects of the broader literary culture in which they were situated, attempts to think of the vernacular, then, not just as an entity or a site but as a condition, mode, circumstance, attribute or aspect of texts and culture which can best be appreciated in terms of the transactions of paratextuality, production, reception, and circulation, each articulation of which produces different but related significance for different readers. As part and parcel of this, it is appropriate that a second 'modern orthodoxy', that is, the term and concept of 'vernacular theology', should be subject to reconsideration. This orthodoxy tends to see in 'vernacular theology' something that opposes or circumvents latinate ecclesiastical/clerical controls

---

[70] Evans, 'Historicizing Postcolonial Criticism', p. 368.

[71] Evans and others, 'The Notion of Vernacular Theory', p. 327.

[72] This trend in scholarship was noted in Evans and others, 'The Notion of Vernacular Theory', p. 317.

over theologizing in the native tongue.[73] Indeed, we can accept that in the later
Middle Ages the business of writing in the mother tongue on matters biblical,
theological, or ecclesiastical could be a fraught experience. This was the era of
the ongoing debate on biblical translation, the Lollard challenge to ecclesiastical authority and clerical control of Scripture, and the ferociously articulated
legal clampdown, in the opening years of the fifteenth century, on religious
dissent and English Bibles by the anti-Lollard Archbishop of Canterbury and
Chancellor of England, Thomas Arundel. The Middle English lives of Christ,
recast from the Gospels with protective layers of interpretation and moralizing,
make for an intriguing contrast and complement with the naked text of the
Wycliffite Bible and affiliated Lollard commentary and polemic.

In the last few years the cultural and textual politics of such religious works
have moved centre-stage in medieval English literary studies. Yet for all the
fascinating and important work focusing on dissent, something vital has been
undervalued: Lollardy and orthodoxy exploited the *same* intellectual terms
and traditions in their approaches to Holy Scripture and theology, and the
Wycliffite Bible translators were impeccably orthodox in their sophisticatedly
scholastic approach to their project, as the prologue to the Later Version of
their Bible shows, and as the seamless adoption of the Bible by so many non-
heterodox fifteenth-century owners proves.[74] Moreover, the tradition of fourteenth-century textual guidance for the spiritually ambitious laity, as studied
by Nicole Rice, lived on into post-Arundelian times which were much more
sustaining of a flourishing and intelligent spiritual culture than has too often
been allowed in modern literary-based scholarship.[75] This book therefore uses
lives of Christ and affiliated works to shed some light on the complexity and
richness of mainstream religious literary culture that has, in the wake of vernacular theology as we have known it in recent years, been somewhat overlooked.

---

[73] Watson, 'Censorship and Cultural Change in Late Medieval England', is the agenda-set-
ting study that largely inspired the vogue for vernacular theology.

[74] See generally Dove, *The First English Bible*; Lawton, 'The Bible', pp. 199–202, and
Johnson, 'The Late-Medieval Theory and Practice of Translation', pp. 127–37. The difficulties
of disentangling the Wycliffite and non-Wycliffite are discussed in Somerset, 'Wycliffite Prose',
pp. 196–97.

[75] For plenteous evidence of this, see in general the essays in Gillespie and Ghosh, *After
Arundel*, and in particular Vincent Gillespie's major reconsideration of the institutional culture
of the Church, 'Chichele's Church: Vernacular Theology in England after Thomas Arundel',
pp. 3–42. See too the essays in Johnson and Westphall, *The Pseudo-Bonaventuran Lives of Christ*,
and Kelly and Perry, '*Diuerse Imaginaciouns of Cristes Life*'.

It would be wrong, though, to deny the considerable intellectual benefits and energy that vernacular theology has brought to the subject area. The allure of it can readily be seen, not least in its being an interesting and attractive combination of terms. As Nicholas Watson points out, it has the advantage of:

> encouraging reflection on the kinds of religious information available to vernacular readers without obliging us to insist on the simplicity or crudity of the information: that is, the term is an attempt to distance scholarship from its habitual adherence to a clerical, Latinate perspective in its dealings with these texts.[76]

Vernacular theology, as conceived here, however, deliberately (if not artificially) keeps Latinity at a distance. Though Watson deploys the term to keep clerical orthodoxy at a distance it is a key part of his historical narrative that vernacular theology was not able so to do for very long, for, tragically, it was, so we are told, stamped on by Arundel's Constitutions and persecuting authorities in the opening years of the fifteenth century. And in the field of religious texts nowhere was the previous 'golden age' occluded more reprehensibly and depressingly (it is alleged) than by Nicholas Love and his *Mirror*, the most important life of Christ of them all.[77] Unfortunately, Love and his work have entered the consciousnesses of many, if not most, modern scholars through Watson's implacably hostile readings of the work (and also through those of his followers). *The Mirror of the Blessed Life of Jesus Christ* (completed by 1410) is still too commonly seen as doing little more than the oppressive work of Arundel and the clerical Latin overculture through the medium of the vernacular and to the detriment of the vernacular. Whether this understanding is sound or not matters greatly, for the *Mirror* survives in more manuscripts than any other medieval English religious prose work outside the Lollard Bible. Moreover, inasmuch as it was publicly mandated against Lollards and heretics for the edification of the faithful by Arundel himself, this was *the* official life of Christ, *the* most institutional literary work of the age, so it is hugely important that modern scholarship is safe and accurate in its interpretation and evaluation of this work, a national set text for this life and the next. Such modern devaluing of Love calls into question the character and the value of the entire *vita Christi* genre and mainstream religious culture as a whole.[78] This issue will be

---

[76] Watson, 'Censorship and Cultural Change in Late-Medieval England', p. 823, n. 4.

[77] Watson, 'Conceptions of the Word', esp. pp. 93–98.

[78] For an interesting recent example of what is at times a rather unsympathetic approach to Love, see Karnes, *Imagination, Meditation, and Cognition in the Middle Ages*, esp. pp. 207–25.

discussed in Chapter 3, 'Translating Meditation for *Men & Women and Euery Age and Euery Dignite of this Worlde*: Nicholas Love's Sovereign *Ymaginacion*.

Watson's narrative is exciting and compelling, and all the more moving and depressing for being a powerfully written story of lost opportunities, of something really impressive and precious snatched away by the remorselessly stifling small-minded Arundel regime. No single development in Middle English Studies has had a greater impact on the discipline in the last two or more decades.[79] Ironically, however, it has begotten its own orthodoxy — a tendency to undervalue or devalue mainstream 'vernacular theology' post-Arundel. This orthodoxy gets some of its appeal and tenacity not just from its own intriguing understanding of Middle English religious texts. It is profoundly connected, in my view, with the ways modern criticism often (mis)understands the textual and cultural relations of Latin and vernacular in terms of the same oppositional concepts of 'contest', 'rupture', and 'displacement', of which I was complaining above, and whose binarism shortchanges the tradition of later Middle English lives of Christ and the richness informing cultural relations between vernacular and Latin.

Why, then, has there been this modern desire to make such a feature of 'vernacular theology' in the first place? Perhaps it is something to do with the attractive idea that certain vernacular devotional works (though, weirdly, not others, like the drama)[80] are definitely intellectually worthy of being called theology — which puts them up there with *bona fide* works of theology in Latin. At the same time, these works, unlike Latin theology, are accessible. What is more, the vernacular, unlike Latin, can be presented as authentic, experiential, and self-liberating (all qualities attractive to modern taste). Moreover, there is ready-made modern value in the qualifier 'vernacular', an invariably positive term, charged with connotations of popular access, freer expression, broader education, even democratization itself, and certainly fair shares for the otherwise-dispossessed and disenfranchised laity. Better still, the vernacular has it both ways, being the underdog but also the historical winner against oppressive Latinity/clerisy. Fair enough, the vernacular *did* rise and *did* oust Latinity from its central cultural functions, and a good thing too, no doubt — although history is littered with some pretty ugly vernacularities. But it is vital, whenever

---

[79] Watson's important retrospective on vernacular theology and the aftermath of his classic 1995 *Speculum* article contains some illuminating modification and qualification of his original position. See '"A Clerke schulde have it if kinde for to kepe counsell"', in Gillespie and Ghosh, *After Arundel*, pp. 563–89.

[80] Crassons, 'Performance Anxiety and Watson's Vernacular Theology', p. 99.

we look at medieval vernacular texts, not to overprivilege their vernacularity as if it were their single most important defining feature or *raison d'être*. When it comes to such contingent and multicontexted phenomena as texts we should be careful about conceiving of the (ever-rising, ever-contesting) vernacular overmuch as an entity or personification with an identifiable agency, autonomy, and agenda, let alone a biography. There is much more to vernacular texts and culture than the vernacular.

There is also more to vernacular theology than texts. In one of its manifestations, it has been boiled down, more or less, to a grouping/genre of Middle English writings, listed at the end of Nicholas Watson's seminal article in *Speculum*. How justifiable and coherent is this group? Are the criteria for it adequately supported or in need of modification?[81] Perhaps we can reconsider this matter rather more fruitfully if we broaden things out to the following question: if there really was such a thing as vernacular theology, does it follow that there was also a 'theological vernacular'? And how should we be assessing what was going on after 1409, when the *langue* of the theological vernacular officially shrank under the shadow of Archbishop Arundel's Constitutions, but the selfsame Constitutions let live and let circulate a residue of pre-Arundelian vernacular theology, which, if it were now authored, would have been somewhat illegal? What are the scope and the significance of the continued ability of the theological vernacular in a so-called Age of Brass?[82] Chapter 4 concentrates on one theologically substantial item of vernacular theology from the period after Arundel: a post-Love mainstream textual touchstone, the *Speculum devotorum* or *Mirror to Devout People*. The *Speculum devotorum* is a life of Christ that self-consciously and programmatically steers a new yet conventional course through the choppy wake of the *Mirror of the Blessed Life of Jesus Christ*.

To get a more animated sense of how such big and awkward issues concerning the two modern orthodoxies matter for modern scholarship (let alone for the medieval materials that are the subject of this book), it may be beneficial,

---

[81] Drama is excluded by Watson: see Crassons, 'Performance Anxiety and Watson's Vernacular Theology', p. 99.

[82] Watson, 'Censorship and Cultural Change in Late-Medieval England', p. 822. See Rice, *Lay Piety and Religious Discipline in Middle English Literature*, 'Conclusion', pp. 133–52, for a consideration of the readerships and circulation of manuscripts of texts of spiritual guidance written in the 1300s. See also the introduction to Nicholas Love, *Mirror*, ed. by Sargent, pp. 75–96, for discussion of the fate of vernacular theology in the fifteenth century and the continued and increasing circulation of fourteenth-century works during this ostensibly oppressive period.

at this stage, to proceed by two brief illustrative examples — two symptomatic moments generated by the two modern orthodoxies. These symptomatic
moments are quite deliberately selected from the key area of Nicholas Love
criticism. I am not interested here merely in disagreeing with what a modern
scholar or two has said about Love's or anyone else's work. I am, more importantly, interested in why such positions were attractive in the first place — and
what is at stake.

Our first symptomatic moment has plenty to do with both modern orthodoxies, though it would be truer to say that it is more explicitly caught up with
the latter-day cult of Vernacular Theology than it is with the modern mythol-
ogy of agonistic binarism. The issue here is Nicholas Watson's condemnation
of Nicholas Love's citation of St Cecilia as the model meditator of the life of
Christ. For Watson, Love's Cecilia is all about vernacular passivity: the *Mirror*'s
authoritarian Latin-language origins mean English is the 'passive recipient' of
structures originating elsewhere and is therefore bereft of 'process'.[83] This, for
a start, smacks of a linguistic essentialism (or sentimentalism, perhaps?) that
overlooks the translinguistic nature of devotional culture. More particularly,
it fails to recognize that by their very nature transactions between reader and
text were unavoidably conducted in the vernacular as a process (however Latin-
influenced). It also rather ignores how Cecilia, as Love translates her, could
have been used genuinely to empower a vernacular reader's spiritual life.

Indeed, Love, following his source, invokes for his audience the model of
this formidable and much-loved female saint, who 'bare alwey þe gospel of
criste hidde in her breste' and meditated on it permanently.[84] To do as Cecilia
does, the reader is told, is to win for the soul salvific skills, strengthening it
against the world, against torment, against vices, and towards the getting of virtues and the performance of penance.[85] Such an enablement, however, is recast
by Watson as a constriction of the vernacular into passivity, gendered *in malo*:

---

[83] Watson, 'Conceptions of the Word', p. 98. A similar argument surfaces in Evans and others, 'The Notion of Vernacular Theory', pp. 322–23, where Love is accused of assuming 'that all
vernacular readers have the same childlike spiritual needs', and of using Cecile as an anti-Lollard
figure: this worryingly overlooks the fact that she is meditating on the Gospel itself, in other
words behaving like a very Lollerwoman taking unmediated liberties with the selfsame *scriptura
sola* and *lex dei* so beloved of the Wycliffites.

[84] Nicholas Love, *Mirror*, ed. by Sargent, p. 11.

[85] Nicholas Love, *Mirror*, ed. by Sargent, pp. 11–12.

> In this model [that is, of meditating on St Cecilia], only Latin is the language of process, of the spirit and of heaven, while, if the mother tongue can give birth to Christ and dispense spiritual nourishment to its users, it can only do so in the crudest sense. Like the birth mothers of medieval biological theory, the vernacular is merely a passive recipient of structures that originate elsewhere.[86]

This statement, a 'passionate misidentification' if ever there was one,[87] forgets the inevitability of process in the process of meditating on the humanity in the vernacular within each soul that meets with Love's *Mirror*. In this case the vernacular and transactions of transcendent textuality can and do go together with each other: what is conceivably 'crude' about reverently and affectively encountering the Sacred Humanity and His teachings, especially if the 'mylke of lyȝte doctryne'[88] will help significantly to get one to heaven? Crudity is too crude a notion for such spiritual sufficiency and intimacy. The birth mothers simile represents the vernacular as oppressively feminized into passivity by an invalid ideology, caricatured as a risible, discredited, historically superseded, and offensive biology. But Love's *Mirror* (let alone the vernacular in general) was never, and could never have been, limited to the role of passive recipient, as Chapter 3 repeatedly shows. Far from it: Love draws on the productive capacities of English language and culture to enable (empower) his audience as meditators and sensitized readers of the Sacred Humanity for their own very considerable benefits. To translate the *Meditationes vitae Christi* into English is to provide it with new vernacular life.

Indeed, the alleged clerical Latinate *elsewhereness* of this translation's origins, which is such an apparent problem in Watson's analysis, is not really a problem at all. By Love's time, this work and its tradition were increasingly at home in England: several versions of the Passion section of the Pseudo-Bonaventuran source had already been vernacularized.[89] The *Meditationes vitae Christi* was, anyway, a truly international text; meditation on the humanity in Latin and in English was also a long-standing tradition. It would be a mistake, then, to see in Love's *Mirror* (for all its historical affiliations with an illiberal establishment)

---

[86] Watson, 'Conceptions of the Word', p. 98.

[87] See the critique of Watson's use of the concept of 'passionate identification' as a means of approaching such texts in Simpson, 'Confessing Literature'. See too Watson's response to the whole of Holsinger's Special Issue: Watson, 'Cultural Changes', and, in particular, his engagement with Simpson on the issue of 'passionate identification' (pp. 134–35).

[88] Nicholas Love, *Mirror*, ed. by Sargent, p. 10.

[89] See Salter, *Nicholas Love's 'Myrrour of the Blessed Lyf of Jesu Christ'*, pp. 102–06.

little more than a spiritually-choking, top-down, inert imposition of matter *from elsewhere*. If it is in any way valid to give Love's *Mirror* a hard time for its alien clerical Latinate structures originating *elsewhere*, what then would we have to do with the Lollard Bible, which steamrollered into the vernacular from a learned Latin *elsewhere*: the home turf of the scholastic elite? Conceivably, the negative press that Love's *Mirror* has endured is driven by an assumption (stemming from both of the 'modern orthodoxies') that a translation which cuts out higher contemplative matter from its source; which gets backed by Arundel; which cautiously renders a mainstream clerical Latin source rather than sourcing itself in the vernacular; which includes anti-Lollard polemic on obedience to the established Church and its practices; which supervises the meditations of its readers; which packages Scripture in protective layers of glossing and preaching; and which breaks no new ground in theological reflection, must be essentially repressive and culturally objectionable. This, however, is too limited and hopeless a view, and this book will challenge and requalify it, especially in Chapter 3.

For our second symptomatic moment we turn to Kantik Ghosh's important book on the Wycliffite heresy which, for all its brilliant overarching narrative and particular analyses, runs into some difficulties (telling in their alliance to the first 'modern orthodoxy') in the claim that, for Love, 'non-scriptural devotional material in his translation must be shown to be as "fructuouse" and as "authentic" as the actual biblical passages':[90]

> The category of 'fruitful' encompasses both the words and deeds of Christ as recorded in the gospels and expositions thereof by holy men and doctors. Discussing John 4: 32 in a passage original to him, and sign-posted as such by a marginal 'N', Love says:
>
> > Miche more gostly fruyt is contenede in þis gospel, þe which whoso desireþ to knowe more fully he sal fynde it in the boke of seynt Austyn vpon þe gospel of Jon, where he makeþ of þe processe of þis gospel a longe processe & clergiale ful of gostly fruite.
>
> The identity of scripture and expositions of scripture assumed in the passage is a general *datum* in the *Mirror*.[91]

Such non-biblical material, rather, amplifies, develops, and elucidates the biblical. Authenticity can only arise in and from the *primum fundamentum* of Scripture itself. The 'gostly fruite' elaborated in a 'longe processe' may

---

[90] Ghosh, *The Wycliffite Heresy*, p. 153.

[91] Ghosh, *The Wycliffite Heresy*, p. 155.

derive from the Gospels, but the 'longe processe' is never really identical with Scripture itself. Exposition should not be mistaken for equivalence, as it seems to be mistaken here, and also later (see below). For exposition, being secondary and dependent, is not the same as the primary biblical text.

So, why the desire to claim that Love follows this 'datum' of identity? Perhaps (to mix metaphors) the *datum* has an academic genealogy in the old binaristic and Gadamerian chestnut of hermeneutics not being able to avoid being like rhetoric, and its concomitant that interpretation paradigmatically displaces or replaces the original.[92] Whether or not this genealogy is the case, what we have here is an erroneous governing assumption, fuelled by the first 'modern orthodoxy', that Love's orthodox agenda of occluding the Lollard Bible inevitably drives him to equate exposition/extrapolation *of* the Bible *with* the Bible, even though Love shows no sign of actually equating the two in this passage or elsewhere.

Whereas Chapter 2 encompasses a range of literary-theoretical categories for the ways in which they are adapted into the vernacular through general ideological transfer and the minute pragmatics of translation, Chapter 3 homes in on one — *forme* or *manere* — and in particular the imaginative *forme* of meditation in Love's *Mirror*, though it reaches out to other vernacular works by the likes of Walter Hilton and the unknown author of the *Cloud of Unknowing* for comparison, contrast, and relevant intellectual context. As we have seen, Love's life of Jesus has been accused of keeping readers from the biblical text with a mere sop of tame meditation. It has also been charged at the same time with preventing mystical ascent, in addition to imposing those allegedly inert latinate structures upon the laity. This chapter questions this commonly accepted position as unduly harsh and fundamentally misconceived. Affective imagining of the life and Passion of Christ was a necessary (and perfectly traditional) gateway towards engaging the Godhead. As such, it featured in the Middle English writings of the *Cloud*-author, Hilton and, of course, Love.

The *Mirror* has also been castigated for spiritually repressive 'dumbing down', but this part of the book shows how Love treats his readers as responsi-

---

[92] See Copeland's fascinating use of the Gadamerian notion that 'interpretation is an act delimited by particular circumstances, by the historically particular situation of the interpreter and his community. This renders the text itself susceptible to circumstances of reception, just as rhetorical arguments are tailored to particular circumstances of time, event, and audience. This first principle leads to a second: the hermeneutical performance assumes a kind of inventional or heuristic force, and becomes an "independent productive act"' (Copeland, *Rhetoric, Hermeneutics, and Translation in the Middle Ages*, p. 70).

ble adults with choices in what and how to imagine. Love's approach to exposition through meditation is part of a larger tradition emphasizing the affective qualities of biblical textuality and its utility for the acquisition of virtues and the facilitating of salvation itself through an affective vernacular theology of hope. We shall see, in this chapter, how the fortifying discourse and theology of hope, whether it is in his paratext or in his inventive treatment of other key passages, and his emphasis on the 'ensaumple of vertues & gude liuyng'[93] found in the life of Christ, profoundly inform his whole enterprise. This chapter therefore pays close attention to how Love translates passages in which strategic changes to the source, his designs on his audience, and his conception of his project, are uppermost — as in his proem's expositions of St Paul's Letter to the Romans and St Augustine's *De agone christiano* (materials not in the original) and in those other places where he re-orientates the *Meditationes vitae Christi* — such as in his version of the Last Supper and in the adapted prayer in which his added polemical 'Treatise on the Sacrament' culminates. Chapter 3 at the same time departs somewhat from the modern academic predilection for seeing the *Mirror* first and foremost in locally English political terms as an anti-Lollard reaction when, arguably, Love was in line with (Lollard-free) mainstream European devotion, as represented, for example, by the *Legenda aurea* and the numerous continental and insular translations of the *Meditationes vitae Christi*, his source. If Lollardy had not existed, he could still have done fundamentally the same thing. (It is telling that he was writing the *Mirror* before Arundel's anti-Lollard legislation.)

This revaluation of Love has implications for the way we may look at successor texts of the fifteenth century. Chapter 4, '"Increasing of Love" in the *Speculum devotorum*: The *Grounde and the Weye to Alle Trewe Deuocyon*', accordingly follows on from Chapter 3 by taking a single text as its focus, the *Speculum devotorum*. This was written quite shortly after Love's *Mirror*, and is an excellent accompaniment to it.[94] It too shows how sophisticated and capable of development the Middle English life of Christ could be. In all probability, it was made for a Birgittine nun of Syon Abbey by a monk of Sheen. The anonymous brother tells us how he nearly gave up his project of translating the *Meditationes vitae Christi* on hearing that a man of his own order, presumably Nicholas Love, had beaten him to it. What in the end he produced is extraordi-

---

[93] Nicholas Love, *Mirror*, ed. by Sargent, p. 9.

[94] For editions, see '*Myrror to Devout People* (*Speculum Devotorum*)', ed. by Patterson, and *Speculum devotorum*, ed. by Hogg.

nary — a life of Christ in the vernacular which is richly Pseudo-Bonaventuran without in fact rendering the *Meditationes* as a main source. Using many sources where the *Mirror* relies for the most part on one, the translator of the *Speculum devotorum* complements Love's approach. Or is he subtly at odds with his illustrious Carthusian predecessor, as it has been alleged, when, for example, he includes meatier biblical and exegetical materials than Love?[95]

Even more than Love's theory-rich *proheme*, the *prefacyon* of the later work displays a nuanced command of the categories and tropes of learned Latin literary theory. In Englishing its materials, the *Speculum devotorum* is a refined and powerful example of *compilatio*, remarkable for the scope and depth of sources and voices deployed, and attentive to telling translational detail. Materials mined by the translator include Peter Comestor's biblical history, Hilton's *Scale*, and a wealth of female visionary and devotional works by such as Catherine of Siena and St Birgitta of Sweden. The ambitiousness and cultural significance of the *Speculum devotorum* are also visible in the fact that its prime sources are the Gospels with the 'doctorys goynge thervpon',[96] and in particular the commentary on the literal sense of the Bible by Nicholas of Lyra, one of the most prestigious scholastic exegetes of the later Middle Ages. Thus, contrary to what has been claimed about post-Arundel literary culture, this orthodox commentator-translator is in fact ready and able to provide direct recourse to Scripture and its literal sense, as prized by the Lollards. The sharp modern distinction, which assumes a malign incompatibility between devout imagination (orthodox pap) and direct use of Scripture (authentic nourishment for the otherwise-cheated laity) is therefore made more open to question by this chapter, especially in the light of the extent to which the Carthusian of Sheen regards and promotes meditation as in effect arising from the literal historical sense of the Bible — a zone of inner voicing where biblical text, authorial intent, and concretely imaginable holy events meet in the shareable interior space of meditating minds.

The next chapter will pave a way towards the more detailed investigation of the two Carthusian lives by sampling a variety of theory and translation practices as witnessed in a range of different types of Middle English *vitae Christi* which are of critical interest in their own right.

---

[95] See Evans and others, 'The Notion of Vernacular Theory', pp. 322–23.

[96] *Speculum devotorum*, ed. by Hogg, p. 9.

Medieval Literary Theoretical Discourse and Translation of Authority in Middle English Lives of Christ

This chapter discusses a variety of lives of Christ for their self-portrayals and their translation practices. It is concerned with what the previous chapter termed 'the first modern orthodoxy', although the discussion of texts is not restricted to this topic. To recap: 'the first modern orthodoxy' all too often regards medieval translation as a matter of Latin-vernacular competition and displacement, and sometimes brings with it the belief that the activity of using literary theory in Middle English is intrinsically at variance with, or is trying to free itself from, overbearing clerical Latin theory and culture. The methodological shortcomings of such attitudes have already had some treatment in Chapter 1. It is also illuminating, however, to examine positive examples of how medieval literary culture, in the form of some Middle English lives of Christ, drew productively on conceptions of literary roles arising from Latin commentary tradition, and on theoretical terms and norms originating in academic prologues: this examination is to be accompanied by discussion of a variety of translation practices. This chapter will therefore try to give an idea of what was possible in the varied repertoire of textual procedures that Middle English translators adopted in a sample of different types of *vitae Christi*, with especial regard to the pragmatic and ideological mutualities of Latin and vernacular culture and texts.

The highly important tradition of the academic prologue has attracted considerable modern scholarly attention. The conventional headings of the

accessus, under which a text of an *auctor* was appraised — *utilitas* (the utility/
value of a work), *intentio* (intentionality), *nomen libri* (title), *modus agendi*
(procedure/style), *ordinatio/forma tractatus* (structure and order of materials),
nomen auctoris (name, life (*vita auctoris*), and status of the author), *materia*
(sources/subject matter) — were accorded a range of vernacular equivalents
and significantly influenced the terminology and ideology of English translators' prologues. The fourteenth century saw this tradition being modified and
sharpened up by an Aristotelian scheme founded on the universally applicable
philosophical grid of the Four Causes. Thus, the efficient cause (*causa efficiens*)
of a work was its author. In the case of inspired texts, the efficient cause could be
duplex, for example God and Man, priest and Holy Ghost. The material cause
(*causa materialis*) was the subject matter/sources of a work. The formal cause
(*causa formalis*) was the form (structure, style, and literary procedures). The
final cause (*causa finalis*) was the objective of text and author, thereby equating
with *utilitas* and *intentio* from the earlier tradition.[1]

The three main roles adopted by the translators — those of the compiler,
the commentator, and the preacher — were seen as being distinct from each
other, but nevertheless related, as if in a continuous hierarchy. St Bonaventure's
systematic definition of a graded continuum of literary roles has aroused significant attention in modern scholarship:

> quadruplex est modus faciendi librum. Aliquis enim scribit aliena, nihil addendo
> vel mutando; et iste mere dicitur scriptor. Aliquis scribit aliena addendo, sed non
> de suo; et iste compilator dicitur. Aliquis scribit et aliena et sua, sed aliena tam-
> quam principalia, et sua annexa ad evidentiam; et iste dicitur commentator non
> auctor. Aliquis scribit et sua et aliena, sed sua tamquam principalia, aliena tam-
> quam annexa ad confirmationem et debet dici auctor.[2]

> The method of making a book is fourfold. For someone writes the materials of oth-
> ers, adding or changing nothing, and this person is said to be merely the scribe.
> Someone else writes the materials of others, adding, but nothing of his own, and

---

[1] For more detailed discussion and examples of the academic literary prologue and academic literary roles, see Minnis, *Medieval Theory of Authorship*, pp. 9–39, 73–117, 160–65;
Hunt, 'The Introductions to the "Artes" in the Twelfth Century'; Minnis and Scott, *Medieval
Literary Theory and Criticism*, pp. 12–36; Johnson, 'Prologue and Practice: Middle English
lives of Christ'; and also Johnson, 'The Late-Medieval Theory and Practice of Translation', esp.
pp. 49–159. For discussion of one of the most elaborate vernacularizations of the Aristotelian
prologue in Middle English, see Johnson, 'Tales of a True Translator: Medieval Literary Theory'.

[2] Parkes, 'The Influence of the Concepts of *Ordinatio* and *Compilatio*', p. 127. This article
has an extensive discussion of the genre of *compilatio*.

this person is said to be the compiler. Someone else writes both the materials of other men, and of his own, but the materials of others as the principal materials, and his own annexed for the purpose of clarifying them, and this person is said to be the commentator, not the author. Someone else writes both his own materials and those of others, but his own as the principal materials, and the materials of others annexed for the purposes of confirming his own, and such must be called the author.[3]

This fourfold definition is a useful generalization and starting point. The 'scriptor' makes a copy. However, actual scribes often modified their texts, changing layout and punctuation to conform with certain preferred readings of the text. The 'compilator' adds materials of others, it is true, but there was much more to the actual practice of compilers than the definition of Bonaventure might seem to offer at first sight. Compilers exercised considerable flexibility in re-dividing and re-ordering materials, which it was up to them to select and combine: these materials may have been presented as being in harmony or, sometimes, at variance with each other. The 'commentator', according to Bonaventure, repeats the words of others, his own words having an ancillary function, that of elucidation. However, actual commentators used their freedom to choose which materials to expound, and, most importantly, they adjudicated and shaped the principal understandings of their texts for their readers to trust. In other words, they were often in the tremendously powerful position of deciding what authoritative texts meant.

The translators certainly did not portray themselves as 'auctores'. However, when they made assertions in their own words without citing a specific source, they might still be writing with some authority, by virtue of the general authority of traditional preaching and of their clerical office of preaching. After all, these translators were clerics working for the profit and salvation of Christian souls, for whom they bore considerable reponsibility and over whom they were meant to be exercising authority. As priests, they expected attentiveness and obedience from their audiences. The preacher can therefore be seen as a special type of commentator. He expounded Christian teaching in the native tongue by the grace of God, Who was conceived of as validating, permitting, and in some degree actually moving him in his office of vernacular biblical and para-biblical exposition. Hence Trevisa's formula: 'such Englysch prechyng ys verrey Englysch translacion'.[4]

---

[3] See Minnis, *Medieval Theory of Authorship*, p. 94, for this translation. For further discussion, see pp. 94–95, and also Burrow, *Medieval Writers and their Work*, pp. 29–31.

[4] Waldron, 'Trevisa's Original Prefaces on Translation', p. 293.

This chapter does not intend to provide a comprehensive inventory of theory in Middle English lives of Christ, though it does aim to give an idea of the range and situational nuance that was possible for theory in the vernacular. A chief intention, then, is to sample a significant variety of different translational moments and episodes in which theory — whether in the form of 'half-changed Latin' or idiomatic terms, ideas, phrases, or attitudes — participates, in interesting or telling ways, in the self-descriptions and in the actual translating practices of a selection of lives in which translational repertoire and theoretical repertoire are often part and parcel of the same cultural impulse. In so doing it will also discuss other features of interest in the texts and in the broader genre of Middle English lives of Christ.

Commentator and Preachers

As we saw in the previous chapter, the *Catholicon* provided the Middle Ages with a serviceable medieval definition of translation as a form of commentary: 'translatio est expositio sententie per aliam linguam' ('translation is the exposition of the significance/teaching/deeper through/by means of another language').[5] The role of the translator as commentator was, according not only to the Bonaventuran schema, but also to common practice, more responsible and prestigious than that of the compiler. Like the compiler, the commentator offered faithful rehearsal of authorities, but he did more because he clarified and explained what was latent in his materials. As a commentator, a maker of an English life of Christ offered exposition developed from Gospel narrative with the intention of edifying his audience. Although the Middle English lives did not actually originate much commentary-material themselves, they were important in bringing such expositions into the vernacular. The commonest expositions were drawn from primary sources, and also from standard commentaries, reworkings of biblical materials, and devotional treatises — such as the *Glossa ordinaria*, Peter Comestor's *Historia scholastica*, Nicholas of Lyra's *Postillae*, the works of St Bernard, the *Legenda aurea*, and many others. Often, a translator would find that the Latin (or French) life from which he was translating had commentary woven into it already. Moreover, even if a life were not made direct from Holy Writ, the very treatment and arrangement of matter in an English life constituted a form of interpretation of the Bible. In having to be a single version, an English life, however indirectly it may have connected with

[5] Joannes Januensis, *Catholicon*, s.v. *glossa* (unfol.).

the Bible, manifested a set of expository decisions concerning Holy Scripture and was therefore responsible to Scripture and, consequently, to God.

The activity of the commentator underwent some important changes during the course of the Middle Ages, and these changes had implications for translators of *vitae Christi*. Whereas the early Middle Ages tended to concentrate on the allegorical senses of the Bible, the emergence in the thirteenth century of an 'Aristotelian' mode of exegesis gave extra priority to the literal sense. For the twelfth-century Neoplatonist William of Conches, the *sententia* was the level of meaning reached only by an effort of commentary. The commentator considered the *sententia* alone: neither grammatical construction nor the exposition of the letter was his concern. Such lower levels, for William, were the business of the gloss:

> Commentum enim est solum sententiam exequens, de continuatione vel expositione litterae nihil agit. Glosa vero omnia illa exequitur.

> A commentary only considers the *sententia*, but has nothing to do with the syntactical structure (*continuatio*) or explanation of the literal text. Indeed, a gloss considers all these things.[6]

Hugh of St Victor, in his *Didascalicon*, a standard text-book of the Middle Ages on reading and exposition, had a similar outlook:

> Littera est congrua ordinatio dictionum, quam etiam constructionem vocamus. Sensus est facilis quaedam et aperta significatio, quam littera prima fronte praefert. Sententia est profundior intelligentia, quae nisi expositione vel interpretatione non invenitur.

> The letter (*littera*) is the proper arrangement of words which we also call construction. The sense (*sensus*) is a straightforward and open interpretation which the letter offers at first sight. The sentence (*sententia*) is a deeper understanding which is discovered in no other way except by exposition or interpretation.[7]

Such definite stratification of levels of meaning, however, had broken down significantly by the time of Nicholas of Lyra in the fourteenth century. Around 1331 he completed his *Postilla* on the literal sense of the whole of the Bible.

---

[6] Cited and translated in Parkes, 'Punctuation, or Pause and Effect', p. 131. The Latin text is cited from Jeauneau, 'Deux rédactions des gloses de Guillaume de Conches sur Priscien', p. 225.

[7] Cited by Parkes, 'Punctuation, or Pause and Effect', p. 131. For the Latin text, see Hugh of St Victor, *Eruditionis didascalicae*, in *Patrologia latina*, CLXXVI (1854), cols 739–838 (III. 9, cols 771D–72A).

For Nicholas, the *sensus literalis* was of paramount importance because it alone was regarded as the basis for the adducing of proof for theological purposes. The literal sense was also the level at which the intention of the inspired human authors of Holy Writ operated. This accounts for Lyra's use of the tell-tale term 'sententia litterae', 'the profound meaning/teaching of the literal sense'.[8] This collocation would have been impossible for earlier exegetes, who would have conceived of *sententia* and *littera* as mutually exclusive levels. Even so, these earlier and the later traditions were not mutually exclusive in their impact on learned culture in the later Middle Ages, and both were available to translators of the lives of Christ. The Wycliffites, rebellious in many ways but orthodox in scholarship, drew readily on Lyra. So too, at the other end of the religio-political spectrum, did the maker of the fifteenth-century Carthusian life of Christ, the *Speculum devotorum*, who was in no way a rebel but energetically used the *Postilla* for the 'lettural vndyrstandynge'.[9] As the level of meaning that referred to the actual events of the *vita* and to what the evangelists meant, the literal-historical level was of huge importance for our translators. It was at this level that they did the greatest share of their interpretative work on the *sentence* of their sources.

When it came to tackling a source, attention to the *sentence*, after the Hieronymic fashion, was central to the theory and ideology of serious medieval translation. *Sententia*, in its many manifestations, demanded expository versatility of the translator. For example, the translator of the Christocentric *Seuene Poyntes of Trewe Love and Everlastynge Wisdom* feels obliged to elucidate 'clergiale teremes' in the vernacular for his audience and to open these terms out for them:

> Ne I translate not þe wordes as þei bene wrytene, one for a noþere, þat is to seye þe englische worde for þe latyne worde — by-cause þat þere beþ manye wordes in clergiale teremes þe wheche wold seme vnsaverye so to be spokene in englische: and þere-for I take þe sentence as me þinkeþ moste opune to þe comine vnderstandyng in englische.[10]

In similar vein, the maker of the *Myroure of Oure Ladye* is typical in giving a greater priority to the *sentence* than to the words, although he tells his reader that he will also labour to keep as close to the words as he can:

---

[8] See Parkes, 'Punctuation, or Pause and Effect', p. 132. For a wide-ranging study of changing exegetical approaches, see Smalley, *The Study of the Bible in the Middle Ages*.

[9] *Speculum devotorum*, ed. by Hogg, p. 9.

[10] '*Orologium Sapientiae*', ed. by Horstmann, p. 325.

Yt is not lyght for euery man to drawe eny longe thyng from latyn into oure Engly-
she tongue. For there ys many wordes in Latyn that we haue no propre englyssh
accordynge therto. And then suche wordes muste be turnyd as the sentence may
beste be vnderstondyd. And therfore though I laboure to kepe bothe the wordes
and the sentence in this boke as farre as oure language wyll well assente: yet some
tyme I folowe the sentence and not the wordes as the mater asketh.[11]

This desire to prioritize *sententia* without leaving the *verba* of the source behind
unrecognizably is typical of many Middle English translators. This same writer
also acknowledges that his renderings will often have to be expansively glossatory or selective in order not only to catch the connotations and nuances of
potentially ambiguous Latin words, but also to accommodate the unfamiliar
contexts which may change such words' meanings from what might normally
be expected:

There is also many wordes that haue dyverse vnderstondynges, & some tyme they
ar taken in one wyse, some tyme in an other, and som tyme they may be taken in
dyuerse wyse in one reson or clause. Dyuerse wordes also in dyuerse scryptures: ar set
and vnderstonde some tyme other wyse then auctoures of gramer tell or speke of.[12]

The most important thing for a translator of the life of Christ was to communicate, teach, and indeed preach the *sentence* of the Word of God to Christians in
need of edification and salvation. We must never lose sight of the fact that these
lives were so often made by priests/preachers. The obligations and techniques
of the commentator were part of the preacher's office, but a preacher addition-
ally had a special relationship with God as an instrument of the divine authority and grace that moved, permitted, and validated his conduct, and which was
also the end of his duties. The preacher, furthermore, had a special duty to his
flock, to whom he should teach the rudiments of the faith and Christian behaviour. For this he was answerable to God.

No wonder, then, that Raymond Lull called preaching 'the highest, the
most difficult, and the noblest office'.[13] The first and greatest preacher was God
the Father, Whom Humbert of Romans dubbed a *magister* as 'Master of all
Preachers', and Whom Christ, the ultimate in human preaching, followed.[14] As
Robert of Basevorn expressed it in his *Forma praedicandi*:

[11] *The Myroure of oure Ladye*, ed. by Blunt, p. 7.

[12] *The Myroure of oure Ladye*, ed. by Blunt, p. 7.

[13] Cited by Rouse and Rouse, *Preachers, Florilegia and Sermons*, p. 61.

[14] Humbert of Romans, 'Treatise on Preaching', ed. by Miller, Prosser, and Benson, p. 250.

God preached [...] to Adam [...]. Afterward He preached frequently through angels, [...] through Moses and some Prophets, [...] through John the Baptist [...]. And at last He Himself, taking on a human soul and body in the unity of substance came preaching the same theme which His precursor had preached before.[15]

To preach, then, was to imitate Christ Himself (the actual protagonist, subject matter and ultimate addressee and mover of the genre in question), of Whom, as the *Speculum devotorum* puts it, 'yhe may thenke how he goth forthe into þe worlde. And precheth þe kyngedome of god, and þe waye to euerlastynge lyfe'.[16] Aquinas called preachers the 'mouth of Christ, and described preaching as 'the noblest of all ecclesiastical functions'.[17] The life of Christ was thus a supreme subject for the literary activity of preachers — and of translators.

A preacher mediated authority to his flock because he knew what to teach, and because he was ordained of God and, officially at least, submitted to His will. Therefore, a preacher could be seen as an instrumental efficient cause, with God as the higher efficient cause. Among the many treatises on preaching we find, in the *Forma praedicandi* of Robert of Basevorn (written *c.* 1322), a conflation of efficient causality and final causality. In his Aristotelian prologue, Basevorn stated that God was the end of the preacher's activity, and at the same time part of the means for effecting that objective. As he says:

> The final cause is designated when it is said: 'The Lord stood with me and strengthened me', for He is my end [...]. He who is also the end may be the efficient cause affecting the whole.[18]

To effect the objective a preacher needed a pure and humble intention, and he needed to be a good man. All manner of problems were held to be possible if this were not so. The later Middle Ages underwent no little anxiety and controversy as to whether the sacrament or sermon of a sinful priest, or a priest of impure intention, actually worked.[19] Comments which the Middle Ages attributed to Thomas Aquinas in a work named *De arte praedicandi* state

[15] Murphy, *Rhetoric in the Middle Ages*, p. 270.

[16] *Speculum devotorum*, ed. by Hogg, p. 166.

[17] Murphy, *Rhetoric in the Middle Ages*, p. 275.

[18] Murphy, *Rhetoric in the Middle Ages*, p. 344. See also Minnis, *Medieval Theory of Authorship*, pp. 161–62.

[19] For a wide-ranging survey of this issue and of the various understandings of how the *officium praedicatoris* was conceived in the later Middle Ages, see Minnis, *Fallible Authors: Chaucer's Pardoner and Wife of Bath*, pp. 36–78.

that 'two things are necessary for preachers, that they may lead to Christ. The first is an orderly discourse; the second is the virtue of good works'.[20] The slippery problem of Chaucer's *Pardoner's Tale*, to which Chaucer characteristically offers no solution, is that an excellent *exemplum* is mis-preached by an evil man with an evil intention.[21] Wycliffe was fiercely strict on this point. He held that preaching had greater priority than the Eucharist. In *De veritate sacrae scripturae*, he wrote that 'predicacio verbi dei est actus solempnior quam confeccio sacramenti' ('the preaching of the Word of God is an act more solemn than the confecting of the sacrament').[22] Wycliffe believed that Holy Scripture could be ruined by a preacher's impure intention:

> Si sensus sacer inscribitur menti sacre, tunc scriptura est sacra, et ut videtur, si mens sit maculata scripturam continens, tunc quedam scriptura, que est diccio peccatoris, est scriptura falsa, licet sit alia prior immaculata.[23]

> If the sacred meaning is written in a holy mind, then that scripture is holy, and so it would seem, if a mind containing scripture were unclean, then that passage of scripture, which is the utterance of a sinner, is now false scripture, even though beforehand it was otherwise immaculate.

Accordingly, the translators of the second version of the Wycliffite Bible portrayed themselves as well-intentioned, morally living men.[24]

It should also always be remembered that the performance of the preacher was permitted and defined not only by the grace of God, but also as it related to the intended profitability of the text to the audience.[25] Alan of Lille accordingly wrote that the preacher should tailor his preaching to his audience, with a view to their social station, wealth, and their sins.[26]

---

[20] Section on Pseudo-Thomas Aquinas, 'De Arte Praedicandi', in *Readings in Medieval Rhetoric*, ed. by Miller, Prosser, and Benson, p. 252.

[21] See the *Canterbury Tales*, in *The Riverside Chaucer*, gen. ed. by Benson, VI (C) 329–968.

[22] John Wycliffe, *De veritate sacrae scripturae*, ed. by Buddensieg, II, p. 156. Translation mine.

[23] John Wycliffe, *De veritate sacrae scripturae*, ed. by Buddensieg, I, p. 287. Translation mine.

[24] See 'Prologue to Wycliffite Bible, Chapter 15', ed. by Hudson, p. 72, where 'good lyuyng' is depicted as necessary to the enterprise of translating the Bible.

[25] *Speculum devotorum*, ed. by Hogg, pp. 1–10.

[26] Alan of Lille [Alanus ab Insulis], 'Compendium on the Art of Preaching', ed. by Miller, Prosser, and Benson, pp. 237–38.

When Carthusians like Nicholas Love and the compiler of the *Speculum devotorum* were obliged to make devotional books they were following a statutory obligation to preach — for the production of pious texts was defined as a remote or indirect form of 'preaching with the hands' as opposed to preaching in the presence of a congregation by means of the voice.[27] Most Middle English Carthusian texts were, of course, translations. John Trevisa, by equating preaching with translation, came up with a similar formula for providing the people with the vernacular teaching of Holy Writ — a formula that programmatically merged preaching and translation into each other:

> Also þe gospel and prophecy and þe ry3t fey of holy churche mot be tau3t and ypreched to Englyschmen þat conneþ [*know*] no Latyn. Þanne [then] þe gospel and prophecy and þe ry3t fey of holy cherche mot be told ham [*to them*] an Englysch, and þat ys no3t ydo bote [*done but*] by Englysch translacion. Vor [*For*] such Englysch prechyng ys verrey Englysch translacion, and such Englysch prechyng ys good and neodful [*needful*]; þanne Englysch translacion ys good and neodfol.[28]

For Trevisa, preaching and translating are both in the same business of sacred exposition. The textual tradition of Trevisa's *Dialogue* accordingly witnesses a tell-tale variant in Caxton's edition of 1482, which designates the Septuagint translators not as 'translatours' but as 'jnterpretours'.[29] Clearly, a belief in translation as interpretation/commentary is at work in the adjustment (or editing) of the text at this point.

Trevisa of course was not alone. Preaching, exposition, and translation were often linked in ecclesiastical officialdom. The Fourth Lateran Council of 1215 stressed the importance of preaching to the masses in vernacular terms that they could understand, and the Decrees of the Council of Oxford of 1222 formalized the commitment of the English church to the production of vernacular manuals, treatises, and narratives. *The Lay Folks' Catechism* of 1357, being a Middle English rendering of Archbishop Thoresby's Latin manual for teaching the laity the rudiments of the faith, is a classic example of this move-

---

[27] Guigo, the fifth prior of the Grande Chartreuse, ordered Carthusian brothers to make holy books: 'though we cannot preach by mouth, we can do so by means of our hands' ('quia ore non possumus, Dei verbum manibus praedicemus'). See the *Speculum devotorum*, ed. by Hogg, introduction, p. xlviii, for the citation of this quotation. For Guigo, see *Guigonis Carthusiae Maioris Prioris Quinti Consuetudines*, in *Patrologia latina*, CLIII (1854), cols 631–758 (XXVIII. 3, cols 693–94); also Guigues I, *Coutumes de Chartreuse*, XXVIII. 3.

[28] Waldron, 'Trevisa's Original Prefaces on Translation', pp. 292–93.

[29] Waldron, 'Trevisa's Original Prefaces on Translation', p. 297.

ment.[30] When, however, vernacular texts of lay education drew on the Bible, they were as a rule not English versions of the Bible in the Wycliffite sense, but selective expositions and extrapolations adapted for particular uses and particular audiences. In general, the nearest the laity got to the Bible text as such was in paraphrases, sermons expounding Latin biblical quotations, or biblical art in churches. The biblical text itself and Bible codices were almost exclusively reserved for the clergy, and even when the laity did have closer dealings with the text of Holy Writ there would most likely be direct or indirect clerical supervision.[31] It was enough, as Langland put it, for a poor man to pierce with a Paternoster the Palace of Heaven.[32] Nevertheless, there survives an immense corpus of religious literature derived from the Bible and from writings and commentary on it, which were intended to provide the non-latinate faithful with edifying *fruyte* of genuine biblical power.

Orm among the Gospel's Words

When it comes to preaching as very translation, Orm and his vernacular exegetical homiletics fit Trevisa's formula perfectly, even though they predate it by some two centuries. Orm's life of Christ, as the work of a preacher, commentator, and translator, merits serious (re)consideration, despite the critical abuse that has customarily been heaped on the *Ormulum* for repetitious dullness and alleged poor quality.[33]

Produced in the twelfth century, the *Ormulum* is the first known Middle English life of Christ; it shows, I would argue, rather more sophistication and a greater measure of academic literary sensibility than has, to date, been generally accepted. His introductory and dedicatory paratext is theory-rich, and strategically deploys the chief categories from the academic prologue in non-latinate native terms and phrases. It even goes so far as to accommodate a concern with *nomen libri* and *nomen auctoris*, for which Orm provides a pair of apposite expositions. The first is of 'Goddspell' (Dedication, ll. 157–84), which is extrapolated into a consideration of the 'godnessess' of Christ (Dedication, ll. 185–320). Explanation for the name of the work is repeated in ll. 1–2 of the

[30] *The Lay Folks' Catechism*, ed. by Simmons and Nolloth.

[31] See generally Rice, *Lay Piety and Religious Discipline in Middle English Literature*.

[32] William Langland, *The Vision of Piers Plowman: A Critical Edition of the B-Text*, ed. by Schmidt, Passus x, ll. 456–59.

[33] See *The Ormulum*, ed. by Holt. Quotations from this work will be cited within the main text of this chapter.

Introduction that follows the table of Latin *incipits*. Orm's concern with proper names is not just a matter of falling in enthusiastically with the decorum and prestige of prologue categories; it also is a foretaste of onomastic expositions in the main body of the work.

At all times with Orm, the *sentence* or 'lare' and the 'frame' (*profit*) or 'sawles nede' are prioritized as the *utilitas* of the work. As he puts it in the Dedication which opens the text:

> Icc hafe wennd inntill Ennglissh
> > Goddspelless hall3he lare
> Affterr þatt little witt þatt me
> > Min Drihhtin hafeþþ lenedd (ll. 13–16)

> I have turned the Gospels' holy teaching into English, according to the little wit that God has lent me.

His *modus agendi* is that he has turned ('wennd') the Gospels' sacred teaching into English. He has, moreover, done so with what 'little witt' God has lent ('lenedd') him. This statement is, however, more than merely topical modesty: that Orm has drawn attention to his abilities as a loan from the Almighty is a reminder that not only are his wits a gift from God for which he can take no credit, but also that they are transient and will evaporate with the selfsame mortality which Christ overcame on humanity's behalf. And in that they are God-given they still demand respect, however modest they may be.

Orm is ever careful to suggest, then, that his work is not a matter of personal ambition or pride. His denial of ownership of ability is matched by his deference to the request of the person who asked him to compose the work. This commitment is performed at the behest ('wille' (Dedication, l. 12)) of a fellow brother, 'Wallterr', who was from the same abbey at Bourne. Orm's *intentio* is thus shared, shaped, and institutionally licensed by a devotional service beyond his single will. The *intentio* and *utilitas* informing such service (and thus the *Ormulum* as a whole), is expressed respectively in the words 'wille' (Dedication, l. 12) and 'frame' (Dedication, l. 18): these two have the objective that English people should learn, follow, and fulfil the teaching of the Gospels:

> Þu [that is, 'Wallterr'] þohhtesst tatt itt mihhte wel
> > Till mikell frame turrnenn,
> 3iff Ennglissh follc, forr lufe off Crist,
> > Itt wollde 3erne lernenn,
> 7 foll3henn itt, 7 fillenn itt
> > Wiþþ þohht, wiþþ word, wiþþ dede. (Dedication, ll. 17–22)

> You [that is, 'Wallterr'] thought that it might well be turned to great profit, if English people, for the love of Christ, would eagerly learn it, and follow it and fulfil it in thought, in word, in deed.

The rather liturgical formula, 'wiþþ þohht, wiþþ word, wiþþ dede' (repeated in the Dedication at l. 120), like the related sequence 'Wiþþ ære [ear] [...], Wiþþ herte [...], Wiþþ tunge [...], Wiþþ dede' (Dedication, ll. 133–36; repeated ll. 309–12), is not just repetitious padding. On the contrary, it emphasizes the nature of the work *as holy work* for his audience, for Orm intends sacred lore to translate not only into English words, but, by extension, into the minds and thence the deeds of his vernacular audience. Such repeated formulae act as periodic incantatory refrains, and should not be miscategorized as undue repetitiousness. They should, rather, be seen as features of structural punctuation marking divisions of expository or thematic treatment, giving the mind of the listener a recognizable sectional pause in which to compartmentalize (and absorb) whichever particular parcel of *materia* and *sententia* has just been heard. Likewise, it would be wrong, for the most part, to criticize Orm for repetition across the broad swathe of his work, because the *Ormulum* consists of sermons to be performed separately on different Sundays. In any case, repetition of what is needful to know is a tried and tested way of teaching — no bad thing, in other words. It should also be remembered that no one in the 1100s or 1200s (or in later centuries) was ever meant to sit down and read the whole of such a text continuously. (Let it not be forgotten either that the liturgy works by repetition.) We have to be careful, then, not to misapply latter-day taste to a text that has its own thought-through historically particular ways.

Such singular ways famously include the remarkably distinctive septenary verse format and the idiosyncratic orthography that were evidently both so important to Orm. The metre, no less than the spelling (so he instructs future scribes), must be accurately copied from the first exemplar, 'þiss firrste bisne' (Dedication, l. 100):

> Wiþþ all swillc rime alls her iss sett,
>   Wiþþ all se fele worrdess. (Dedication, ll. 101–02)

> With the very same verses as set down here, with identical words.

It is highly significant that Orm makes this demand for his *ipsissima verba* to be preserved down to the last detail. His intent is not primarily to protect the integrity of his text in terms of its manuscript transmission: it concerns another matter — an issue of intervernacular performativity.

Intriguingly, it would appear that at Bourne Abbey, Orm, an Anglophone, was surrounded by French-speaking Normans who might not have had a good grasp of English, but who may nevertheless have been in the position of having to read out the *Ormulum*'s Gospel expositions to the locals: hence the insistent assistance of the relentlessly phonetic spelling, the punctuation, and the accents in Orm's text.[34] This, however, is not necessarily evidence of resistance to the Norman yoke, or of a culturally oppositional otherness. It is important here to be aware of what was culturally shared. Orm's use of standard Latin sources and hermeneutic conventions in his paratext and self-commentary show a common western European educated heritage in action — a heritage open to Normans and English alike. Orm's English text, for all its intensely native look (he uses Saxon divines like Aelfric and Wulfstan and there is precious little sign of French vocabulary in his text), is thoroughly imbued with its Latin sources and with the latinate tradition that he, like his fellows at Bourne, carried round in his bones. It would therefore be unwise to believe that Orm was deaf to the influence or needs of his Francophone brothers, who, despite the tensions and abuses attendant on the Norman Conquest, were also in the European main-stream and in whose holy institutional enterprise he shared. The text itself, part of that larger enterprise, shows us that Orm and Brother Walter (whose French name is a tell-tale sign that he was indeed a French-speaker) had in common not only the culture of Bourne Abbey, but also the project of seeing this work come to fruition. The temper, discipline, values, and expectations of this insti-tution must have had some shaping effect on the nature and common purpose (that is, the *materia*, *intentio*, and *utilitas*) of the *Ormulum*. That French words are notably absent from Orm's English is not necessarily evidence of the irrel-evance, ignoring, or casting aside of a Francophone milieu: indeed, there is no latinate diction either in this clearly culturally latinate clerical text. There must, then, have been a Francophone context for the *Ormulum*.

There is something rather touching about the idea of Orm assisting his French brothers, however ventriloquially, to communicate holy lore to the locals. Here, rather than being a site of 'fissure' or antagonistic competition, a major language boundary is a joining-place of collaboration for a higher cause. It should also be remembered that any priest-preacher worth his salt or his immortal soul is going to be more interested in getting his holy message across to his flock than in making some point about language politics (although Orm's decisions with

---

[34] For a convincing and fascinating argument about Orm's francophone context and preparation of his text for French-speakers, see Worley, 'Using the *Ormulum* to Redefine Vernacularity'.

orthography are of real political significance in the way they address a linguistic divide). After all, Orm is performing a most sacred duty for Christian souls under the watchful eye of the Almighty, Who will judge and reward his textual labour for the moral and spiritual obligation and privilege that it is.

Orm accordingly stresses that the book is written through the motive and permissive grace of God, 'all þurrh [*through*] Cristess hellpe' (ll. 26; and restated in similar words, Dedication, l. 90). This is precisely what one might expect of a duteous priest-preacher in his *officium praedicatoris*: he is subject to, guided by, and licensed by the grace of God in the form of the second person of the Trinity, the subject of this devout work. Orm has an entirely conventional view of the divinely ordained power and authority of the preaching priest, whose *officium* requires assent, obedience, love, and even praise from the laity, even if the priest himself is morally defective:

> 7 te birrþþ lufenn wel þin preost
> 7 lutenn himm 7 lefftenn,
> Ʒet forrþenn þohh he nohht ne beo
> Swa god man summ himm birrde. (ll. 6140–43)

And you should love your priest well, and bow [that is, defer] to him and exalt him, even though he may not be as good a man as he should be.

A bad man is still a valid priest (though if he does not repent and reform he will be drawn 'till helle' (l. 6149)). Here, Orm takes care to clarify that the preaching and the authority of the *Ormulum* are safeguarded in advance by the ordination of those who will preach it (whoever they may be) as well as by the grace of God that helped in the making of the book.

As for the manner of translating, the Gospels from the 'messeboc' [*mass book*] (Dedication, l. 31) have been assembled in one English book — 'sammnedd' [*gathered together*] (Dedication, l. 29) — thereby making a harmonic compilation following the life of Christ and the Church year. It is important to understand that the harmony of the Gospels is an informing principle behind the whole work. In the Preface subsequent to the Dedication, Orm advertises the concept of Gospel harmony by reworking the standard exposition of the Gospel as the four-wheeled waggon of 'Amminadab' and 'Salemann' (ll. 1–104). When one Gospel is being preached or expounded, the other three are necessarily in agreement and within intertextual reach.

The *Ormulum* reflects traditional preaching on the Gospel in church; it therefore has an equally conventional *modus agendi* by which its *materia* is treated. Firstly, a theme is announced, then a biblical passage is referred to, and after this it is rendered; this is followed by preacherly exposition, normally at length. Orm describes his sequence of exposition:

> 7 aʒʒ affterr þe Goddspell stannt
>   Þatt tatt te Goddspell meneþþ,
> Þatt mann birrþ spellenn to þe follc
>   Off þeʒʒre sawle nede. (Dedication, ll. 33–36)

And always after the Gospel is placed what the Gospel means — which must be expounded to the people for their souls' necessity.

He will present the Gospel text, and then expound it for the particular needs of his audience.

Orm makes an interesting distinction between the two types of 'wordess' which he has 'ekedd' [*added in*] 'Amang Goddspelless wordess': those that fill up the verse, and those which are there for the purpose of elucidation:

> Icc hafe sett her o þiss boc
>   Amang Goddspelless wordess,
> All þurrh me sellfenn, maniʒ word
>   Þe ríme swa to fillenn;
> Acc þu shallt findenn þatt min word,
>   Eʒʒwhær þær itt iss ekedd,
> Maʒʒ hellpenn þa þatt redenn itt
>   To sen 7 tunnderrstanndenn
> All þess te bettre, hu þeʒʒm birrþ
>   Þe Goddspell unnderrstanndenn. (ll. 41–50)

I have in this book, entirely on my own account, set many words amongst the Gospels' words in order to fill out the verses; yet you shall find that my words, wherever they are added in, are able to help those who are reading it to see and understand all the better how they ought to understand the Gospel.

In the manner of the Bonaventuran commentator he takes responsibility for the words he adds for elucidation, for, as he puts it, these words are 'ekedd' 'all þurrh me sellfenn'. Expository sources put to use include the *Glossa ordinaria*, the Pseudo-Anselmian *Enarrationes in Mattheum*, and even Old English works by the likes of Aelfric and Wulfstan.[35] The extent to which commentary-mate-

---

[35] See the important article by Morrison, 'Sources for the *Ormulum*'. For the *Enarrationes in Matthei Evangelium* (misattributed under the name of Anselm of Laon), see *Patrologia latina*, CLII (1854), cols 1227–1500. See also Morrison, 'Orm's English Sources'; Morrison, 'New Sources for the *Ormulum*', and Morrison, 'A Reminiscence of Wulfstan'.

rial is kept apart in the order of vernacular exposition maintains some distinction between text and gloss. The primacy of the Gospels as the wellspring of the *Ormulum* is also warranted by a table of properly referenced Latin *incipits*, to which he draws attention (Dedication, ll. 335–42).

It is a truism of Orm Studies that the work contains an unusually vast amount of preacherly exposition of Gospel *materiae*. The sheer stupefying scale and alleged dullness of this are the most familiar and long-standing features of Orm's image in academe as an heroic garden shed obsessive. Our Brother of Bourne, however, is not so chronically dull as some would have it: his intelligence and agility in expounding 'lare', it may be argued, have not been accorded enough recognition; for he draws on his Latin commentaries with genuine care, sometimes preferring one to another, and at other times conflating them thoughtfully with nuanced skill.[36]

A good idea of Orm's behaviour as a commentator can be gained from the homily on the three temptations of Christ in the desert, which is, ostensibly, an exposition of Matthew 4. 5, but which discusses a different order of temptations to be found in Luke 4. 5. This same discussion is to be found in the *Glossa ordinaria* at the appropriate place in the commentary on each of the Gospels, but Orm's actual wording is closer to Pseudo-Anselm.[37] But, it should be said, Orm's choice of wording from one commentary does not preclude influence from other concordant commentaries. Though he generally draws on the *Glossa ordinaria*, his use of a concordant Pseudo-Anselmian wording could most credibly have been encouraged and/or underwritten by the *Glossa* itself, which twice authorizes the Pseudo-Anselmian interpretation. The fact that his discussion of the order of the three temptations is closer in wording to Pseudo-Anselm may mean no more than that he used Pseudo-Anselm's words as opposed to someone else's, which might just as easily have been used. It could also mean that there was something positively preferable for him in the choice that he made.

So, Orm was not merely writing with recourse to commentaries as separate entities: it would appear that he was writing intertextually and nimbly with commentary-tradition pulsing through his veins. By the same token, he, and indeed any translator of a life of Christ or of another authoritative work, may respond with particular complexity to connexions, canonicity, or hierarchy within commentary-tradition, such as when, paradoxically, the words of a translation may come from one commentator, but the *auctoritas* and *sententia* for

---

[36] See generally Morrison, 'Sources for the *Ormulum*'.

[37] Morrison, 'Sources for the *Ormulum*', p. 431.

drawing on them may come from another. This brings a specifically medieval and academic dimension to the Hieronymic tradition of translating not word-for-word but according to the choices required and allowed by the *sentence* of the work and by the *utilitas* conceived for any given audience or readership.

Juggling commentaries purposefully, then, is something of which Orm seems well capable, but what about his actual translating of the biblical text on which he preaches? To put it mildly, Orm has not enjoyed a reputation as a translator of notable linguistic, narrative, or doctrinal subtlety. In some first steps of revaluation, then, let us examine his rendering of the literal-historical sense of the passage in Matthew's Gospel where Jesus wishes to be baptized by a reluctant John the Baptist:

> Tunc venit Jesus a Galilæa in Jordanem ad Joannem, ut baptizaretur ab eo. Joannes autem prohibebat eum, dicens: Ego a te debeo baptizari, et tu venis ad me? (Matthew 3. 12–14)

> Then came Jesus from Galilee to the Jordan to John, for He would be baptized by him. John, however, fended Him off, saying: 'I ought to be baptized by You — and You come to me?'[38]

SECUNDUM MATHEUM XIX
Venit IHC a Galilea in Jordanem ad Johannem ut baptizaretur.

> Unnderr þa daȝhess, alls uss seȝȝþ
>   Maþeow þe Goddspellwrihhte,
> Comm Jesu Crist off Galileo
>   Fra Nazaræþess chesstre
> Till flumm Jorrdan, till Sannt Johan
>   Þær he stod follc to fullhtnenn,
> 7 Crist ta wollde fullhtnedd beon
>   Att Sannt Johaness hande;
> 7 Sannt Johan droh himm o bacch
>   7 nolde he Crist nohht fullhtnenn,
> 7 seȝȝde; naȝȝ, lef Laferrd, naȝȝ,
>   Ne darr i þe nohht fullhtnenn;
> Me birrþ beon fullhtnedd att tin hannd,
>   Þin blettsinng tunnderrganngenn,
> 7 tu, min Laferrd, cumesst her
>   Att me to wurrþenn fullhtned? (ll. 10648–63)

---

[38] Translation mine.

> In those days, as Matthew the Gospel-maker tells us, came Jesus Christ from Gallilee and the town of Nazareth to the River Jordan to Saint John who was standing there baptizing people. And Christ too wished to be baptized at Saint John's hand; and Saint John drew himself aback, and would in no way baptize Christ, and said, 'No, dear Lord, no — I dare not baptize You: I should be baptized at Your hand to undergo Your blessing. And you, my Lord, are coming here to be baptized by me?'[39]

Orm takes care to identify in English which of the four evangelical *auctores* is being translated: note that Matthew is represented here as saying ('seʒʒþ') the narrative rather than writing it. This orality is more suitable for a live congregation, many of whom may not have been able to read, but all of whom would have been able to comprehend, through their ears, the opened lore of the evangelists.

Orm's translating is reasonably smooth, and contains small additions that clarify and, to a subtle extent, dramatize the Gospel text. 'Unnderr þa daʒʒhess' (taken from the opening of Mark's Gospel at 1. 9) is also an idiomatic expansion of 'tunc', and the mention of Nazareth and Galilee is additional information true to the historical level of the text (and also comes from Mark 1. 9), reminding us that the Lord has definitively left home to commence His work (we must never forget that the exposition of the Gospel is the exposition of events). The words 'Þær he stod follc to fullhtnenn' are additional too. With a certain emphasis gained from the alliteration, they advert to John's practice of mass-baptism and make the implicit point that when Jesus chose to be baptized He humbled Himself as a man in the sight of many.

The dependent clause 'ut baptizaretur' is turned into a main clause, 'Crist ta wollde fullhtnedd beon', which, connected to its predecessor with '7', highlights narrative sequentiality, as also does the shift into lines of verse with strong caesuras (the caesuras being represented in Holt's edition by indented lineation), each of which marks a progression. The word 'ta' ('too') brings out the point that Christ wishes to be one of the crowd. This wish, the will of the incarnate God exhibiting His humanity and His divine condescension, is brought out in particular by Orm's choice of the word 'wollde', which has no explicit equivalent in the Latin. This word — indeed this whole line — is echoed in the antithetical and doubly negated '7 nollde he Crist nohht fullhtnenn', which renders 'prohibebat eum'. The Latin 'prohibebat' would normally just carry a notion of prevention and forbidding (as in the *Catholicon*'s definition in terms of *interdicere*, *contradicere*, and *uetare*),[40] but here Orm shows himself open to the classical

---

[39] Translation mine.

[40] Joannes Januensis, *Catholicon*, s.v. *prohibeo*, unfol.

Latin sense of keeping someone or something at a distance: hence his 'Sannt Johan droh himm o bacch'. This motion of drawing back is all the more ritually significant when we take it into account that Orm has just portrayed John statically as *standing* in the river ('Þær he *stod* follc to fullhtnenn'), which is not in Matthew. The two references to hands ('Att Sannt Johaness hande'; 'att tin hannd') are, in turn, not simply a case of idiomatic Englishing: by complementing each other they elucidate the physical circumstances of a providential yet intimate drama of binaries implicit in the Vulgate Gospel text.

When John 'draws back' in the English, he is given a string of cumulatively negative English words with which forcefully to object to Jesus's wish: 'naȝȝ, lef Laferrd, naȝȝ, | Ne darr i þe nohht fullhtnenn'. The collocation 'lef Laferrd', which confirms John's love, subordination, and obedience, mitigates the preceding and succeeding uses of the otherwise rebellious 'naȝȝ [...] naȝȝ', whilst at the same time the word 'darr' advocates (and excuses) his refusal as a matter of fearfulness rather than as one of culpable disobedience. Orm's John demonstrates with these very few words (all added to the Vulgate with theological decorum by the translator) that he possesses true *reverence* — that devout quality which medieval religious tradition defined as a distinctive composite of the love and fear of God. In alignment with his reverence, John presents himself as being excused by an over-riding obligation to be baptized and blessed by his 'Laferrd': 'Me birrþ beon fullhtnedd att tin hannd': note the decorum with which the Baptist does not dare to oblige Jesus Himself.

In translating this passage Orm works discriminatingly and provides his congregation with a sound preparation for the expository teaching that will follow; he has given them a feeling for the literal sense of the Vulgate text and for the historical events to which it refers. Without taking liberties with the *sensus literalis*, Orm's Englishing clarifies, enlivens, and highlights what matters in the Gospel. All in all, he does deliver on his stated aims in his 'academic prologue', and satisfies its key categories. Perhaps we should be tempted to acknowledge a shocking truth: as the work of a preacher-translator in the learned tradition, the *Ormulum* is, dare it be whispered, interesting.

Meditative Texts and Learned Glosses: *Love's* Mirror

That Nicholas Love's *Mirror* is interesting is beyond denial nowadays. There is, however, significant disagreement about the worthiness of his project, his agenda, and the kind of translator he was. What cannot be disputed, however, is that Nicholas Love drew knowingly and strategically on a comprehensive repertoire of academic literary discourse, which he naturalized into words and action in his English *translatio* of his source. The next chapter of this book discusses how inventively and significantly Love used the materials and methods of the commentator, not just to interpret and repackage, for his own ends, the Latin *prohemium* of his *auctor*, but also to deploy and to shape new materials that he added to his *proheme* before he started rendering the words of the Pseudo-Bonaventuran prologue.

The following passage, taken from Love's *proheme*, is a brief but representative example of the idiomatic facility with which Love articulates theoretical terms and categories. Here he discusses the tradition of Scripture and other holy writings, of which the genre of the *vita Christi*, for unlearned Christians especially, is the supremely edifying instance:

> þe whiche scripture [i.e. biblical text] ande wrytyng [i.e. parabiblical commentary, hagiography, devotional matter] for þe fructuouse matere þerof steryng specialy to þe loue of Jesu ande also for þe pleyn sentence to comun vndirstondyng semeþ amonges oþere souereynly edifiyng to symple creatures.[41]

The 'matere', with its 'pleyn (full and comprehensible) sentence', is 'fructuouse'. The *utilitas* is the profit to be gained in stirring to the love of Jesus and the edification of simple souls. '[F]ructuouse matere' simultaneously considers *materia* and *utilitas*: Love often inter-relates and combines prologue-paradigm categories *ad hoc* like this, as and when it suits his discussion. There is a similar idiomatism, as we shall see later, in his negotiating of theoretical categories in his discussion of his own activity, for example in the care he takes to point out, concerning the *ordinatio/forma tractatus*, that the *Mirror* may be read according to the days of the week or the Church year.[42]

Love's prohemial discourse is articulated in the idiolect of the commentator, but what does this commentator-translator do when it comes to treating his sources? We will now discuss an example of how his fluent negotiation of source text and standard biblical commentary advances his aim of producing a vernacular meditative *vita Christi*. The point of this discussion is not solely to say something worthwhile about Nicholas Love alone. It more particularly serves as one example among several in this chapter of the varied and productive repertoire to be found in translations of the life of Christ that were made in and around the academic tradition.

---

[41] Nicholas Love, *Mirror*, ed. by Sargent, p. 10.

[42] Nicholas Love, *Mirror*, ed. by Sargent, pp. 12–13.

The following extract from the *Mirror* shows how Love treats the beginning
of the Pseudo-Bonaventuran meditation on the Passion on the morning before
Christ was taken.[43] The Latin narrates the manner of Christ's going into the
garden with His disciples to pray. As a deft compiler-commentator, Love does
not limit himself merely to Englishing the literal sense of the source. Rather he
modifies it according to what he sees as a more useful, complete, affective, and
authoritative treatment of this particular section, more responsive to commentary-tradition and, at the same time, to the genre of the meditative life of Christ.

The first thing to notice is the 'B.N.' in the margin.[44] Although it might
stand for 'bene nota' it could also mean that Nicholas Love's authority is com-
mixed with that of Pseudo-Bonaventure, in line with his practice as earlier
explained in a Latin note at the start of the text.[45] It should be noted that this
passage is in a different position in the original: perhaps Love here is highlighting a compiler's responsibility for transposing material. In any case, it transpires
that Love has indeed made significant changes to the *Meditationes* by deploying
material from the Vulgate itself. These changes, refracted through, or accompanied by, orthodox commentary tradition, are of such a quality and degree that
perhaps in their own right they might merit an 'N' to be juxtaposed with the
'B.' Below are the corresponding passages from Pseudo-Bonaventure and Love:

> Reassume igitur meditationes istas a principio passionis, et prosequere per ordinem
> usque in finem, de quibus, sicut mihi videtur, modicum tangam: tu vero, ut placet,
> exerciteris in amplioribus, ut et tibi Dominus ipse dabit. Attende ergo ad singula,
> ac si praesens esses; et cerne eum attente, cum a coena exiens, sermone completo, in
> hortum cum discipulis suis vadit. Ultimo nunc intra, et perpende quomodo affec-
> tuouse, socialiter et familiariter eis loquitur, et ad orationem hortatur; quomodo
> etiam ipse pusillum, id est, per jactam lapidis progrediens, humiliter ac reverenter
> positis genibus orat Patrem. Hic parumper subsiste, et mirabilia Domini Dei tui
> mente pia revolve.[46]

> Make use of these general meditations, then, and follow through in order from the
> beginning of the passion to the end. I will touch upon those events as I see fit. But
> as it pleases you, and as the Lord will grant it to you, enlarge on the scenes more
> fully. And so notice every detail as if you were present.

[43] The following discussion revises materials from my article, 'Johnson, 'Prologue and
Practice: Middle English lives of Christ', pp. 78 and 82.

[44] Nicholas Love, *Mirror*, ed. by Sargent, p. 161.

[45] Nicholas Love, *Mirror*, ed. by Sargent, p. 7.

[46] *Meditationes vitae Christi*, ed. by Peltier, p. 600.

Watch him attentively, when once his sermon was over, he left the supper and walked to the garden with his disciples. This will be the last time they will accompany him. Focus on how affectionately, affably and intimately he spoke to them and urged them to pray. Then watch how he proceeded a little farther — about a stone's throw away — fell to his knees and in reverent humility prayed to the Father.

At this point, pause a while, and with a loving mind think back on the wonders of your Lord.[47]

Go we þan now to þe processe of his passione, takyng hede & makyng vs in mynde as present, to alle þat foloweþ. And first beholdyng how after þe processe of þe gospell of seynt John, oure lord Jesus after þat worþi sopere was done, and þat noble & fructuose sermone endet whereof it is spoken in þe next chapitre before, went with his disciples ouer þe watere of Cedron in to a ȝerde [yard] or a gardyne, in to þe which he was wonte ofte siþes [accustomed often] to come with hees disciples, & there he bade hem abide and praye.

And forþermore takyng with him hese þre speciale secretaries [confidants], þat is to sey Petur & James & Jone, & tellyng hem þat his herte was heuye and sorowfulle vnto the deþ: badde hem þere abide & wake with hym in praieres.

And so a litel ferþer fro hem, as aboute þe space of a stones cast vpon a litel hille: mekely and reuerently knelyng vpon hese boþe knene [both His knees] made his praiere to þe fadere, deuoutely in manere as it foloweþ after.

Bot here abide we a litel while, & take we hede with a deuout mynde of þis wondurfulle dede of oure lord Jesu, soþely worþi to be hade in inward soroufulle compassion.[48]

There are important differences between Love and Pseudo-Bonaventure. The second Latin sentence, 'tu vero, ut placet, exerciteris in amplioribus, ut et tibi Dominus ipse dabit', is cut by Love. It is not biblically necessary. The *Meditationes* does not state that Christ 'went with his disciples ouer þe watere of Cedron'. This is inserted into the *Mirror* directly from the Gospel of St John 18. 1: 'trans torrentem Cedron', as is 'was wont ofte sithes to come with hees disciples', which reflects John 18. 2: 'quia frequenter Jesus convenerat illuc cum discipulis suis' ('as Jesus often came there together with His disciples').[49] In citing John's name, Love acknowledges these additions.

---

[47] For a modern English translation of the *Meditationes vitae Christi*, I have used John de Caulibus, *Meditations on the Life of Christ*, trans. by Taney, Miller, and Stallings-Taney, p. 239.

[48] Nicholas Love, *Mirror*, ed. by Sargent, p. 161.

[49] *The Vulgate New Testament with the Douay Version of 1582 in Parallel Columns* (London: Bagster and Sons, 1872), p. 151. Modern English translation mine.

Pseudo-Bonaventure's Jesus talks to His disciples. We are not told in the Latin what He says, but only how He says it: 'affectuouse, socialiter et famili-ariter' ('affectionately, affably and intimately'). These attractive ways of Jesus's speaking are worthy of meditation, but they have only imaginative status and are not biblically authentic. Love exercises his right not to mention them. His Christ follows the Vulgate more closely, with sadder scriptural words that enter the English text, as we shall see a little later.

In the *Mirror*, Peter, James, and John are specified as confidants. In the *Meditationes vitae Christi* they are not even mentioned. The words of Jesus to them, albeit reported, are the words of the Vulgate, for Love adds that the 'thre special secretaries' are told by Him that His heart is heavy and sorrowful unto the death, and are asked to stay and wake with Him in prayers:

MATTHEW 26. 37–38

Et assumpto Petro, et duobus filiis Zebedaei, coepit contristari et moestus esse. Tunc ait illis: Tristis est anima mea usque ad mortem; sustinete hic, et vigilate mecum.[50]

And taking Peter and the two sons of Zebedee, He began to be sorrowful and mournful. Then He said to them: 'My soul is sorrowful even unto death; abide here, and watch with me'.

MARK 14. 33–34

Et assumit Petrum, et Jacobum, et Joannem secum: et coepit pavere et taedere. Et ait illis: Tristis est anima mea usque ad mortem: sustinete hic, et vigilate.[51]

He took with Him Peter and James and John, and He began to be fraught and weary. And He said to them: 'My soul is sorrowful even unto death; abide here, and watch with me'.

These added materials from Matthew and Mark are not, unlike the excerptions from St John's Gospel, acknowledged. Love acquires the disciples' names from the two evangelists, but the interesting addition, 'his thre special secretaries', is not from the Vulgate. It is to be found, however, in orthodox commentary in the *Glossa ordinaria* and in Lyra's *Postillae*, all of which were commonly included in Bible codices.[52] The enormous availability and authority of these works, given their interlinear and marginal cohabitation with the Vulgate text,

---

[50] *The Vulgate New Testament*, p. 40.

[51] *The Vulgate New Testament*, p. 69.

[52] Citations from Nicholas of Lyra, *Postilla literalis*, ed. by Leontorius henceforth follow quotations in the main text of this chapter.

make for an influence measurable in inches and page-turns. The standard inter-linear gloss on Matthew's 'Et assumpto Petro, et duobus filiis Zebedaei', 'qui-bus secretiora manifestaret' (to whom He would reveal His privities) (fol. 80ʳ), feeds into Love's rendering. However, consultation also of the exposition and vocabulary of Lyra's *Postilla litteralis* provides further illumination of deftly complex source-use:

¶ ET ASSUMPTO PETRO ET DUOBUS FILIJS ZEBEDEI. Isti enim tres erant magis familiares ipsi christo: et ad eius secreta magis admittebantur quam alii. Ratio autem tacta est supra xvii. (fol. 80ʳ)

¶ AND TAKING PETER AND THE TWO SONS OF ZEBEDEE. These three, truly, were themselves the great familiars of Christ, and they more than others were admitted to His intimacies. The reason for this is touched on above with regard to Chapter 17.

These three especially were Christ's 'familiares'. The words 'tres' and 'secreta' emerge in Love's 'þre speciale secretaries'. It is worth bearing in mind here that Lyra refers his readership back to his earlier discussion of the three confidants in his examination of Matthew 17, in which is to be found a more detailed exposition proceeding from a Vulgate text very similar to the later passage in Matthew 26. This more detailed exposition also contains strong similarities to Love's rendering, including the word 'specialis', as in 'speciale' in the *Mirror*:

¶ ASSUMPSIT PETRUM ET IACOBUM ET IOHANNEM FRATREM EIUS. Isti enim tres sunt assumpti ad videndum gloriam future resurrectionis propter pre-rogatiuam eminentie specialis inter alios. (fol. 53ᵛ)

¶ HE TOOK PETER AND JAMES AND HIS BROTHER JOHN. These three, truly, on account of the prerogative of their special eminence amongst the others, were taken so that they could see the glory of the future resurrection.

The notion of having confidants is linked by Lyra to the very words of Jesus, words which Love closely reports *ad verbum* (see above):

¶ SUSTINETE HIC ET VIGILATE MECUM. tanquam amici speciales qui debent in angustijs amicis assistere. (fols 80ʳ–80ᵛ)

¶ ABIDE HERE, AND WATCH WITH ME. Just as special friends who ought to assist friends in distress.

The *sentence* and vocabulary of these concordant expositions (for instance, 'spe-ciales') interconnect with, and re-inforce, each other. Love's rendering, moti-vated by them, is a vernacular concentration of them.

In the light of this, the earlier addition, 'ouer þe watere of Cedron', noted above, invites further investigation. In commentary-tradition Cedron was associated with Christ's sorrowful heart. Lyra in the *Postilla moralis* expounds Cedron as 'sad mourning/sorrow/grief': 'trans torrentem cedron. qui interpretatur tristis meror' ('across the rushing stream of Cedron, which is to be interpreted as sad grief/sorrow'; fol. 235ᵛ). Other, earlier, commentators would appear to lend this understanding a weight of tradition, which increases the likelihood of Love responding to it. Rabanus Maurus, for example, in his *Commentaria in libros Machabaeorum*, interprets the name suitably sadly: 'Interpretatur autem Cedron tristitia, sive moeror, sive dolor' ('Cedron, however, is to be interpreted as sadness, or grief/sorrow or anguish/distress').[53] The exposition of Hugh of St Victor, in *De claustro animae*, is similar: 'Cedron interpretatus tristi vel moeror' ('Cedron interptreted as sad or grief/sorrow').[54] Incontestably, Love's addition was motivated by an exegetical association of Cedron with Christ's sorrowful heart and as a crossing-point to the inexorable yet willed *dolor* of the Passion. Love's addition of Christ's sorrowful heart evidently spurred another addition, the torrent of His passional sadness which is Cedron. This is paralleled by his addition to the Latin at the close of this passage, which attempts by instruction to translate the same sadness to the meditating interiority of the reader: 'soþely worþi to be hade in inward soroufulle compassion'.

Such alterations and additions make this passage significantly different in content, tone, and devotional burden from the *Meditationes vitae Christi*. The English text is more biblically grounded (and therefore authoritative), affective, and suitable for its intended readers and hearers. The *utilitas/profyte* of Love's inserted burst of Gospel-harmonizing, which is substantially commentary-motivated, is that it forms a more densely and emotively expounded version closer to vital biblical events desirable to be known for the purposes of understanding and sympathizing with the 'processe of his passion'.

Moreover, Love provides, better than does the *Meditationes*, the necessary context for Jesus's subsequent solitary praying for Himself at the beginning of His Passion. The Englishman stresses factually but affectively the Humanity of Christ when he has Jesus tell His 'secretaries' of His sorrow unto the death and

---

[53] Rabanus Maurus, *Commentaria in libros Machabaeorum*, in *Patrologia latina*, CIX (1852), cols 1125–1256 (xv, col. 1211).

[54] Hugh of St Victor, *De claustro animae*, in *Patrologia latina*, CLXXVI (1854), cols 1017–1182 (bk IV, col. 1146).

asks them to 'wake with him in praieres'. This poignantly contextualizes, and is echoed in, Jesus's subsequent lone praying in His agonized Manhood — such praying being an utterly mortal form of discourse with His mortality its subject and motivation.[55] Also, Love's reader/hearer, once told of Christ's intimately human heart being 'heuye & sorowfulle vnto the deþ', becomes in turn another 'speciale secretarie', simply by being present in the very process of reading or hearing. The subsequent instruction 'Bot here abide we a litel while, & take we hede' cannot but be followed by such a reader, who is necessarily *there* as a confidant in the imaginative *mise-en-scène*.

This is not the only example of commentary-motivated addition from the Gospels in Love's *Mirror*. The account of the thief who blasphemed Christ, 'Pendet inter duos latrones [...]. Alii blasphemant, dicentes' ('He hangs between two thieves [...]. Some blaspheme [Him], saying') becomes:[56]

> And ȝit more ouere, he hangeþ by twix two thefes, of þe whech þat oneʒ blas-phemeþ & tempteþ him to impacience. And þerwiþ oþer blasphemene & skornyng seyene [...].[57]

This, Salter observes, has a parallel in Luke 23. 39: 'Unus autem de his, qui pendebat, latronibus, blasphemabat eum, dicens [...]' ('One, however, of these thieves who was hanging there, blasphemed Him, saying [...]').[58] However, she does not account for the residue of other words in Love's text that are not in the original: these concern the tempting of Christ to impatience, that is, '& tempteþ him to impacience'. If Lyra in his commentary on this Gospel in his *Postilla moralis* is consulted, however, we do find reference to patience (fol. 181ʳ). We come yet closer to Love's rendering, though, if we turn to the *Postilla literalis* and the *Glossa ordinaria*, not for what either has to offer as regards the Gospel of Luke, but for their comments on the corresponding passage in Matthew 27. 40. The *Glossa* reads thus: '¶ SI FILIUS DEI ES. Si insultantibus cedens descenderet de cruce: virtutem patientie non demonstraret' ('¶ IF YOU ARE THE SON OF GOD. If, ceding to these insults, He were to descend from the cross, He would not demonstrate the virtue of patience') (fol. 85ʳ). Lyra follows this: 'si autem tunc de cruce descenderet | virtutem patientie non demonstraret'

---

[55] Nicholas Love, *Mirror*, ed. by Sargent, pp. 162–65.

[56] *Meditationes vitae Christi*, ed. by Peltier, p. 606.

[57] Nicholas Love, *Mirror*, ed. by Sargent, p. 176.

[58] Salter, *Nicholas Love's 'Myrrour of the Blessed Lyf of Jesu Christ'*, p. 311; *The Vulgate New Testament*, p. 118 (translation mine).

('If, however, He were then to descend from the cross, He would not demonstrate the virtue of patience') (fol. 85ʳ).

It is telling that Love added some translated words from one Gospel but other translated words from commentary on another Gospel. This goes to show how the Gospels' *sentence* was regarded as harmonious, to the extent that commentary on each was accorded possible interchangeability. This passage and the previous passage robustly represent the complexity and flexibility with which commentary-tradition could be used by a Middle English translator of this genre. It is not unthinkable that such renderings might in part have sprung from Love's familiarity with standard glosses and not solely from his physical consultation of a glossed Bible. In any case, as with other, previously-discussed, additions to a Latin original, this instance shows not just the inextricability of biblical text and gloss, but also that a medieval translator of a life of Christ, even when he is not ostensibly tackling the Bible at first hand, but at second hand through a meditative reworking like the *Meditationes vitae Christi*, is reading and treating his ostensible source through a universal original, the Gospel and its commentary-tradition. Love is certainly not alone in doing this.

Notions of translation as displacement and as competition would not carry us forward very far here in explaining Love's workings in these passages. Neither would any attempt to underplay their academic nature. The scholarly technicalities of excision, transposition, rephrasing, and insertion are in no way at odds with affective textuality or meditation — nor do they compromise the spiritual or moral dignity of the reader or hearer. The cross-lingual intertextual flexibility with which Love treats his *matere* is nimble; he negotiates the *Meditationes*, the Vulgate, and commentary with serious literary aims in mind. The *Mirror* embodies a productive translational partnership of Latin and English, and of Holy writ and parabiblical textuality, or as Love puts it concisely in his *proheme*, 'scripture and wrytyng'.[59]

Opening Latin: The Speculum devotorum

The fifteenth-century Carthusian meditative life of Christ, *Speculum devotorum*, was written for a Birgittine sister of Syon Abbey by a brother of Sheen. Like Love's *Mirror*, it has a long and self-consciously academic *prefacyon*.[60] All the major categories are covered. The translator claims purity of *entent*; invokes

[59] Nicholas Love, *Mirror*, ed. by Sargent, p. 10.

[60] *Speculum devotorum*, ed. by Hogg, pp. 1–11.

the authority of his prior and of divine grace as licensing and moving factors in the production of the work;[61] declares the 'profyte' of the work to be the edifying of souls, the gaining of virtues, spiritual knowledge, and sweetness in grace. It provides wisdom, comfort in adversity, the very company of Christ Himself, and all things necessary to spiritual health — and, as is also stated in Love's *Mirror*, it outdoes all hagiography.[62] Our Carthusian even goes to the extent of inventing a new *nomen libri*, 'A Mirowre to deuout peple'.[63] As for the *materia*, it is the life of Christ as witnessed in the Bible, the Doctors of the Church (especially Nicholas of Lyra and Peter Comestor), and a variety of 'approved' holy women.

It is of literary-theoretical interest here, then, that *materia* from commentators is considered, in part, as a function of *modus agendi* — for these are the materials with which the monk of Sheen expounds his primary material, the life of Christ (Lyra is especially useful for helping the translator uncover the *sensus literalis* of the Vulgate):

> Ferthyrmore gostly syster ȝe schal vndyrstande that þe grounde of the boke folowynge ys þe gospel and þe doctorys goynge thervpon, & specyally I haue folowyd in þys werke tueyne [*two*] doctorys of the whyche þat one ys comunely called the Maystyr of storyis [*Master of Histories*] and hys boke in englyisch the scole storye that othyr Maystyr Nycholas of Lyra þe whyche was a worthy doctur of dyuynytee & glosyde alle the byble as to the lettural vndurstandynge [*literal sense*], & therfore I take these tueyne doctorys most specyally as to thys werke for they goo neryste to the storye [*history/historical events*] & to the lettural vndyrstandynge of eny doctorys that I haue red; notwythstandynge I haue browgth inne othyr doctorys in diuerse placys as to the moral vertuys, & also sum reuelacyonys of approuyd wymmen, & I haue put nothynge too of myne owen wytt but that I hope maye trewly be conseyuyd be opyn resun & goode conscyence for that I holde þe sykyrest [*surest*].[64]

Note that, as a humble compiler, the maker of this work adds nothing of his own unless it is 'conseyuyd be opyn resun & goode conscyence': the former, 'opyn resun', is self-authorizing through its self-evidential nature, and the latter, 'goode conscyence', exculpates him automatically through purity of *entent*. He is also eloquent about the *ordinatio* of his work and the use of features of layout

---

[61] *Speculum devotorum*, ed. by Hogg, pp. 2–4.

[62] *Speculum devotorum*, ed. by Hogg, pp. 5–8; Nicholas Love, *Mirror*, ed. by Sargent, p. 11.

[63] *Speculum devotorum*, ed. by Hogg, p. 5.

[64] *Speculum devotorum*, ed. by Hogg, pp. 9–10.

and structure — such as the table of memorizable chapter headings made for the benefit of the reader (this shall be discussed in greater detail later in this chapter).

The monk of Sheen's practice of translating shows the same academic temper, and he is clearly capable of using the same range of expository methods that Love deploys in the passages on Christ in the garden — and more. But first, by way of approach, there is something to be said for looking beforehand at another, earlier work, Richard Rolle's Psalter, which combines a thoroughly academic prologue with a very regular translation method. This takes the form of an expository sequence, which commences with quotation and then close translation of the Latin text, followed by moral and spiritual exposition thereof. In this approach it shares points of similarity with the *Speculum devotorum*.

In his glossatory translation of the Psalter, Rolle claims that he is attempting to follow the letter, and only circumlocutes when he has no other choice:

> In þis werk I seke no strange Inglis, bot lightest and comunest and swilke þat es mast [*that which is most*] like vnto þe Latyn.[65]

His *entent* is to provide the reader without Latin with as close an experience as possible of the original, together with orthodox commentary and affective extrapolation. His method of opening the Psalter has two main stages: firstly, an 'interlinear-style' verbal gloss-type rendering, which allows the original to cast a literalistically latinate shadow in the vernacular; and, secondly, a more open translation together with expository (and devotional) extrapolation of the *sentence*, based in general on the *catena* of Peter Lombard:[66]

> In þe translacioun I folow þe letter als mekil als [*much as*] I may, and þare I fynde na propir Inglys I folow þe witte of þe word, so þat þai þat sal [*those who shall*] rede it, þam thar noght dred errynge. In expounynge I folew haly doctours.[67]

His approach can be exemplified by a typical expository sequence from Psalm 3:

> *Voce mea ad dominum clamaui et exaudiuit me de monte sancto suo.* 'With my voyce I cried til [*to*] oure Lord and he me herd fra his haly [*holy*] hille.' Voyce of hert, þat

---

[65] Richard Rolle, *English Writings*, ed. by Allen, p. 7.

[66] Richard Rolle, *English Writings*, ed. by Allen, pp. 125–26, where Allen points out that Rolle did not, it would appear, borrow outside Peter Lombard, and probably formulated some of his own expositions. Hodgson, *The Sanity of Mysticism*, pp. 151–88, finds possible use of St Augustine's *Enarrationes*. Hodgson's alleged discovery is cited in Alford, 'Richard Rolle and Related Works', p. 42.

[67] Richard Rolle, *English Writings*, ed. by Allen, p. 7.

es, grete ȝernynge of Goddes luf, sounes bifore Crist. His praier he calles cryinge, for the force of fire of luf [*love*] es in his saule, þat makis his prayer to thrille heuen. And so he herd hym fro his haly hille, þat es, of his rightwisnes [*righteousnesness*], for it es rightwise byfor God to help hym þat es in angwys [*anguish*] for his luf.[68]

Such a reliance on Latin glosses permeates medieval translation and is to be found also in non-biblical and non-devotional translations, notably those dealing with the most prestigious and authoritative sources, for example Chaucer's and Walton's translations of Boethius,[69] and Gavin Douglas's Scots version of Virgil, the *Eneados*. These too drew on commentary and its methodology in the best manner of the age. Chaucer turned to Trevet's commentary, some Remigian glosses, and the French translation of Jean de Meun (itself an academic rendering). Walton benefited from Trevet and Chaucer's *Boece*. And in his 'wlgar Virgill' Gavin Douglas used commentary material from Ascensius and Servius.[70]

The *Speculum devotorum*, however, is not quite so patterned and systematic in its treatment of sources, though it does still observe the different layers of close rendering, of moral and spiritual exposition, and of prayerfulness (*lectio*, *meditatio*, *oratio*). In this work there is also great variety in the types of *materia* drawn on, and in the translator's treatment of them. This repertoire, for all its breadth, is governed by a unity of *entent* articulated through the formal cycle of *lectio*/narration, meditative explication, and prayerful exhortation. Sometimes the rendering of sources is periphrastic; sometimes sources are conflated. On occasions, the monk of Sheen is selective in choosing a meaning that meets his aims, and he accordingly suppresses other options. At other times, the rendering, be it of Gospel matter or of other materials, is almost verbatim.

In the first two chapters of the *Speculum devotorum* there is a practice of quoting the Latin of the Vulgate, then translating it closely; this is followed up sometimes with a more open rendering of the literal sense, extrapolating in the manner of the commentator for the purposes of developing meditation and an understanding of the biblical events.

---

[68] Richard Rolle, *English Writings*, ed. by Allen, pp. 8–9.

[69] See my essay. Johnson, 'Walton's Sapient Orpheus', pp. 139–68; Gleason, 'Clearing the Fields: Towards a Reassessment of Chaucer's Use of Trevet', and also Minnis, '"Glosynge is a glorious thing": Chaucer at Work on the *Boece*', pp. 106–24. See also generally Machan, *Techniques of Translation: Chaucer's Boece*, for Chaucer's use of Trevet, and also Copeland, 'Rhetoric and Vernacular Translation in the Middle Ages'. See too Johnson, 'Walton's Heavenly *Boece* and the Devout Translation of Transcendence'.

[70] Bawcutt, *Gavin Douglas*, pp. 92–127.

In our next example, we see how the translator of the *Speculum devotorum*, in contrast with the routine practice of Love and many others, includes (like Rolle) Latin biblical quotations in his text before expounding them — but he does so in his own way. In this case, the Latin Vulgate quotations are not deposited in the text by the compiler as the chief *materia* then to be expounded: sometimes they are deployed as instruments to gloss and explain other parts of the Bible and the *vita*: this is a particularly empowering and fruitful form of vernacular commentary-translation. As part and parcel of the same operation, the maker of the *Speculum devotorum* uses a fairly recent Middle English work for authoritative comment and as a means of conveying such biblical Latin into his work.

This intriguing procedure occurs in the first chapter of the *Speculum devotorum*, where the Creation and Fall are expounded, ever with a view to the coming of Christ and the Redemption of Man — as one would expect of a life of Christ. The passage in question deals with the nature of the Creation, and, in particular, with how Adam was made by God:

> ...& in the sexte daye he made the firste man the whyche ys callyd Adam, & he made hym of sclyme [*slime*] of the erthe as to the body as we rede in the fyrste boke of holy wryt þe whyche ys callyd genesys where hyt ys wryte thus: Formauit dominus deus hominem de limo terre; thys ys to seye: Oure lorde god made man of the sclyme of the erthe.[71]

The text and its location in the Bible are properly cited. The translation is close, and easy enough for a vernacular reader to understand — the only addition being the traditional formulaic prefixing of 'oure' to 'dominus deus', in 'oure lorde god'. The next segment of translating is, after a close rendering of the Vulgate, accorded a second, more *opyn* rendering that clarifies the literal sense:

> Et inspirauit in faciem eius spiraculum vite; thys ys to seye: And he inspyryd in hys face þe spyracle of lyf, þe whyche ys no more to oure vndyrstandynge opyn but that he made & put in the same body that he hadde formyd of the erthe a resunnable [*rational*] spirit.[72]

The transliterative latinate words 'inspyryd' and 'spyracle' would scarcely make the meaning of the source clearer for the intended sister of Syon, let alone a wider vernacular audience, and so a more glossatory comment is necessary —

---

[71] *Speculum devotorum*, ed. by Hogg, p. 22.

[72] *Speculum devotorum*, ed. by Hogg, p. 22.

with the English writer making the point that a rational soul was combined
with a body made of the slime of the earth. There is then a further gloss on this
subject:

> a resunnable spiryt, the whyche ys of thre pryncipal mygthtys [*powers*], þat ys to
> seye of Mynde, Resun, & wylle, to the lyknesse of the holy trynytee, the whyche ys
> oo [*one*] parfyth [*perfect*] god.[73]

This particular gloss is not taken from a Latin commentary. It comes from a
vernacular work, the *Scale of Perfection* of Walter Hilton.

> The soule of a man is a liyf, made of thre myghtes — mynde, resoun, and wille — to
> the ymage and the likenes of the blissid holi Trinité.[74]

In the Cambridge manuscript of the *Speculum devotorum* the Canon of
Thurgarton is designated 'Maistre Walter Hilton',[75] that is, conceivably as a
magister — which status in the hierarchy of textual authority is second only to
that of a fully-fledged *auctor*. The forty-third chapter of Book I of this Middle
English Master's text treats of the excellence and dignity which man's soul first
had, and of the beastly wretchedness it lapsed into at the Fall. The *Speculum
devotorum* carries on the same trajectory through further citation of Genesis,
this time without recourse to Hilton:

> for hyt ys wryte in the forseyde boke of genesys thus: Et creauit deus hominem ad
> ymaginem et similitudinem suam; thys ys to seye: And god made man to hys owen
> ymage and lyknesse, vndyrstondyth as to the soule.[76]

Before long, however, Hilton's text is picked up again verbatim. The tenor of
this whole chapter, whether it is using Hilton or not at any given point, is generally consonant with the *sententia* of the *Scale* on the beastly nature of the
Fall, though the *Speculum devotorum* seems to stress beastliness rather more
than its vernacular predecessor. Further related material from Hilton, discussing the nature of original sin, is accordingly used to round off the chapter; yet,
at first sight, one could be forgiven for thinking that the *Speculum devotorum*
is not drawing on a work like the *Scale*, but extrapolating independently from

---

[73] *Speculum devotorum*, ed. by Hogg, p. 22.

[74] See Walter Hilton, *The Scale of Perfection*, ed. by Bestul, II. 43.

[75] This is noted in the variants and not included by Hogg in his edited text; see *Speculum
devotorum*, ed. by Hogg, p. 29.

[76] *Speculum devotorum*, ed. by Hogg, pp. 22–23.

Scripture. Paradoxically, however, the very Latin of the Psalter, here used for the purpose of commentary on Genesis, has its immediate source not in the Vulgate but in a recent vernacular work. What is remarkable in this case is that this Carthusian uses Hilton on the Vulgate in the same way that he (or Love or Orm) uses standard academic Latin commentary like the *Glossa ordinaria* or Lyra:

> Of þys fallynge of the fyrste man Dauyd seyt in the sautyr thus: Homo cum in honore esset non intellexit, comparatus est iumentis insipientibus, et similis factus est illis; thys ys in englyisch: Man whenne he was in worschype vndyrstode hyt not, & therfor he loste hyt; he ys lykened to vnwyse bestys [*beasts*], þat ys, to vnresunnable bestys be carnal beholdynge, & made lyke to hem in bestly louynge of hymself & othyr creatures vycyusly.[77]

This draws on Hilton:

> for as David seith in the sautier: *Homo, cum in honore esset, non intellexit; comparatus est iumentis, et similis factus est illis* (Psalms 48. 21). A man whanne he was in worschipe, he knewe it not, and therefore he loste it and was maad like to a beest.[78]

The words 'louynge of hymself & othyr creatures vycyusly' comes from a statement of Hilton's a little earlier: 'Adam synnede, chosynge love and delite in himsilf and in creaturis'.[79]

It is worthy of note that a vernacular work has attained the functional status of a learned commentary, deployed to produce and adjudicate authoritative meaning. Such confidence in the *auctoritas* of vernacular texts would indicate that a similiar authority was conceivable for the *Speculum devotorum* itself. In the cases of both vernacular texts, however, such authority does not owe itself to fantasies of vernacular autonomy, nor does it comprise a brave shaking off of colonizing latinity, for it springs continuously and connectedly from the wellhead of Latin Scripture and its accompanying commentary tradition.

The monk of Sheen then reminds his audience that an angel threw Adam and Eve out of Paradise to live in sorrow on earth and to suffer death. Having mentioned this terrible price for original sin, the chapter closes suitably, with further recourse to the *Scale* in the form of a reminder of how Christ's Passion, which constitutes the climax of the *Speculum devotorum*, restored humanity:

---

[77] *Speculum devotorum*, ed. by Hogg, p. 28.

[78] Walter Hilton, *The Scale of Perfection*, ed. by Bestul, II. 43.

[79] Walter Hilton, *The Scale of Perfection*, ed. by Bestul, II. 43.

Alle thys was for the fyrste synne of man the whyche ys callyd orygynal; for the whyche synne as Hylton seyt we mygth neuyr haue be sauyd thowgth we hadde neuyr doo othyr venyal ne deedly, but only thys that ys called orygynal for hyt ys the fyrste synne, & that ys nothynge ellys but lesynge of þe rygthwysenesse þe whyche we were made inne but yf oure lorde Ihesu cryste be hys precyouse passyon hadde delyueryd vs & restoryd vs aȝen.[80]

And wite thou wel, though thou hadde nevere doo synne with thi bodi deedli ne venyal, but onli this that is callid origynal — for it is the first synne, and that is not ellis but the loesynge of thi rightwisenesse whiche thou were maad inne — yit schuldest thou nevere have ben saaf yif oure Lord Jhesu Criste bi His precious passioun hadde not delyvered thee and restored thee agen.[81]

There is a significant change of address from Hilton's use of the second person to the Carthusian's use of the first person plural. Although this work was written for one nun, it also entertained the possibility of a larger circulation, as the title *A Mirror to Devout People*, envisages.

Further evidence of the repertoire of the maker of this work will be discussed in Chapter 4. The point of this particular example has been to show another particular modality of resourcefulness, another Middle English maker of a life of Christ variously combining Latin and Middle English whilst performing different types of translating, from close literalism to expansive elaboration of *sentence*.

A Tale of Christ: Translating and Genre in the Passion of Our Lord

The later Middle Ages sustained a considerable tradition of scriptural exegesis paying particular attention to the literary features of the Bible.[82] The exegete who did not take into account the stylistic forms and the very literariness of the Bible might be led into interpretative error. There emerged in the later Middle Ages an enhanced understanding of the variety of genres within the Bible. Alexander of Hales, St Bonaventure, Thomas Aquinas, and many others appraised and taught the multiform styles and modes of Holy Scripture, its 'modes' (in Latin its 'modi'), whose function was to move the will. Such modes

---

[80] *Speculum devotorum*, ed. by Hogg, p. 29.

[81] Walter Hilton, *The Scale of Perfection*, ed. by Bestul, II. 43.

[82] See Minnis, *Medieval Theory of Authorship*, pp. 118–40, for a discussion of the variety of forms found in the Bible by medieval commentators.

included the narrative, exhortative, preceptive, disputative, deprecative, lauda-
tory, oratory, exemplificative, revelatory, prophetic, and figurative.

Medieval clerics, then, were well aware of the place and power of style and
genre for affective and hermeneutic purposes, and it is to a creative indirectly
expository use of genre that we turn next. This case, so different from the other
lives discussed in this chapter, is nevertheless ideologically in tune with them.
It elaborates *sentence* by refracting it edifyingly and intriguingly through a
genre that was normally a very long way from the Bible, from learned literary
thought, and from academic commentary. Nevertheless, it is a *bona fide* life
of Christ, and its dealings with doctrine, devotion, and the Gospel are substantial, inventive, and compelling — and could not have been accomplished
without a conventional foundation of academic learning underneath it. As
such, it invites critical attention, especially as the text has enjoyed precious
little appraisal at all.

The *Passion of Our Lord* in Oxford, Jesus College, MS 29 (*c.* 1285–1300
or earlier?) is an accurate and fast-moving Gospel harmony.[83] It does not
contain homiletic expansion or expository digression. It does, however, play
most pointedly with the genre of the *chanson de geste* in order to reinforce the
authority and meaning of Christ's life, and to provide emotionally intelligible
materia for its intended audience. At the opening of the work the audience is
told that this 'lutele tale' ('little tale')[84] is about neither Charlemagne nor his
twelve retainers, but about Jesus (and, by implication, His twelve disciples).
Here, Christ may be imagined — yet must not be miscategorized — in terms
of the *chanson de geste* and all the transient worldly chivalry and proud heroics
that Charlemagne and such tales represent. The Christ of the *Passion of Our
Lord* thereby outdoes and diplaces 'karlemeyne' (l. 3)[85] and all other human
heroes, but He does it through His 'mylde [...] dede' ('mild [...] deeds')[86] and,
above all, His Passion.

Time and time again in this work, the poet-translator exploits the popular attractiveness of the *chanson de geste* in order to engage, defamiliarize, and
refresh pious understanding: a very distinctive and energetic mode of *expositio
sententiae*. To take one notable example, he charges a familiar feature of heroic

---

[83] *An Old English Miscellany*, ed. by Morris, pp. 37–57. For dating of the scribal hand of
the manuscript, see Hill, 'Oxford, Jesus College MS 29, Part II', p. 271.

[84] *Passion of Our Lord*, in *An Old English Miscellany*, ed. by Morris, l. 1.

[85] *Passion of Our Lord*, in *An Old English Miscellany*, ed. by Morris, l. 4.

[86] *Passion of Our Lord*, in *An Old English Miscellany*, ed. by Morris, l. 41.

narrative, the dastardly business of the betrayal of one's lord, with extra significance when he applies it to the case of Jesus, Judas, and His comitatus of disciples: 'Ac on hyne bitrayede. þat et of his brede' ('but one betrayed Him, who
ate of his bread').[87] Outside the Gospel, these words would simply point to a
treacherous and disloyal transgression against lordly hospitality and generosity.
Here, however, it also refers, inventively and edifyingly, to the Last Supper.

Christ passes a wine-sop to Judas to identify His treacherous follower. In a
sacramentally adjusted replay of the blblical scene, the wine-soaked bread, the
very stuff of the Host as well as of good hosting, represents the actual body
and blood betrayed. Judas's offence against his lord's hospitality is sharpened
shockingly with eucharistic irony, and provokes the self-damning despair that
blasphemes the Holy Ghost and, by tradition, consigns Iscariot to Hell.[88]

Christ's announcement to the assembled party of His impending betrayal
is a model of courtesy. He breaks the news with 'veyre chere', politely dropping
the bombshell that one amongst their fellowship ('yuere') at this very table will
betray Him, capping the news with a threat and prediction all the more chilling
for being so gentle and genteel:

> At the schere þursday. as ye mawen ihére
> Þo vre louerd wes isethe. to his supere.
> He byheold abute. myd swiþe veyre chere.
> And seyde to his disciples. þat þo myd him were.
> On scal me bitraye. þat nv is vre yuere.
> Iwis hym were betere. þat he ibore nere.[89]

On Holy Thursday, as you may hear, when Our Lord was seated at His Supper, He
beheld what was about Him with such fair countenance, and said to His disciples,
who were with Him: 'One who is now our companion shall betray Me. Surely, it
were better for him he had never been born'.

Note in these lines the very long run of -ere end-rhyming; this stylistic heightening accompanies thematic heightening. Just like a king or lord who looks
'abute', surveying his courtiers or comitatus before addressing them, Jesus
would alight on individuals as His gaze moves around, making each disciple
feel isolated in so doing. At the same time He also re-inforces the status and

---

[87] *Passion of Our Lord*, in *An Old English Miscellany*, ed. by Morris, l. 44.

[88] The faithful poet, in contrast with Judas, puts his text in the way of divine grace by but-
tressing his *narratio* with prayers for it (ll. 19, 547–52, 691–706).

[89] *Passion of Our Lord*, in *An Old English Miscellany*, ed. by Morris, ll. 89–92. Translation mine.

responsibility of the group as a group (that is, the Church as a collectivity), by incorporating them all in His (omniscient) view. He speaks to them not in anger but with a mildness which of itself is terrifying, given what is at stake, whilst simultaneously showing courtesy, aristocratic *sangfroid*, courage, and a social graciousness sourced in divine grace. The shock of this betrayal is the greater because it is revealed with mildness rather than forthright condemnation. The message jars with the manner of delivery, but there is a deeper, positive point to this: Christ is always mild to those those who, like His disciples (and like the pious audience of this work), want to serve Him, however much (like Peter, the other disciples, and the poet's audience) they may on occasions fall short and let Him down terribly.

In routine colloquial use the locution *better for him that he had never been born* is a common threat leading to some ghastly vengeance or punishment inflicted by the offended party. Here, closely following the Gospels, it is the prelude to Iscariot's actual sin.[90] These words, however, are no threat, even though they unavoidably feel threatening. They disclose Christ's foreknowledge of Judas's choice of sin, despair, and an infernal destination. A man foreknown to damnation has no benefit in ever having been alive in the first place. No wonder the Disciples are so terrorized. The same chilling words are also an indication of Christ's gracious acquiescence in His own betrayal. At the same time, they are a sign that His divine will is guiding the providential process of the Passion towards its inevitable conclusion:

> Euerych lokede to oþre. hi were sore of-dredde.
> Hi nuste neuer bi hwich of heom. he hit iseyd hedde.
> Þo queþen his disciples. on after on.
> Louerd hi seyden alle. hwo is so hardy mon.
> Þat durre þe bytraye. of vs everyuch on.
> We willeþ to þe deþe. alle myd þe gon.[91]

Everyone looked at each other; they were mightily terrified. They had absolutely no idea which of them He had said this about. Then uttered His disciples, one by one, 'Lord' (they all said) 'who is so bold a man that he would betray You? Every one of us — we would all go to the death with You'.

The words 'hardy' and 'durre' normally denote desirable qualities of heroic courage: it is interesting here that the disciples do not seem to regard this

---

[90] Matthew 26. 24.

[91] *Passion of Our Lord*, in *An Old English Miscellany*, ed. by Morris, ll. 95–100. Translation mine.

betrayal first and foremost as a moral error but as an act provoking fear at cross-ing a ruler — a blunder of foolish boldness, as so often committed by the big-mouthed and vainglorious knights who strut their way to fame or ruin in the *chanson* genre. Decorously but hastily (like the *beot*-swearers on the eve of the Battle of Maldon), the disciples re-affirm their vow to endure to the death with their lord, a familiar boast of the would-be loyal follower about to be put to the test, but here, as the audience knows from the familiar Bible story, about to fail and bewail. However, Christ, the victim, for all the dread in the room, is self-contained in a blessed heavenly bliss that outdoes and overgoes the worldly imperturbability of the heroes of *geste* tradition:

> Þo seyde vre louerd crist. þet is ful of blysse.
> Nymeþ gode yeme. þat ye nouht ne mysse.
> Hwam ich biteche þat bred. þat ich on wyne wete.
> He me schal bitraye. to nyht er he slepe.
> He hit bitauhte iudas. þat alle hit myhte iseo.[92]

Then said Our Lord, Who is full of bliss. 'Pay good attention, so that you miss nothing at all: He whom I give the bread I wet in wine shall betray me tonight before he sleeps'. He gave it to Judas, so that all might see it.

There is theologically freighted dramatic irony here, for this is the beginning of the process of the Passion, the unhappiest yet most blessed event in history. For all that Christ is about to experience (and to represent for humans) the supreme unhappiness, He is nevertheless 'full of bliss', as the source of eternal bliss, its wellhead. Judas departs, appropriately enough, into the darkness to do the shameful deed. The newly wretched Iscariot is soon labelled as a lone out-cast, bereft of the companionship of the *comitatus*: 'Al hym seolf one. nedde he nenne yuere' ('All himself alone, he had no companions at all').[93]

Clearly, this life and Passion is most unlike, for instance, Love's *Mirror*, the *Ormulum*, or the *Stanzaic Life of Christ*, or many other lives in the way it ver-nacularizes the Gospels. It is not, however, merely eccentric or popularizing. It should be seen as healthy evidence of the formal and functional diversity of the Middle English life of Christ. Although it may use popular idiom it is far from being without high seriousness, and far, too, from being unscholarly: Elizabeth Salter noted how accurately the words of Jesus and the Jews are translated, and how closely the Gospel account is followed — to the point of the work being

---

[92] *Passion of Our Lord*, in *An Old English Miscellany*, ed. by Morris, ll. 101–05. Translation mine.

[93] *Passion of Our Lord*, in *An Old English Miscellany*, ed. by Morris, l. 114.

classifiable as a genuine Gospel harmony.[94] The *Passion of Our Lord*, then, is not a text that takes its chivalric or Christological liberties and obligations lightly. With its own affective design on its audience, it translates and 'spiritually re-honours' the *chanson de geste* and its complex generic values tactfully in order to make a freshly intuitive and richly serious *expositio sententiae* of the Gospels. The *Passion of Our Lord*, then, is morally, spiritually, and artistically, a substantial work worthy of consideration alongside the more palpably learned and prestigious vernacular *vitae Christi*.

Compilers and Compiling

Many translators of Middle English lives of Christ were compilers. The ubiquitous, utilitarian, and flexible medieval literary genre of *compilatio* was concerned essentially with the accessible presentation of authoritative materials according to the needs of the users of the book. Though he must not corrupt his materials the compiler nevertheless exercised the right to choose, exclude, re-order, expand, condense, repeat, highlight, juxtapose, and contradistinguish *materia* as he saw fit.[95]

Translator-compilers were, like anyone else treating biblical and theological materials, affected by developments in habits of exegesis in the thirteenth and fourteenth centuries. At this time commentary-tradition, as exemplified by the works of such schoolmen as Albert the Great, Thomas Aquinas, and Nicholas of Lyra, increasingly emphasized the literal sense of the human authors of Holy Scripture as it developed throughout the whole work. Authorial intention and argument became more palpably the criteria of appraisal.[96] Works were therefore assessed as being constructed of discernibly and deliberately organized parts. Compilers were therefore permitted to re-arrange parts of authoritative works and combine them with the materials of other writers when the context allowed or required. They therefore worked by selecting materials, dividing them (*divisio*), and re-arranging them in a justifiable order (*ordinatio*) with a particular utility.[97] Such *divisiones* and *ordinationes*, as in the case of Love's *Mirror*, were perhaps made more manifest by the use of tables, running titles at

[94] Salter, *Nicholas Love's 'Myrrour of the Blessed Lyf of Jesu Christ'*, p. 75.

[95] See in general Parkes, 'The Influence of the Concepts of *Ordinatio* and *Compilatio*', and Minnis, *Medieval Theory of Authorship*, pp. 191–210.

[96] Minnis, *Medieval Theory of Authorship*, pp. 73–74.

[97] Parkes, 'The Influence of the Concepts of *Ordinatio* and *Compilatio*', pp. 127–131.

the tops of pages, underlining, colour, marginal annotation, paraph marks, and
other features of scholarly textual organization.

The tradition of 'translation as compilation', though profoundly shaped by
the ways of academe, is quite often rather informal when it draws on learned
theory. It tends frequently to be idiomatic and indirect, even when it clearly and
knowingly accommodates key theoretical categories. Such a spirit informs the
earliest fourteenth-century translation of the Passion-section of the Pseudo-
Bonaventuran *Meditationes vitae Christi*, the *Meditations on the Supper of our
Lord, and the Hours of the Passion*, a work in which there is considerable con-
densation, cutting, expansion, and abridgement. At the beginning of his work
the translator refers to his effort as a compilation that shall move, teach, and
save his unlearned 'congregacyun' through meditation on the Passion:

> For þou shalt chaunge þy chere a none,
> Or elles þyn herte ys harder þan stone.
> Y wyl þe lere [*I will teach you*] a medytacyun
> Compyled of crystys passyun;
> And of hys modyr, þat ys dere,
> What peynes þey suffred þou mayst lere.
> Take hede, for y wyl no þyng seye
> But þat ys preued [*proved*] by crystes feye [*faith*],
> By holy wryt, or seyntes sermons,
> Or by dyuers holy opynyons.
> Whan þou þenkest þys yn þy þoȝt
> Thyr may no fende noye þe with noȝt [*No fiend may harm you with anything*].[98]

The translator takes care here to accommodate, in concisely idiomatic fashion,
key categories from the scholastic prologue, pointing out that the *modus agendi*
of the work is compilatory, cheer-changingly affective, and meditative; that its
materia concerns Jesus's and Mary's sufferings, and that its *intentio/utilitas* is
to edify the soul and fend off fiends.[99] He also makes it clear, as a conscientious
compiler, that, by founding his work on the Bible and orthodox interpretation,
he is not at odds with authority.

Many of the great and standard medieval works were also great compila-
tions. Alongside a plethora of reference works, preachers' manuals, and col-
lections of *distinctiones* there were texts like the *Historia scholastica* of Peter
Comestor (sacred history), Ranulf Higden's *Polychronicon* and Bartholomew's

---

[98] *Meditations on the Supper of Our Lord*, ed. by Cowper, ll. 4, 13–22.

[99] Allen, 'The *Manuel des Pechiez* and the Scholastic Prologue'.

De proprietatibus rerum, the *Speculum maius* of Vincent of Beauvais (encyclo-
paedia), the *Catholicon* of Joannes Januensis (dictionary), the *Legenda aurea* of
Jacobus a Voragine (collection of holy lives), and, of course, Gospel harmonies.
Lives of Christ were necessarily in their turn re-ordered, reorganized compila-
tions too: they combined four distinct but equally authoritative Gospels.[100] The
late-fourteenth century translator of *Oon of Foure*, a rendering of the *Unum ex
quattuor* of Clement of Llanthony, engages with a tradition of Gospel harmony
numbering, among others, St Augustine's 'boc of acording of þe four gospel-
eis' (*De consensu evangelistarum*). It indicates the desirability of making one
of four, 'for not alle gospeleres seyn alle þingis, & þo þingis which þei seyn
þei seyn not alle þingis bi kindeli ordre in her place'.[101] 'Kindeli ordre' is 'ordo
naturalis', the actual historical sequence of events. This was distinguished from
'ordo artificialis', an artificial order of narration, which may at times be more to
a writer's purposes. Not all Gospel events were recorded in each Gospel; therefore Christians needed to be shown how they could be harmonized from the
different accounts, not only for copiousness of knowledge but also as a demonstration of the real harmony existing between all four evangelists.

The preoccupations of *Oon of Foure* are also to be found in Chaucer's prologue to the *Tale of Melibee*, as a precedent for his own literary practice as a
compiler and translator — a telling sign that the exemplarity of Gospel harmony had penetrated deep into secular territory in becoming a licence for textual variation:

> 'Gladly', quod I, 'by Goddes sweete pyne!
> I wol yow telle a litel thyng in prose
> That oghte liken yow, as I suppose,
> Or elles, certes, ye been to daungerous [*hard to please*].
> It is a moral tale vertuous,
> Al be it told somtyme in sondry wyse
> Of sondry folk, as I shal yow devyse.
>   'As thus: ye woot that every Evaungelist
> That telleth us the peyne of Jhesu Crist
> Ne seith nat alle thyng as his felawe dooth;
> But nathelees hir sentence is al sooth,
> And alle acorden as in hire sentence,
> Al be ther in hir tellyng difference.
> For somme of hem seyn moore, and somme seyn lesse,

---

[100] See *The Ormulum*, ed. by Holt, I: 'Icc hafe sammnedd o þiss boc | Þa Goddspelless neh
alle' (Dedication, ll. 29–30).

[101] Quoted in Salter, *Nicholas Love's 'Myrrour of the Blessed Lyf of Jesu Christ'*, pp. 76–77.

> Whan they his pitous passioun expresse —
> I meene of Mark, Mathew, Luc, and John —
> But doutelees hir sentence is al oon'.[102]

The accounts of the four evangelists differ because some say more and some say less. However, there is no contradiction among them. Their meaning is all one. The Gospels were conceived of as complementary, each evangelist performing a necessary task contributing to a satisfactory whole. They provided the most prestigious example possible to Chaucer — and to makers of lives of Christ — of the feasibility and desirability of treating a weighty subject or text legitimately in different ways.

St Augustine was one of the most authoritative of the many commentators on the harmony of the Gospels, upon which there was an extensive literature, including his own *De consensu evangelistarum*, as cited by the English translator of Clement of Llanthony.[103] In Book I, Chapter II, section iv, Augustine gives a forceful and lucid assessment of the relative roles and harmony of the evangelists;

> Et quamvis singuli suum quemdam narrandi ordinem tenuisse videantur, non tamen unusquisque eorum velut alterius praecedentis ignarus voluisse scribere reperitur, vel ignorata praetermisisse quae scripsisse alius invenitur; sed sicut unicuique inspiratum est, non superfluam cooperationem sui laboris adjunxit.

> And however they may appear to have kept each of them a certain order of narration proper to himself, this certainly is not to be taken as if each individual writer chose to write in ignorance of what his predecessor had done, or left out as matters about which there was no information things which another nevertheless is discovered to have recorded. But the fact is, that just as they received each of them the gift of inspiration, they abstained from adding to their several labours any superfluous conjoint compositions.[104]

Or, as the *Speculum devotorum* pithily puts it in invoking Gospel harmony to justify his own addition to the genre, 'that one leuyth anothyr supplyeth' ('that which one leaves another supplies').[105]

---

[102] *Canterbury Tales*, in *The Riverside Chaucer*, gen. ed. by Benson, VII, 936–52. See also The discussion of this text in Minnis, *Medieval Theory of Authorship*, p. 167.

[103] See the English translation in *The Works of Aurelius Augustine, Bishop of Hippo*, ed. by Dods, VIII: *The Sermon on the Mount. The Harmony of the Evangelists*, trans. by William Findlay and S. D. F. Salmond (1873), pp. 133–504.

[104] See Augustine, *De consensu evangelistarum*, bk I, ch. II. 4, col. 1044, and Augustine, *The Harmony of the Evangelists*, ed. by Dods, trans. by Findlay and Salmond, pp. 141–42.

[105] *Speculum devotorum*, ed. by Hogg, p. 4.

No one evangelist, then, offers a final and comprehensive treatment of the life of Jesus, yet each Gospel is worthy and necessary. Similarly, each rendering of the life of Christ compiled in English was regarded as profitable, but did not claim to be the final treatment. Each Middle English life was limited to, and justified by, its particular intention and structural distinctiveness. For example, the translation of *Unum ex quattuor* is intended specifically to show the harmony of the four Gospels' narratives; Nicholas Love's *Mirror* is a devout series of meditations on the humanity of Christ which is intended to stir the devotion of *simple soules*. It is divided into sections for the days of the week, and can also be used according to the times of the Church year. *The Miroure of Mans Saluacioune* emphasizes, through typological exposition, the life of Christ as a fulfilment of the Old Testament.[106] *The Early Version of the Northern Homily Collection* is designed to provide unlearned English people with an understanding of the Sunday Gospels.[107] The *Stanzaic Life* is, likewise, structured according to the Church year. The *Meditations on the Supper of our Lord, and the Hours of the Passion* takes account of the canonical hours.[108] The *Speculum devotorum* has thirty-three chapters to the worship of the thirty-three years of Christ's life on earth.[109]

Though a compiler may not assert, he is permitted to alter the structure of his sources: such alteration may have a profound effect on the original and present considerable creative opportunities. Change is normally effected, however, in order to re-orientate the work for another audience, often one of lesser sophistication than that of the original. A good example of such re-orientation of structure is *The Seven Poyntes of Trewe Loue and Euerlastynge Wysedame*, an English reworking of the *Orologium sapientiae* of Henry Suso, a devotional treatise on the wisdom, love and Passion of Jesus.[110] Suso's two books and twenty-four chapters are compiled into seven chapters, or 'poyntes' (as set out in a table of *capitula* at the beginning of the work) with much abridgement, conflation, and cutting out of repetition. The new compilation is written for

---

[106] Salter, *Nicholas Love's 'Myrrour of the Blessed Lyf of Jesu Christ'*, pp. 62–63, 96–97. For editions of this work, see *The Mirour of Mans Saluacioun[e]*, ed. by Henry, and *Miroure of Mans Saluacionne*, ed. by Huth.

[107] *English Metrical Homilies from Manuscripts of the Fourteenth Century*, ed. by Small, pp. 4–5; Salter, *Nicholas Love's 'Myrrour of the Blessed Lyf of Jesu Christ*, pp. 81–84.

[108] For this work, see *Meditations on the Supper of Our Lord*, ed. by Cowper.

[109] *Speculum devotorum*, ed. by Hogg, p. 1.

[110] '*Orologium Sapientiae*', ed. by Horstmann.

a devout woman; there have been cuts to *clergiale* material, and preservation only of the matters which will edify the intended readership. There is to be no redundant rendering:

> Butte for als miche as in þe forseyde boke þere beþ manye maters and long processe towchynge [*discourse concerning*] him þat wrote hit and oþere religiose persones of his degre, þe whiche, as hit semeþ to me, were lytel edificacione to wryte to ȝowe, my dere ladye, 7 to oþere deuowte persones þat desyrene þis drawynge owt in eng-lische: þere-fore I leve seche [*such*] materes 7 take onelye þat me þinkeþ edifiyng to ȝowe.[111]

The new symbolic but thematically functional *ordinatio* of the Seven Gifts of the Holy Ghost is declared. The compiler has exercised his freedom to change it according to his *entent*:

> I folownot [*sic*] þe processe of þat boke [*I do not follow the sequence of that book*] in ordere, but I take þe materes in-sindrye [*individually*], as þei acordene to mye pur-pos [...] ¶ And þus, considerynge alle þe processe of þe forseyde boke [...] after mye symple vnderstandyng hit may be comprehendet as in effecte in to VII poyntes þat longene [*pertain*] to þe trewe loue of owre lorde Jhesu, aftere þe VII ȝifftees [*gifts*] of þe holye goste.[112]

This new *ordinatio*, although it occurs at the level of *forma tractatus*, manifests an expository decision. 'Materes', however closely translated, now take their context and meaning from those Seven Gifts. This does not mean to say that the *sentence* of the original is in any way being undermined. The compilers' *manere* is, on the contrary, informed by respect for the original and a desire to release its potential in a new milieu, and his *modus exerptoris* (that is, the compilatory mode of the excerptor) is at one with that of faithful translation in wishing to communicate what is most useful for the target audience.[113] Similar situational flexibility in the application of *ordinatio* is shown in the rescheduling of parts of Love's *Mirror* in Longleat House MS 14. In this codex is evidence that Love's readers (or those who supervised them) devised a Lenten reading plan consist-ing of a sequence of passages suited to the devotional season.[114]

---

[111] 'Orologium Sapientiae', ed. by Horstmann, p. 325.

[112] 'Orologium Sapientiae', ed. by Horstmann, p. 325.

[113] For discussion of the *modus excerptoris*, see Minnis, *Medieval Theory of Authorship*, p. 192.

[114] See the introduction to Nicholas Love, *Mirror*, ed. by Sargent, p. 133. See also the codi-cological work on this by Ryan Perry (to whom I am grateful for details of this manuscript feature), on the Queen's University Belfast-University of St Andrews Arts and Humanities

Sertayn Þyngus of Ihesu Criste on a Rowe:
The Encyclopedic Stanzaic Life of Christ

The late fourteenth-century *Stanzaic Life of Christ* is a life for all seasons. A didactic and scholarly work, it was probably compiled into English at St Werburgh's Abbey, Chester.[115] In this text of over 10,000 lines, *auctores* are cited, and materials and themes clearly divided, subdivided, and often enumerated — all under the organizing principle of the *vita* as articulated through the cycle of the Church year.

The prologue to the *Stanzaic Life* shows what the writer thinks he is doing as a preacher, compiler, commentator, and translator, and how and why. As a 'loosened' academic prologue, written with vigour and ease, it conforms to the priorities of its Latin forebear without rehearsing the standard latinate terminology. That another Middle English prologue, in its own particular way and for its own particular ends, is so fluently idiomatic as a variation of the type, is further evidence of the flexible 'naturalization' of this highly portable cultural form.

The prologue opens with a preacher's confidence in gaining grace from Christ Himself for making this book:

> He ȝeue [*gave*] me grace sumwhat to say
> To botene [*cure*] hem [*them*] þat ben to blynde
> Here lyfe to rule in good aray,
> Thorwe lore þat I in þis boke fynde. (ll. 5–8)

'He ȝeue me grace sumwhat to say' indicates that this particular clerk believes that his instrumentality is licensed and guided by God's grace, and that his free will is accordingly upraised. He claims that he is authorized to select and communicate that which will 'botene', that is, 'cure': such is the *utilitas* of the book. By translating he is not reporting the mere words in English form. Rather, his *officium* is to choose, evaluate, import, and expound the *sentence*, the 'lore þat I in þis boke fynde'. However, such finding is not the ultimate *intentio* of the work, for its readers, on apprehending the 'lore', are expected subsequently to rule their lives 'in good aray'. Reader response is reader responsibility. Just as a translator needs a good intention and moral worthiness on his own part, so too

Research Council's *Geographies of Orthodoxy* project website.

[115] See the introduction to *A Stanzaic Life of Christ*, ed. by Foster, p. xiv. Line numbers of this work will from now be inserted after quotations in the main text. Some of the following discussion draws passim on Johnson, 'Prologue and Practice: Middle English lives of Christ', pp. 83–85.

does the intended ideal (but real-life) reader, the so-called 'worthy wyght' who asked for the translation to be made:

> A worthy wyght wylned at me [*a worthy individual desired of me*]
> Sertayn þyngus for to showe,
> Þat in Latyn wrytun saw he,
> In Englissh tonge, for to knowe
>
> Of Ihesu Cristes Natiuite
> And his werkus on a rowe,
> To the whiche by good Auctorite
> He myghte triste [*trust*] 7 fully knowe. (ll. 9–16)

The translator has been requested by this worthy layman to 'showe', that is, 'expound'/'clarify'/'demonstrate' in English, 'Sertayn þyngus' that he has seen written in Latin, so that he will be able thereby to know about Christ's 'werkus on a rowe' according to the divinely sanctioned, exegetically harmonized order of the *vita* and the Church Year. 'Auctorite' is the means by which he might 'triste' and 'fully knowe'; it has the double power of being trustworthy and true, as the meeting point of obedient faith and absolute knowledge.

The translator describes his *modus agendi* (*manere*):

> And myne Aucteres fully rehersynge,
> On the whiche I founde my lessoun. (ll. 19–20)

The 'Aucteres' who are the sources of this work, and who adjudicate the meaning of Christ's life, are to be fully rehearsed. Such is necessary to 'lessoun', the interpretative reading of 'Aucteres' and of their teaching. This statement advertises the decorum of the compiler-commentator at work. 'Aucteres' are necessary, not only for the purposes of writing truly and safely — they also demand a priori to be communicated, translated, known, believed, and acted upon. Just as the translator's 'lessoun' is founded on such 'rehersynge', so should all readers in their turn exercise their minds and their faith, and take heed of the content. As a true *compilatio* this text demands the diligent exercise of *lectoris arbitrium*:

> Ther-fore þat redeþ here wyth-ynne,
> Rewarde [*consider/regard*] þe mater of euery resoun,
> And trewe wyttenesse, as haue I wynne,
> Writen he shal fynde redy boun [*at hand*]. (ll. 21–24)

It is vital that the reader considers 'þe mater of euery resoun', that is, the subject matter of every argument or case; for a 'resoun' is not simply a leaden fact. The *Stanzaic Life* is a thinking layman's encyclopaedic life of Christ — a compendious compilation of highly ordered and subdivided explications and Christological, ecclesiological knowledge scheduled to the life-shaping *ordinatio* of the Church year. It demands to be thoughtfully absorbed, and its rationales and ordering of knowledge understood soundly. Each of the divisions and subdivisions of which this *vita* is made is presented as one in a series of ordered reasons, points, modes, or justifications. Rendered into the native tongue and duly expounded, each part is accordingly safeguarded by being labelled and sourced in 'Aucteres', with 'wyttenesse names wryten þere-on' (l. 28).

Drawing mainly on the *Legenda aurea* and Higden's *Polychronicon* — and therefore also on the army of *auctores* cited within these sources — the *Stanzaic Life* is a variation on Aquinas's catchphrase *sapientis est ordinare*. Each well-shepherded section and subsection is accorded a Latin header or cue. These coordinate and highlight all the controlling divisions and connective tissues of *materia*. It is fitting and academically reassuring that these are consistently and meticulously rehearsed by the compiler in the dignity of the learned tongue, and not just put into contemporary English, especially as so many of them constitute individual *auctoritates* in their own right. The *Stanzaic Life*'s use of Latin provides visual evidence of sound *ordinatio*, trustworthy subsequent translating, and proper use of commentary-materials. It allows and encourages the poet to render an idiomatic version with the Latin as a safety-net. This translator looks two ways at once at his double audience of clerks ('lettert men') and laity ('lewet men'), accommodating, dividing, ruling, and deferring to both text and audience, and catering for learned and unlearned:

> that I in Latyn thenke to say,
> for lettert men that sitten by
> to conferme this in gode faye. (ll. 3466–68)

> In Latyn as I shal specify,
> And after in Englisch more verray
> for lewet men that her ben by. (ll. 7150–52)

Though strongly and selfconsciously rooted in 'Aucteres' and 'Auctorite', the *Stanzaic Life* does not lose itself in receding into Latin materials. On the contrary, the Latin legitimizes and strengthens the English text. Indeed, it would be true to say that just as the Latin of the *Stanzaic Life* is *in-eched* (that is, inserted) into the Middle English text, so from another angle it also seems that the Middle English is *in-eched* into the Latin. This is a symptom of Latin-English and lay-clerical mutuality rather than rupture, competition, or displacement.

The invincible energy and stamina with which the translator-compiler of this *vita Christi* presses on with his labour of rendering, ordering, and dividing is exhausting to behold. For example, in the Nativity section (ll. 701–1128), we are told that what is to be noted is that Christ's Nativity was miraculously done, multiply shown, and usefully exhibited. No sooner does the first of these divisions of materials get going than it subdivides itself into the five signs that show us that Mary was indeed a virgin, these being: Isaiah's prophecy (ll. 729–32); Aaron's rod (ll. 733–44) and Ezechiel's vision of Heaven's gate (ll. 745–56); Mary's marriage to Joseph (ll. 757–64); the drying-up of the prying hand of the midwife who wanted to test Mary's maidenhood (ll. 765–80); and, fifthly, the catch-all category of many other miracles — such as temples and images falling down (ll. 781–88). The second division of 'miraculous showing' enumerates the different combinations of old, new, and eternal (ll. 797–824), and the uniting of all kinds of opposites — God, man, mother, maid, human heart, and true faith — that are significant to Christ's being born (ll. 825–40). The third division of 'miraculous showing' (ll. 841–72) rehearses the different ways by which humans have been engendered — ending with Christ's birth of woman without man. And it goes on. The whole performance is like this.

If anyone were to search this piously divisive and excursive *vita Christi* for the Passion of Our Lord, then s/he would seek without finding — most notably in the Passion section itself. This work is not like other 'narrative' lives. Instead, it tells us that Christ's Passion was characterized by a trio of bitterness, scorning, and needfulness/fruitfulness. Each feature of this triad enjoys further subdivisions.Within the same Passion section there are also lively digressive biographies of Pontius Pilate (ll. 6433–6816) and Judas Iscariot (ll. 6817–7052). There is, then, not much affective content in this work, although emotive spirituality is not wholly absent: there are, for example, compassionate addresses written by St Bernard — one to Christ (ll. 5897–5904) and another in the voice of Christ to man (ll. 5930–48).

The demonstrably rationalizing apportionment of knowledge and the repeated declaration of reasons for divisions of *ordinatio*, then, encourage and require the reader/hearer of the *Stanzaic Life* to think obediently and attentively through the *materia* according to its divisions, orders, and joins. This text answers questions that the reader does, and does not, know that s/he wishes to ask. It also teaches that the lore of Christ is that which is contained and controlled by this very text's overarching institutional and divine design. The *ordinatio* in itself signals authority, wisdom, and comprehensiveness. This work's encyclopaedic appropriation and ordered control of schematized knowledge (though it is no *Speculum maius*, by a long way) — be it historical, natural, mythological, geographical, physiological, mathematical, cosmological, or whatever — constitute a self-proving vehicle of truth that elucidates the meaning of human life and dynamically taxnomizes its solving Christology. Christ is thus formatted through the discourses and structures of human knowledge, and human knowledge is reciprocally formatted through Christ. The modern editorial *nomen libri* of this work is the *Stanzaic Life of Christ*, but inasmuch as it consists of the ordered lore of Christ, perhaps it might better be called *Sertayn þyngus of Ihesu Criste on a Rowe*.

Negotiating Structures and Lectoris arbitrium: Nicholas Love and the Speculum devotorum

Prologues of lives of Christ routinely explain why the structure of a translation is as it is, and what the procedures and benefits of the work are for the reader. *Compilatio* is the most reader-centred of all medieval literary genres, predicated as it is on the needs and the morally responsible free choice (*lectoris arbitrium*) of the users of the book.[116] *Compilatores* expected that diverse readers would use books differently from each other, and that any one reader might change-ably negotiate material in different ways on different occasions. Selective use, variable order, different motivations for use, and a range of reader-capabilities were the factors that a compiler, thinking about the pragmatics of reading and the vagaries of readers, would take into account in preparing his *ordinatio/forma tractatus*. He would also think about the *ordinatio* as a truth-bearing or symbolic principle of organization — be it in accord with the *temporale* and the Church year, the seven gifts of the Holy Ghost, the seven days of the week, the seven deadly sins, the thirty-three years of Christ's life, or whichever other vari-ous structures and authorized patterns of human knowledge might serve their turn on any given occasion.

Nicholas Love, in his *proheme*, gives instruction on how his book may be used according to the days of the week, and the times of the Church year. He certainly made sure, in support of this *ordinatio*, that his *Mirror* went into the world with a rich apparatus of chapter headings, running titles, table of contents, attribution of sources, use of initials to distinguish his own words from those of the *Meditationes*, and so on. The source for these instructions, however, is not the *prohemium* of the original; it is, intriguingly, right at the end of the Latin work. These instructions are more effective, and more likely to be applied, transposed, as they are by Love, to a position *before*, not after, the

---

[116] For discussion of *lectoris arbitrium* see Minnis, *Medieval Theory of Authorship*, pp. 201–02.

meditations themselves. Clearly, Love is taking up an idea from the source and applying it on his own account (as the responsible and assertive marginal 'N.' at this point in the text seems to declare) to the *ordinatio* and *forma tractatus* of his *Mirror*:

> Meditationes vero sic divide, ut die Lunae incipiens, procurras usque ad fugam Domini in Aegyptum. Et eo ibi dimisso, die Martis, pro eo rediens, mediteris usque ad apertionem libri in synagoga; die Mercurii exinde, usque in ministerium Mariae et Marthae; die Jovis abinde, usque ad passionem; die Veneris et Sabbati, usque ad resurrectionem; die vero Dominica, ipsam resurrectionem, et usque in finem; et sic per singulas hebdomodas facias, ut ipsa meditationes tibi reddas familiares.[117]

> Divide the meditations as follows:
>
> On Monday, start at the beginning (of the Lord's life), and go as far as the Lord's flight into Egypt; then stop at that point.
>
> On Tuesday, resume there, and meditate as far as his opening of the Book in the synagogue.
>
> On Wednesday, proceed from there to the ministry of Mary and Martha.
>
> On Thursday, go from there to the passion and the death.
>
> On Friday and Saturday, go as far as the resurrection.
>
> Finally, on Sunday, meditate on the resurrection itself up to the end of his earthly life.
>
> Follow this schedule every week of the year, so that you famialiarize yourself with those meditations.[118]

> And for als mich as þis boke is dyuydet & departet in vij parties, after vij dayes of þe wike, euery day on partie or sume þerof to be hade in contemplacion of hem þat hauen þerto desire & deuocion: þerefore at þe Moneday as þe first werke day of þe wike, bygynneþ þis gostly werke, tellyng first of þe deuoute instance & desire of þe holy angeles in heuen for mans restoryng, and his sauacion, to stire man amongis oþer þat day specialy to wyrshipe hem, as holy chirch þe same day makeþ speciale mynde of hem. Also not onelych [*only*] þe matire of þis boke is pertynent & profitable to be hade in contemplacion þe forseide dayes, to hem þat wolen & mowen [*wish it and are may do so*]: bot also as it longeþ to þe tymes of þe ȝere, as in aduent to rede & deuoutly haue in mynde fro þe bigynnyng in to þe Natiuite of oure lorde Jesu, & þere of after in þat holy feste of Cristenmesse, & so forþ of oþer matires as holy chirch makeþ mynde of hem in tyme of þe ȝere.[119]

[117] *Meditationes vitae Christi*, ed. by Peltier, p. 629.

[118] John de Caulibus, *Meditations on the Life of Christ*, trans. by Taney, Miller, and Stallings-Taney, p. 332.

[119] Nicholas Love, *Mirror*, ed. by Sargent, p. 13.

Love's reader might, or more likely might not, be able, in practical terms, to digest the whole book in a single week. If not, it might be possible to read or hear one chapter, or some portion thereof, on a designated weekday in accordance with the *ordinatio* taken up by Love from the Latin. This would maintain a disciplined rhythm, tracing, however incompletely or intermittently, the whole trajectory of Christ's life in manageable weekly cycles, and would keep the *affecciouns* of the reader better in touch with the complete life and thus the whole humanity of His Person, culminating with the Passion and Resurrection. Alternatively, and with the same selectivity, the cycle of the Church year could also be used flexibly to schedule the reading or hearing experience. The reader could also switch between the two schemes, and it is even recommended at the end of the *Mirror* that s/he can 'take þe partes þerof as it semeþ moste confortable and stiryng to his deuocion, sumtyme one & sumtyme an oþere'.[120] All such *ordinationes* are a matter of free reader choice (*lectoris arbitrium*) and responsibility. It is fitting that a Latin instruction signalling flexibility of *ordinatio* should itself become, through being translated, an example of the same in textual action. This literary act of Love's is another species of translation — instantiated in another empowering and fruitful meeting of the roles of the translator and compiler.

In company with the *Mirror*, the *Speculum devotorum* makes considerable deliberations in its prologue about its *ordinatio*. In particular, it discusses the table of chapter headings, that it, like the *Mirror*, deploys at the beginning of the book, or, more accurately in this case, just before the narrative but after the prologue; for the compiler of the *Speculum devotorum* refers his reader forward to the 'tabyl', where can be seen the full *ordinatio* of the life and Passion. Presumably, at this point, a reader might well thumb forward to the table and see immediately the scope and nature of the work. Whether or not the 'gostly syster' did this, the compiler intends her to read the 'tabyl', because he puts it between the *prefacyon* and the start of the first chapter. He evidently meant it to be used frequently as an integral part of the work, which has thirty-three chapters to honour the thirty-three years of Christ's life:

> For I haue dyvydyd the boke folowynge in thre & thyrty chapetelys to the worschype of the thre and thyrty ȝere that oure sauyoure lyuyde in erthe; & I haue sette þe tytyllys of hem alle in a tabyl aftyr thys prefacyon afore the boke that hosoeuere [*whosoever*] lykyth to rede hyt maye see schortly there alle the matere [that is, *materia*] of the boke folowynge & rede where hym lykyth best, & that he mygthte þe

---

[120] Nicholas Love, *Mirror*, ed. by Sargent, p. 220.

sonnyr [*sooner*] fynde that he desyryth moste, & the bettyr kepe hyt in mynde, &
also redylokyr [*more readily*] fynde hyt yf hym lyste to see hyt aȝen; notwythstondynge hyt were best hoso mygth haue tyme and laysyr [*leisure*] therto, to rede hyt
alle as hyt ys sette.[121]

This is not just a description of the *forma tractatus*, or *divisio*. This passage instructs on use: this 'tabyl' will help the reader to preview, choose, and
return to materials; it will also assist the memorial absorption and retention of
'matere'. The intention behind each 'tytyll' to reveal 'alle the matere of the boke'
harmonizes with the *Catholicon*'s definition of *capitula*, which 'breviter capiant
et contineant aliquam sententiam' ('they briefly capture and contain a measure
of the *sententia*'): each heading contains in short some worthwhile teaching to
found in each chapter.[122] The 'tabyl' has the further function of providing the
reader with an abbreviated 'at-a-glance' version of the whole book, as well as
compressed versions of individual chapters. These could also act as preparatory
prompts to future reading. As such, the 'tabyl' can 'stand in' for fuller *matere*,
as is also the case in Love's *Mirror* and the *Miroure of Mans Saluacioune*.[123]
Furthermore, the 'tytyllys' may have enough mnemonic power to re-invigor-
ate old experience, which in reality cannot exclude other experience of other
vitae Christi or of the tradition of Passion meditation beyond the *Speculum
devotorum*. Such complementary experience is in no way at odds with what the
compiler intended, for he himself recognizes the harmonic intertextual diversity of treatments of the life of Christ, which are meant to be inter-related, not
kept apart — or seen as vying with each other.

The 'tabyl', a common feature of the literary genre of *compilatio*, invaluably
enhances the usability of this work and, most importantly, reader-choice, 'that
he mygthte þe sonnyr fynde that he desyryth moste'. The word 'desyryth' is particularly suitable because it invokes the language of devotional stirring. Also,
the book is not made for one reading but for multiple re-use, 'yf hym lyste to
see hyt aȝen'. It is indicative of the compiler's respect for, and expectations of,
lectoris arbitrium, that he deals first with the matter of reader-choice, and only
afterwards appends a consideration of those who might read all the book *in
ordine naturali*: 'notwythstondynge hyt were best hoso mygth haue tyme and

---

[121] *Speculum devotorum*, ed. by Hogg, pp. 1–2.

[122] Joannes Januensis, *Catholicon*, s.v. *capitulum*, unfol.

[123] Nicholas Love, *Mirror*, ed. by Sargent, pp. 3–6; and see the *Miroure of Mans Saluacionne*,
ed. by Huth, ll. 10–13, where the translator tells us that he has listed the chapters in his proem,
so that the reader may, in effect, bear the whole book away.

laysyr therto, to rede hyt alle as hyt ys sette'. In any case, both methods of reading (as with Love's double scheme) are commendable.

Moreover, the thirty-threefold 'tabyl' glorifies Christ each time it is consulted, be it in part or whole. Each single 'chapytyll', as one thirty-third, witnesses to the whole life in a way that a sevenfold division into days of the week (as in the Passion narratives and the *Meditationes vitae Christi* and the *Mirror*) does not. Moreover, though there is a certain comprehensiveness in the treatment of Christ's life in works such as the *Legenda aurea* and the *Stanzaic Life of Christ*, each individual *divisio* in these works does not in itself reflect the wholeness of the *vita* with the same rhetoric of number invoked by the *Speculum devotorum*. One wonders if the monk of Sheen was seeking to complement or overgo Bonaventure and Love and the 'festal' lives through an enhanced *ordinatio* drawing on the primariness of the life itself rather than the secondariness of the constructed forms and cycles of Holy Church.

It is also tempting to conjecture, all the usual caveats about numerological over-interpretation notwithstanding, that there may be a connection between this *ordinatio* and the threes and ones at the heart of the instruction at the end of the *prefacyon*, an instruction to pray at the beginning, middle, and end of the life, thereby enhancing the work's simultaneous divisibility and its unity by two threes (that is, thirty-three?), three Paternosters and three Aves, and a one (a Creed). The main caveat here is that, even though it is credible that a medieval reader may choose to read some or all of this into the text, the compiler does not make such an intention clear, for he chooses to highlight the betokening of the Holy Trinity, Mary, the Saints, and his own sins:

> ¶ Also I haue prayde ȝow in the fyrste chapetele of the boke folowynge and by ȝow or eny othyr devout seruaunt of god that maye aftyrwarde be the grace of god rede the boke folowynge to seye thre Pater noster, thre Aueys, & a crede to þe worschype of the holy trynytee the whyche ys oo verry god, of oure lady, & of alle þe seyintys & for goode grace þat ys necessarye in redynge of the sympyl medytacyonys folowynge, & also for the forȝeuenesse of the synnys of the fyrste wrytare of hem, & the same prayere I haue askyd aȝen abowte the myddyl afore the passyon, & also in the laste ende in betokenynge þat the holy trynytee ys the begynnynge, the mydyl, & the ende, of alle goode werkys, to whom be alle worschype ioye & preysynge now & wythoute endynge, Amen.[124]

These three prayers seemingly apply an equal valorization to the Passion and the whole life, from beginning to end. Yet at the same time, in that the Passion

---

[124] *Speculum devotorum*, ed. by Hogg, pp. 10–11.

is the only individual part of the life specified, it is also, rather paradoxically, singled out against and above the rest of the *vita*.

Though this book is designed to give the reader maximum flexibility, the writer expects of his readership what he expects of himself, a pure intention and genuine diligence:

> ¶ Also the medytacyonys folowynge be not to be red negligently, & wyth hasty-nesse but dylygently & wyth a goode avysement [*consideration*] that þe redare maye haue þe more profyte therof, for hyt ys bettyr to rede oo [*one*] chapetele dylygently & wyth a goode delyberacyon thanne thre wyth negligence & hastynesse, for ȝe schul not consydere how myche ȝe rede, but how wel.[125]

If the reading is inattentive or over-hasty, then it will be without 'profyte', that is, without *utilitas*. A 'goode delyberacyon' is vital for a meditative text which makes considerable demands on the concentration and, particularly, on the sensory and reasoning functions of the imagination. Degree of frequency and of diligence of reading are paramount: 'the oftyr and dylygentlokyr he lokyth therinne [*the more often and more diligently he looks therein*], the more grace schal he fynde': the more, the better.[126] It is up to the reader 'how wel' she does. The compiler thus includes a notion of variable degree of *utilitas* in his *prefa-cyon* — different potentials and value for different episodes of behaviour.

Conclusion

This chapter has discussed how, in some intriguing instances, which are often of wider significance, medieval literary theory goes native and 'middlebrow' in what translators say and do in a range of Middle English lives of Christ. We have seen how some lives variously exploit the discourse of the academic prologue and utilize the clerkly literary roles of commentator, compiler, and preacher in their functionally diverse approaches to translating. We have also seen a remarkable variety of relations between what theory-influenced pro-logues say and what translators actually do with their sources, be they the Gospels, or learned commentaries, or earlier Middle English texts — from literalistic Englishing and the unpacking of the intended literal sense of the source(s) through to elaboration of the *sententia*. We have also seen some of the different tactics translators use to influence the reception of their works and the

---

[125] *Speculum devotorum*, ed. by Hogg, pp. 8–9.

[126] *Speculum devotorum*, ed. by Hogg, p. 7.

behaviour of their readers. And, it must also be said, in all these activities the complex and co-operative mutuality of Latin and English has repeatedly been seen to be productively at work at the cultural as well as at the textual level.

Consequently, the rather misleading and distracting modern conception of translation as displacement/competition/rupture looks restrictive and not too robust. Translations can be sites of juncture and collaboration rather than fissure — especially when a translator is clearly on home territory both in Latin and the vernacular. The idea also, that theoretical terms are positively stripped of their previous latinate affiliations by being brought into English textual culture clearly does not go very far when there is clear continuity and little or no antagonism between Latin and English.

That Latin or technically latinate terms become naturalized idiom and start to look different from how they originally looked is not necessarily a marker of discontinuity either: this apparent difference can go hand-in-hand with ideological connectedness and portability. This should be no surprise, given that idiomatic negotiation of literary-theoretical categories was also carried out in Latin itself. The notion that the vernacular had an agenda of evading 'colonial' Latinity, in any case, finds little support, then, in the ways in which our translators were at home with Latin and English languages, texts, and readers: this is merely a function of them being at home with themselves and their own redistributive capabilities.

The texts highlighted for particular attention in this chapter are not merely witnesses for a vernacular theoretical literary sensibility: they are all worthy of attention in their own right. Orm, then, is more theoretically aware and interesting than hitherto thought (indeed, the same goes for most other writers discussed in this chapter); moreover, he is capable of being an intelligent and resourceful translator. Nicholas Love and the maker of the *Speculum devotorum* are deft commentator-translators and negotiators of *ordinatio* — as is the maker of the *Stanzaic Life of Christ*. And the translator of the racy Gospel harmony known as the *Passion of Our Lord* turns out also to be inventively nimble in repurposing the discourse of the *chanson de geste* in order to communicate intuitively apprehensible matter of moral and spiritual necessity.

The next chapter, on Nicholas Love, focuses on a work that has in modern times been condemned for keeping readers from enjoying the fruits of Scripture, and for stopping the layperson from ascending to contemplation. It has also been accused of being the oppressive tool of an Arundelian clerical Latinity that would dumb down theological latitude amongst the people. These issues will be subject to some reconsideration. There is also much more to this text than polemics and politics. Love's *Mirror* may be a highly local text with a highly politicized agenda, but it is also, more broadly, not only a remarkable mainstream vernacular response to a Latin work of international importance but also a monument of English translation and crafted prose. The ways Love translates some strategically important parts of his text are particularly telling and demand critical attention, and it is to Love's translational strategies and their pragmatics that we turn now.

Translating Meditation for 'Men & Women & Euery Age & Euery Dignite of this Worlde': Nicholas Love's Sovereign *Ymaginacion*

The previous chapter considered how the terms and ideology of learned literary thought affected a range of Middle English lives of Christ (and thereby textual culture at large). It did so by investigating how and why writers adopted and adapted academically derived theory and attitudes in their own statements about the nature of their activities, and also in the details of translating that are a nuanced and pragmatic measure of such attitudes at textual work. The current chapter stays with the business of translating, this time focusing on a vitally important aspect of mainstream spiritual tradition — how to imagine and meditate on the Sacred Humanity of Christ.

When it comes to Nicholas Love, the topic of imagining the Sacred Manhood has been a fraught one. In the first chapter of this book we saw how Love has somewhat been cast as the *bête noire* of orthodoxy who prevented spiritual ascent in the laity. It would of course be folly to deny that Love was other than a conservative who believed in lay obedience to the clerics of Holy Church, and who thought that lay speculation on matters theological should go no further than the clergy's public teachings on matters of faith and doctrine. At the same time, like many in English and European mainstream devotion, he firmly encouraged contemplative ascent in those capable of it. He was also confident in the power of his *Mirror* to help all souls towards a foretaste of heaven and salvation itself: no mean ambition. Accordingly, at the very start of his work he brandishes the Apostle Paul's famous *auctoritas* from Romans 15. 4:

> all thynges þat ben written generaly in holi chirche ande specialy of oure lorde Jesu cryste þei bene wryten to oure lore [*for our instruction*] that by pacience and conforte of holi scriptures we haue hope that is to say of the Life & Blysse that is to come in anothere worlde.[1]

We shall see, in this chapter, how the fortifying discourse and theology of hope (whether it is in Love's paratext or in his inventive treatment of the Last Supper) and his emphasis on the 'ensaumple of vertues & gude liuyng' (p. 9) to be found in the life of Christ, profoundly inform his whole enterprise, right down to telling details of translation. Therefore, after looking at how Love fits into the medieval tradition of imagining the Sacred Humanity, I shall examine how he defines and sets up his project in his *proheme*. For our purposes, the most important aspects of his paratext are his co-option of *auctoritates* from the Apostle Paul and St Augustine: the line of approach and the details of the way Love translates these two signal much about his overall strategy and his understanding of what he wishes to do with the *Mirror*, and this is reflected in trajectories of nuanced change he makes to the *prohemium* of his Latin source, the *Meditationes vitae Christi*, a work believed, of course, in the Middle Ages to have been composed by St Bonaventure.[2] These changes tell us much about Love as a skilled and resourceful translator: this is of critical value in its own right. Above and beyond this, such translational changes in Love's *proheme* and elsewhere in the *Mirror* (as with the Last Supper, the *Ave Maria*, and

---

[1] Nicholas Love, *Mirror*, ed. by Sargent, p. 9. Quotations from this work will be cited within the main text of this chapter.

[2] See the *Meditationes vitae Christi*, ed. by Peltier, p. 510. This edition is used by Sargent for his edition of the *Mirror* because it is apparently closer to the version of the Latin source Love used than the text in the modern edition (John de Caulibus, *Meditaciones vitae Christi*, ed. by Stallings-Taney). The days when St Bonaventure could be called the author of this work are long gone, but the ineradicable association of the *Meditationes* with the great progenitor of Franscisan spirituality has left it with a permanent 'Pseudo-Bonaventuran' identity, despite the fact that John de Caulibus, a Franciscan of San Gimignano, has in modern times generally been credited as the author of the work, held to have been written originally by him in Latin. Recently, however, Sarah McNamer has claimed that the earliest version was in Italian, and probably made by a woman; see McNamer, 'The Origins of the *Meditationes vitae Christi*'. Peter Tóth and David Falvay have, however, challenged this and unearthed a new contender for some kind of authorial role in the genesis of this work: one James of Cortona; see Tóth and Falvay, 'New Light on the Date and Authorship of the *Meditationes vitae Christi*'. For a modern edition of the Passion section see *Meditaciones de passione Christi*, ed. by Stallings.

the Susonian prayer he chooses to close the whole operation) reconfigure the conditions for reading the book, for the relationship between Love and his readers/hearers, and for the relationship between the earthly and the divine. Individually and in co-ordination, details of translational reorientation disclose much about Love's ambitions for his work's broader cultural impact. It is through such details that we can see something significant in how he makes and manages a linguistically generated imaginative topography for the interiorities of the users of this meditative work. Too little attention has been paid by recent scholarship to this central feature of his enterprise. This chapter attempts to pay the *Mirror* a measure of such attention.

Before this, however, some basic information about this monumental work. The *Mirror of the Blessed Life of Jesus Christ* was written before 1410 by the Carthusian Prior of Mount Grace, Nicholas Love.[3] Extant in some forty-nine known manuscripts and nine early printed versions, it was one of the most successful English books of the fifteenth century.[4] There is no dissent among modern scholars as to its great popularity and prestige. In a publication of 1981 Elizabeth Salter could safely claim:

> Margaret Deanesley's statement, made in 1920, 'Love's *Myrrour* [...] had an interesting history and was probably more popular than any other single book in the fifteenth century' [...] has been substantially reaffirmed and extended by more recent research upon the *Myrrour* and related treatises.[5]

More recently, Michael Sargent has reaffirmed Deanesley's view, although one should point out the vastly greater numbers of manuscripts of the Wycliffite Bible.[6] The *Mirror* is also rightly seen as not only prime evidence for a broaden-

---

[3] The major study of the *Mirror* is still Elizabeth Salter, *Nicholas Love's 'Myrrour of the Blessed Lyf of Jesu Christ'*. Excellent contextual information on a full range of topics is to be found in the introduction to Sargent's edition. See also Ghosh, 'Nicholas Love'. See also the essays on the Carthusians and their culture in Luxford, *Studies in Carthusian Monasticism*; also Brantley, *Reading in the Wilderness*, and Cré, *Vernacular Mysticism in the Charterhouse*.

[4] See Sargent, 'Bonaventura English: A Survey of the Middle English Prose Translations', p. 153. For surveys of manuscripts and codicological discussion, see the introduction to Nicholas Love, *Mirror*, ed. by Sargent, pp. 96–158, and the Queen's University Belfast-St Andrews *Geographies of Orthodoxy* Arts and Humanities Research Council project web site <http://www.qub.ac.uk/geographies-of-orthodoxy/>.

[5] See Salter, 'The Manuscripts of Nicholas Love's *Myrrour of the Blessed Lyf of Jesu Christ* and Related Texts', p. 115.

[6] See Sargent, 'Bonaventura English: A Survey of the Middle English Prose Translations', p. 151.

ing audience for vernacular devotional prose in the later-medieval period but also a factor in developing it.[7]

As well as enjoying an enduring popularity, Love's *Mirror* had considerable prestige and authority. In many copies is included a *memorandum* which records that around 1410 the *Mirror* was licensed by Archbishop Arundel and commended and mandated for the edification of the faithful and the confutation of all false Lollards and heretics (p. 7). Thus it can be said that the *Mirror* was the 'official' Middle English life of Christ, especially given the Church's policy of frowning on the circulation of vernacular Bibles amongst the laity. As late as 1532, Thomas More, in opposing the the Bible translator William Tyndale, recommended, alongside Hilton's *Scale of Perfection*, the Middle English rendering of the *Imitation of Christ* and Love's *Mirror* as proper and profitable reading-matter for pious Christians. He advised 'redynge of suche englysshe bookes as moste may norysshe and encrease deuocyon. Of whyche kynde is Bonauenture of the lyfe of Cryste, Gerson of the folowynge of Cryste, and the deuoute contemplatyue booke of Scala perfectionis wyth suche other lyke'.[8] The *Mirror* took pride of place in English religious textual culture from the time of Arundel right up to the eve of the Reformation.

Love's work is a translation of the Pseudo-Bonaventuran *Meditationes vitae Christi*, an imaginative series of meditations following the order of Christ's life. The *Meditationes* enjoyed immense success and influence throughout Europe.[9] The editor of the medieval Irish version of this work eloquently acknowledges its massive importance:

> The *Meditationes* has been variously referred to as a Life of Christ, a biography of the Blessed Virgin, the fifth gospel, the last of the apocrypha, one of the masterpieces of Franciscan literature, a summary of medieval spirituality, a religious handbook of contemplation, a manual of Christian iconography, one of the chief sources of the mystery plays.[10]

In the view of Michael Sargent, it 'was probably the most influential as well as the most popular of early Franciscan devotional writings. Indeed, one might say that the *Meditationes* had an importance in late medieval spirituality compara-

---

[7] See Salter, *Nicholas Love's 'Myrrour of the Blessed Lyf of Jesu Christ'*, p. 16, and the introduction to Nicholas Love, *Mirror*, ed. by Sargent, pp. 75–96.

[8] Thomas More, *The Confutation of Tyndale's Answer*, ed. by Schuster and others, p. 37; also O' Connell, 'Love's *Mirrour* and the *Meditationes vitae Christi*', pp. 3, 42.

[9] See Salter, *Nicholas Love's 'Myrrour of the Blessed Lyf of Jesu Christ'*, pp. 39–46.

[10] See *Smaointe Beatha Chríost*, ed. by ó Maonaigh, English appendix, pp. 325–26.

ble to that of the *Imitation of Christ* in the *devotio moderna*.[11] It was so important that it was translated into many vernaculars including French, Italian, Swedish, Spanish, Dutch, Bavarian, Catalan, Bulgarian, Irish, and English.[12] Sarah McNamer has also recently reminded us that 'it is widely agreed that the work now known as the Pseudo-Bonaventuran *Meditationes vitae Christi* was the single most influential devotional text written in the later Middle Ages'.[13]

There are many manuscripts of the work in England containing the Latin original.[14] Also, an indication of the authority and spiritual power accorded to the work in the late medieval period is to be gained from the fact that an indulgence of forty days was granted between 1452 and 1457 by the Archbishop of York, the Bishops of Durham and Carlisle and the Suffragan Bishop of York (who was also Bishop of Philippopolis) to any person devoutly reading a single chapter of the work.[15] Apart from the success and prestige of the Latin original and of Love's version, the importance of the *Meditationes vitae Christi* in medieval English culture can be gauged through the fact that there are several extant versions of the Passion section and three lives of the Virgin and Christ, all Englished in the fourteenth century.[16]

The *Meditationes vitae Christi* consists of a series of meditations following the events from the debate of the council in heaven concerning Man's restoration right through to the sending of the Holy Ghost to the Disciples. Though it is a work containing much meditative material there is also a considerable homiletic element. As regards its first intended audience, it was written for a Poor Clare's spiritual, moral, and contemplative benefit. The tone of the work is appropriately intimate. The 'dilecta filia' is drawn closer to biblical events as if she were present or even a participant, and this is done in order to gain more efficaciously the multiple benefits of affective experience, be it moral *fruyte* from the most exemplary of exemplary lives or, for those capable of the journey, a pathway towards higher contemplation.

---

[11] See Sargent, 'Bonaventura English: A Survey of the Middle English Prose Translations', p. 148.

[12] See Salter, *Nicholas Love's 'Myrrour of the Blessed Lyf of Jesu Christ'*, pp. 44–46; Sargent, 'Bonaventura English: A Survey of the Middle English Prose Translations', pp. 148–51.

[13] McNamer, 'The Origins of the *Meditationes vitae Christi*', p. 905.

[14] Sargent, 'Bonaventura English: A Survey of the Middle English Prose Translations', pp. 149–51.

[15] Sargent, 'Bonaventura English: A Survey of the Middle English Prose Translations', p. 154.

[16] See Salter, *Nicholas Love's 'Myrrour of the Blessed Lyf of Jesu Christ'*, p. 103, and the *Geographies of Orthodoxy* project web site.

The *Meditationes vitae Christi* is a work not only imaginative and dramatic but also instructive and authoritative. Its sources are the Bible, patristic texts, and earlier works of revelation and meditation. More indirectly, but just as importantly, with regard to general influences and milieu, 'it seems, in many ways', according to Salter,

> to gather up the varied elements of Franciscan piety, and express them as a whole. Behind it lies the mystical theology of St. Bernard and St. Bonaventure, no less than the simple but profound faith of St. Francis of Assisi. But in its marked stress on the emotional aspect of the Life of Christ as against theological issues, it allies itself with that part of Franciscan activity which aimed at popularising the great devotional themes set by the foregoing centuries.[17]

Love's *Mirror* reflects circumstances of composition and intended audience different from those of the *Meditationes vitae Christi*, and this can be seen most explicitly in his prologue, or 'proheme' as he calls it (pp. 9–13). As a Carthusian, he was obliged to make devotional books. The devotional book which Love chose to make in the vernacular had as its purpose the stirring of devout souls, lay and religious, men and women, to the love of God, hope of heaven, and to good living, as well as providing this widened audience with orthodox teaching on the life of Christ. Love carefully supervises the meditating imaginations of his readers and hearers, and explains biblical events to them in clear English authoritatively, intimately, and affectively.[18]

It would be wrong, however, to emphasize too much the narrowly political intentions and uses of the *Mirror*. Although he indubitably includes significant amounts of anti-Lollard polemic (and closes the work with a highly orthodox treatise on the Eucharist), Nicholas Love, beyond all question, produced a work which could service a generally mainstream, affective, instructive doctrinal intention and utility for clerks and laity alike, with the stress on the relatively unlearned.[19] Such intentions are reflected in the exclusion of the more

---

[17] Salter, *Nicholas Love's 'Myrrour of the Blessed Lyf of Jesu Christ'*, pp. 42–43.

[18] For Sargent's discussion of how Love makes changes to his source for the purposes of re-orienting the exercise of meditation on the Sacred Humanity, see the introduction to Nicholas Love, *Mirror*, ed. by Sargent, pp. 54–75. Recent work on this aspect of Love's treatment of the *Meditationes vitae Christi* has been done by McNamer, *Affective Meditation and the Invention of Medieval Compassion*, esp. pp. 207–25; also Karnes, 'Nicholas Love and Medieval Meditations on Christ', and Karnes, *Imagination, Meditation, and Cognition in the Middle Ages*, esp. pp. 128–49. See also Perry, '"Some sprytuall matter of gostly edyfycacion".

[19] For the main examples of anti-Lollard polemic and glossing in Nicholas Love, *Mirror*, ed.

difficult theology and advanced contemplative materials of the original, and of passages that address themselves more to the circumstances of the enclosed religious.[20]

More than is the case in his source, Love clarifies the rudiments of meditating on the Sacred Humanity, starting by telling his audience that imagining the life of Christ is indeed permissible and suitable for all, and something to be commended. Unsurprisingly, he has lower expectations of his readers and hearers than does Pseudo-Bonaventure, who reminded his 'dilecta filia' that St Francis achieved perfection in Jesus through contemplation of His life; that contemplation by its very nature could purify her by gradual steps, and that Jesus Himself might take over from the author as her teacher and guide. Moreover, contemplation may make her soul catch fire and enable her to distinguish the false from the true (*Meditationes vitae Christi*, ed. by Peltier, p. 510).

All this is omitted by Love, for such things are unlikely to happen to members of his intended audience; but there is no slight against them here. The level at which he proposes to work is more needful to more people. Appropriating another *auctoritas*, allegedly from St Bernard, Love states that the imagining of the Manhood of Christ is particularly suitable for his audience, who can only imagine bodily images and are unlikely to proceed beyond corporeal thought and discourse, but will still find things profitable to them:

> To þe which symple soules as seynt *Bernerde* seye contemplacion of þe monhede of cryste is more likyng [*pleasing*] more spedefull [*efficacious*] & more sykere [*trustworthy*] þan is hyȝe contemplacion of þe godhed ande þerfore to hem is pryncipally to be sette in mynde þe ymage of cristes Incarnacion passion & Resurreccion so that a symple soule þat kan not þenke bot bodyes or bodily þinges mowe [*may*] haue somwhat accordynge vnto is [*his*] affecion where wiþ [*with which*] he maye fede & stire his deuocion. (p. 10)

For Love's readers and hearers, contemplation of the Sacred Humanity is more 'likyng' ('pleasing'), 'spedefull' ('efficacious'), and 'sykere' ('trustworthy') than contemplating the Divinity. It is 'likyng', as his discussion of potential tediousness in the 'epilogue' at the end of the text indicates (p. 220), because there has

---

by Sargent, see. pp. 132, 137–38, 142, 220–01, and the 'Treatise of the Sacrament', pp. 223–39, esp. 235–39. See also Sargent's discussion of anti-Wycliffism in his introduction, pp. 54–75.

[20] For examples of statements regarding exclusion or curtailment of theological, contemplative, and expository passages or materials otherwise aimed at the enclosed religious, or likely to be wearisome by continuance or unsuitable for *simple soules*, see pp. 43, 47, 72, 75–76, 85–86, 105, 118–19.

to be an element of attraction in order to teach and move effectively. Secondly, meditating on the Divinity, as opposed to the Humanity, would not be 'spede-full' for his intended audience because they need to be saved more than they need to practise mystical athletics in the here and now. Thirdly, the close preacherly supervision and support of the imagination in the *Mirror* (and in the source) and the relative lack of ambiguity in a moralized historical narrative of Jesus's life are more 'sykere' — not fraught with the dangers of misinterpreta-tion, pride, and delusion endemic to enterprising higher contemplation. Love's work is also trustworthy in providing guaranteed spiritual benefits arising from the *ymaginacion* of Christ's life. By this humble (but not necessarily unambi-tious) mode of imagining, hope, love, and understanding will be stirred in sim-ple souls, who should be able to grasp 'sykerly' the sacredly exemplary nature of Christ's life, suffering, death, and rising again. It is not actually necessary for salvation or devotional health to generate imaginative intercourse with Jesus Himself in meditation, as commended in the Latin original (*Meditationes vitae Christi*, ed. by Peltier, pp. 510–11) — and as pursued with such personal com-petitiveness by Margery Kempe — although it is definitely a good thing, if it happens. The *Mirror*'s audience's 'affeccions', however, will be stirred Godwards in hope by the likenesses narrated to them. To this end the fundamental affec-tive images of Incarnation, Passion, and Resurrection will 'work' for anybody. The *Mirror* is, then, about inclusiveness, reliability, accessibility, and effica-ciousness: to see in it a master-narrative of undemocratic dumbing down and diversion from the Bible is largely, though not wholly, beside the point.

The Rewle of Diuerse Ymaginacions: Gostly Substances

Before discussing the *Mirror* in detail, it is necessary to understand Love's con-cept of *devout imaginacioun*, the traditional principle informing the sacred imagining and meditation on Christ's life that constitutes the *modus agendi* of his work.[21] We should also discuss the relationship between *devout imagi-*

---

[21] The recent monograph by Karnes, *Imagination, Meditation, and Cognition in the Middle Ages*, takes an interest in the area, but it concentrates on St Bonaventure's understanding of 'the cognitive underpinnings of meditation'. What emerges, however, is that 'no author of gospel meditations in the period appears to have shared Bonaventure's fascination', so it is not easy to see how, despite this, 'Bonaventure's successors in the genre announce his influence on their work above all in their untroubled assumption that imagination's considerable powers render it capable of transporting a meditant from Christ's humanity to his divinity' (p. 141), especially when one can see plenty of other clerks in the Pseudo-Dionysian tradition who clearly exerted

nacioun and Love's 'take' on higher forms of contemplative spirituality: this is especially important because his reputation has been assailed by accusations of hindering the spiritual progress of his readership/audience and infantilizing them, at the same time as selling short the contemplative and spiritual reach of his Latin source, the Pseudo-Bonaventuran *Meditationes vitae Christi*. One just has to look, however, at what Love actually says and does to see that this is often inappropriate or over-harsh. If we start at Love's own explanation of his approach to, and of his choices in, shaping his new English life of Christ, we can see that he makes fluent and easy use of medieval theory of imagination and the norms of contemplative literature, and is by no means as obstructive to individual piety as some would have it.

Medieval Latin and English analogues concerning imagination and contemplation are relevant for the modern scholar in illuminating Love's own approach. The works of Hilton and the *Cloud*-author are particularly helpful because they, like the *Mirror*, are mainstream and similarly self-reflective in their treatment of meditation on the life of Christ and the workings of the imagination.[22] Furthermore, Love actually had some acquaintance with the works of Hilton, whom he admires and warmly recommends as the maker of a 'next text' for those who would proceed further in *gostly* work. As imaginative writers, Love, Hilton, and the *Cloud*-author assumed that they knew, and endeavoured to cultivate, the capacities of their intended or likely readers, and, though their target-audiences differed, all three shared the same attitudes about what kinds of imagination and contemplation were suitable for their specific purposes.

Approbation for meditating on the Sacred Humanity is visible, for example, in Book II of Hilton's *Scale of Perfection*, when a tripartite scheme of love, somewhat resembling the three degrees of contemplation, previously defined in

influence in the area: I will be citing such Latin and vernacular works in order to give context to Love. For an illuminating analysis of 'devout imaginacioun' with reference to Love and later drama, see Beadle, '"Devoute ymaginacioun" and the Dramatic Sense'.

[22] For the works of the *Cloud*-author, see *The Cloud of Unknowing and Related Treatises*, ed. by Hodgson. See also the more accessible edition, *The Cloud of Unknowing and The Book of Privy Counselling*, ed. by Hodgson; *Deonise Hid Diuinite and Other Treatises on Contemplative Prayer*, ed. by Hodgson. There is also a serviceable online TEAMS edition, *The Cloud of Unknowing*, ed. by Gallacher, at <http://www.lib.rochester.edu/camelot/teams/cloufrm.htm>. See too the online TEAMS edition of Walter Hilton, *The Scale of Perfection*, ed. by Bestul. Michael Sargent is in the process of completing for EETS a new critical edition of Hilton's *Scale*. For relevant context on the tradition of imagining the Sacred Humanity, see Minnis, 'Affection and Imagination in the *Cloud of Unknowing*'. The broader context of medieval theory of imagination is set out by Minnis, 'Memory and Imagination'.

Book I, is invoked.[23] The first and lowest level is the love of God by faith alone, and the second is the knowledge of God gained by thinking imaginatively on His Humanity. This category applies to the *Mirror*. The third and highest stage is when the intellect comprehends perfect love with knowledge of God's divinity, albeit that the divinity is still united to His Humanity, this being the only manner in which the divinity can be apprehended by humanity on this earth.

The key point to bear in mind here is that the only route to the Godhead is via the Manhood: such would be the route taken by any of Love's audience willing and able to progress further, or who, in the course of using the *Mirror*, may be blessed enough to feel the *gostly sweetnes* that the Carthusian envisages as happening to some of his readers and hearers. Hilton may have been writing for a rather different audience than Love was, but he and Love are in total accord:

> Neverthelees unto sich soulis that kunne not thenken on the Godhede goostli [*cannot meditate spiritually on the Godhead*], that thei schulde not erren in here devocion, but that thei schulden ben conforted and strengthed thorugh sum manere inward bihooldynge of Jhesu, for to forsake synne and the love of the worlde — therfore oure Lord Jhesu tempereth His unseable light of His Godhede, and clothid it undir bodili liknesse of His manhede, and scheweth it to the innere iye [*eye*] of the soule and fedeth it with the love of His precious flesch goostli, […] oure Lord Jhesu in His Godhede is a spiret [*spirit*], that mai not be seen of us lyvand in flesch [*while alive in the flesh*] as He is in His blissid light. Therfore we schulle lyven undir the schadwe [*shadow*] of His blissid manhede as longe as we aren here [*are here*].[24]

Nearly all people were likely to be *simple soules* to some degree, including the powerful and non-stupid Ricardian and Lancastrian magnates who were the early users of this book, as well as high-powered theologians like Thomas Netter who knew and advertised his own contemplative limitations.[25] Each of these people, as Love puts it, who 'þat kan not þenke bot bodyes or bodily þinges

---

[23] Walter Hilton, *The Scale of Perfection*, ed. by Bestul, II. 30. For an examination of the influence upon Hilton and the *Cloud*-author of standard medieval theory of imagination, see Minnis, 'Affection and Imagination in the *Cloud of Unknowing*', esp. pp. 351, 355–56. I have drawn generally on this still-important article because, in locating and illustrating the theoretical context of the works of these two vernacular imaginative writers, it provides a vital context, I would argue, for Love.

[24] Walter Hilton, *The Scale of Perfection*, ed. by Bestul, II. 30.

[25] Mishtooni Bose pointed out in a paper at the International Medieval Congress, Leeds, 2006, that Netter, despite being a leading orthodox theologian and Carmelite monk, was very open about his own inability to rise high in contemplation.

mowe [*may*] haue somwhat accordynge vnto is [*his*] affecion where wiþ [*with which*] he maye fede & stire his deuocion' (p. 10), may not ascend to mystical heights, but s/he will know Jesus and love Him. In the words of Hilton:

> thei kunne not thenke on Jhesu ne love Him Godli, but as it were al manli and fleschli aftir the condicions and the liknes [*likeness*] of man. And upon that reward thei schapin al her werkynge, in here thoughtis and in here affeccions. Thei dreden Him as man, and worschipen Hym and loven Hym principali in manli ymagina-cioun, and goon no ferthere.[26]

Such simple souls think of God by anthropomorphizing Him, fearing, lov-ing, begging mercy from Him, and worshipping Him as they would a man.[27] When loving Him they do so with an image in mind of His life and Passion on earth, as in the *Mirror*. This is not as excellent as loving the spirit, but it is still excellent, and is not untouched by grace. The *Cloud*-author may have aimed his works at 'parceners [*co-heirs/partakers*] in þe hieȝst [*highest*] pointe of þis contemplatiue acte',[28] but he approved of the kind of audience Love sought, even though he was not writing for them: 'ȝe, þouȝ al þat þei be ful [*although they are very*] good men of actiue leuyng, ȝit þis [*yet this*] mater acordeþ noþing to hem'.[29] For the House of God has many mansions, as Hilton pointed out: some of these are for the perfect contemplatives who gain the highest heavenly rewards, and some of them are for the simpler souls.[30]

In harmony with this thematic image, *The Book of Privy Counselling* (in all probability also written by the anonymous author of the *Cloud of Unknowing*) declares the Manhood of Christ to be the door through which Christians are brought to the 'goostly fode [*food*] of deuocioun'. This is enough, in fact, to save them, whether they contemplate the Godhead as advanced mystics, or, more 'simply', behold the suffering of the Manhood:

> Þei entren by þe dore [*door*], þat in beholdyng of þe Passion of Criste sorowen here wickydnes, þe whiche ben cause of þat Passion, wiþ bitter reprouyng of hemself [*themselves*], þat deseruid & not suffrid, & pite & compassion of þat worþi Lorde, þat so vili [*vilely*] suffrid & noþing deseruid; & siþen lifte up here hertes to þe loue & þe goodnes of his Godheed, in þe whiche he vouchedsaaf to meke hym [*humble*

---

[26] Walter Hilton, *The Scale of Perfection*, ed. by Bestul, II. 30.

[27] Walter Hilton, *The Scale of Perfection*, ed. by Bestul, II. 30.

[28] *The Cloud of Unknowing and Related Treatises*, ed. by Hodgson, p. 2.

[29] *The Cloud of Unknowing and Related Treatises*, ed. by Hodgson, p. 2.

[30] Walter Hilton, *The Scale of Perfection*, ed. by Bestul, I. 44.

himself] so lowe in oure deedly manheed [*mortal humanity*]. Alle þees entren bi þe dore, & þei scholen be saaf [*shall be safe/saved*]. & wheþer þei gone inne, in þe beholdynge of þe loue & þe goodnes of his Godheed, or oute, in beholdyng of þe peyne of his manheed, þei scholen fynde goostly fode of deuocion inowȝ, soffisaunt [*enough, sufficient*] & aboundyng to þe helþe & sauyng [*saving/salvation*] of here [*their*] soules, þof al þei [*although they*] comen neuer ferþer inwardes in is liif.[31]

That 'þei scholen be saaf' ('scholen' having at this time a sense of inevitability like the modern word 'must') should not be overlooked. Nor should it be overlooked that the beholding of both the Godhead and of the Manhood yields a sufficiency of devotional nourishment, 'goostly fode of deuocion inowȝ'. The business of 'simply' getting saved puts all other considerations of the spiritual life truly under the shade of the Manhood: this applies to all sublunary, as-yet-unsaved, free-willed sinners: everyone. Unless one knows how to be a devout *simple soule* first there is no point to any other spiritual ambition. Just as Hilton very definitely asserts the unique, tremendous power of meditating on the humanity of Christ, Love finds morality, edification, and a true ground for a saving devotion for his audience in meditations of the Sacred Humanity.

For Hilton, those who want to go on to higher contemplation must pass through this stage of meditating on the Sacred Humanity: 'til thyn herte be mykil yclensid [*much cleansed*] from sich synnes thorugh stedefaste trouthe and bisi [*busy/diligent*] biholdynge on Jhesu Crist in praieres and in othir good werkes, thou mai not perfightli have goostli felynge of Hym'.[32] This is the truest way to ghostly feeling of God. Likewise, the *Cloud*-author cannot see a way to ghostly feeling for anyone who has not started here:

Neuerþeles ȝit [*yet*] ben þees [*are these*] faire meditacions þe trewest wey [*way*] þat a synner may haue in his begynnyng to þe goostly felyng of himself & of God. & me wolde þenk [*it would seem to me*] þat it were inpossible to mans vnderstondyng — þof al [*although*] God may do what he wil — þat a synner schuld com to be restful in þe goostly felyng of himself & of God, bot if he first sawe & felt by ymaginacion & meditacion þe bodely doynges [*bodily doings*] of hymself & of God, & þerto sorowed for þat þat were to sorowen, & maad ioie for þat þat were to ioien. & whoso comeþ not in bi þis weye, he comeþ not trewly; and þerfore he mote [*must*] stonde þeroute [*thereout/outside*].[33]

[31] *Book of Privy Counselling*, in *The Cloud of Unknowing and The Book of Privy Counselling*, ed. by Hodgson, p. 91.

[32] Walter Hilton, *The Scale of Perfection*, ed. by Bestul, I. 15.

[33] *Book of Privy Counselling*, in *The Cloud of Unknowing and The Book of Privy Counselling*, ed. by Hodgson, p. 90.

This statement about the *matere* and *manere* of a vital and sovereign genre, the *vita Christi*, has implications for the utility of the *Mirror*, because a more advanced mystic might have a use for the work as a first step in meditative exercise, for, as Hilton maintains, God in Himself can never be grasped by the imagination, though, with grace, an increasingly proficient beginner may move from 'manli' to 'gostli affeccions'.[34] Yet, he warns, we should never fall into the falsehood of separating the Humanity from the Divinity. This cautioning is a very important part of the tradition of imagining the Sacred Humanity, for Love too is emphatic that we should never believe the Manhood to be in reality sundered from the Godhead, but only parted 'in manere' provisionally for the purposes of devout imagination (p. 159).

Likewise, with a similar theoretical self-awareness on the topic of the equally provisional nature of imagining the incorporeal things of heaven by means of corporeal human discourse, Love takes a text-book approach in easy accord with Gallus in his Pseudo-Dionysian commentaries and with Richard of St Victor in his contemplative writings:[35]

> wherefore it is to vndirstonde at þe bygynyng as for a pryncipal & general rewle of diuerse ymaginacions [*divers imaginings/meditations*] þat folowen after in þis boke þat þe discriuyng [*describing*] or speches or dedis of god in heuen & angels or oþere gostly substances bene [*are*] only wryten in þis manere, & to þis entent þat is to saye as devoute ymaginacions & likenessis styryng [*stirring*] symple soules to þe loue of god & desire of heuenly þinges. (p. 10)

---

[34] Walter Hilton, *The Scale of Perfection*, ed. by Bestul, II. 35.

[35] Thomas Gallus, also known as 'Vercellensis', Victorine Abbot of St Andrews, Vercelli from 1219 to the year of his death, 1246, expounded many Pseudo-Dionysian works, including *De mystica theologia*, *De divinis nominibus*, both of the *Hierarchies*, and some of the letters. The expositions of most relevance to vernacular English meditative literature are his brief commentary, or *Glossa* on *De mystica theologia* (1232), misattributed to John the Scot under whose name (Joannes Scotus) it is printed in *Patrologia latina*, CXXII (1853), cols 267–84; a fuller version of the same, the *Explanatio* (1241), and the *Extractio*, a paraphrase of the work. He also wrote another *Extractio* on *De caelesti hierarchia*. For extensive quotation and examination of these works and Richard of St Victor, *Benjamin minor*, *Patrologia latina*, CXCVI (1855), cols 1–64, as it applies to Hilton and the *Cloud*-author, see generally Minnis, 'Affection and Imagination in the *Cloud of Unknowing*'. The introduction to *The Cloud of Unknowing and Related Treatises*, ed. by Hodgson, pp. xxx–xlix, discusses the English writer's debt to Gallus, whom in *Deonise Hid Diuinite* he openly acknowledges as a chief source, the *Cloud*-author having 'moche folowed þe sentence of the Abbot of Seinte Victore, a noble & worþi expositour of þis same book' (ed. by Hodgson, pp. 119–28, at p. 119). For edited, translated, and commented extracts from the Latin tradition, see Minnis and Scott, *Medieval Literary Theory and Criticism*, pp. 165–96.

This overarching and transferrable rule puts the layperson into the field of meditative *imitatio clerici*, but the statement comes with its own warning: even if it becomes second nature to imagine fluently the events and discourses of heaven, the devout soul must never forget that such imagining is being carried out from solid earth by a carnal mortal. Such corporeal likening is permissible as long as it is acknowledged as being no more than imaginative, as the *manere*, the *modus agendi/forma tractandi* befitting this kind of text. Through imagining, then, the *affectus* is moved to desire those unknowable incorporeal things and to further love of God. Grosseteste, for example, commenting on *De mystica theologia*, identifies the necessarily earthly element in the anagogic passages of the Bible, which uses symbols and imaginative similitudes for the benefit of humans, which is why theologians necessarily write imaginatively when writing of God.[36]

The same applies to writers of meditations on heavenly events. Love, like much medieval commentary-tradition on Pseudo-Dionysius's *De caelesti hierarchia*, sees anagogical corporeal imagery as raising up the soul of the reader 'to loue & desire gostly inuisible þinges, þat he kyndly knoweþ not' (p. 10). This exercise gives the meditating imagination a limited but workable idea of celestial phenomena, such as angels, whom Love needs to portray in his narrative. In his *Extractio* on *De caelesti hierarchia* Gallus gives an interesting parallel to the *Mirror* when he describes the imaginative mode that is used for the representation of the angels:

> Neque enim possibile est nostrae menti sursum excitari ad illam immaterialem imititationem et contemplationem caelestium hierarchium, nisi ipsa mens nostra (secundum conditionem praesentis caecitatis) utatur manuductione signorum materialium [...] nobis autem sub signis sensibilibus in Scripturis traduntur.[37]

> For it is not possible for our mind to be uplifted to that immaterial imitation and contemplation of the heavenly hierarchies, unless that same mind, in line with its present blindness, employs the guidance of material figures [...] imparted to us in the Scriptures under the guise of forms accessible to the senses.[38]

When Love in his turn comes to describe angels and events in heaven he is accordingly most careful to elucidate their mode of existence and to draw attention to their imaginative status. In the first chapter of the *Mirror*,

---

[36] Discussed by Minnis, 'Affection and Imagination in the *Cloud of Unknowing*', p. 343.

[37] Cited by Minnis, 'Affection and Imagination in the *Cloud of Unknowing*', p. 334.

[38] Minnis and Scott, *Medieval Literary Theory and Criticism*, pp. 174–75.

'¶ A deuout meditacione of the grete conseile in heuen for þe restoryng of man & his sauacione' (pp. 15–19), a short instruction in the original telling the reader to understand the chapter not literally, but figuratively, 'hoc autem non proprie, sed appropriate intelligas' ('you should, however, understand this not literally but figuratively'; *Meditationes vitae Christi*, ed. by Peltier, p. 511), is greatly expanded into theatrical directions and a strategic justification of devout imagination:

> And þus was termynet & endet þe grete conseil in heuen for þe restoryng of man & his sauacion.
>
> ¶ Þe which processe sal [*narrative shall*] be taken as in liknes & onlich [*only*] as a manere of a parable & deuoute ymaginacion, stiryng man to loue god souereynly for his grete mercy to man & his endless gudnes. [...]
>
> ¶ And þus mykel [*to this extent*] & in þis maner may be seide & þought by deuoute contemplacion of þat [*what*] was done aboue in heuen byfore þe Incarnacion of Jesu⸱ now go we done to erþe [*down to earth*], & þenk we how it stode [*stood*] wiþ his blessed modere Marie. (p. 19)

Great care is taken in defining and licensing the degree and the modality of the imaginative act open to both writer and reader: 'þus mykel & in þis maner may be seide & þought'. The words 'abouen' and 'done' are used by Love to indicate a physicalized 'up/down' imagining of heaven and earth. The *Cloud*-author famously inveighs against the literalistic and unduly credulous use in meditations of such directionally and physically orientated words, like 'in' and, in particular, 'up': 'Bot now þou mayst not come to heuen not bodely, bot goostly. & ȝit it schal be so goostly þat it schal not be on bodely maner: nowþer upwardes ne donwardes'.[39] Likewise, Love stresses that the going 'done' from heaven to earth in meditation is purely imaginative.

Both Love and the *Cloud*-author work in an authoritative tradition of imaginative devotional writing, a tradition that frequently reminds its readers to be aware of the artifice intrinsic to representing the incorporeal as corporeal, and to filling in the gaps where the Bible is silent. A case in point is Love's flagging-up, in this very passage, of the medieval theoretical concept of parabolic discourse, which here he applies to the provisional combining of dissimilars in the representation of the heavenly in terms of the earthly: 'Þe which processe sal be taken as in liknes & onlich as a manere of a parable & deuoute ymaginacion' (p. 19). If we turn to the most authoritative medieval dictionary, we

---

[39] *The Cloud of Unknowing and Related Treatises*, ed. by Hodgson, p. 61. See also p. 63 for the same topic.

see that the *Catholicon*, citing Hugutio of Pisa, defines *parabola* as a similitude or comparison of dissimilar things: 'parabola id est similitudo siue comparatio ex dissimilibus rebus' ('*parabola* is a similitude or comparison of dissimilar things').[40] Here, therefore, Love is warning that dissimilars entertained in meditative imagining of heavenly things should not be believed to be equatable in reality. With this caveat understood, the imagination is all the more licensed and free to move on and to engage in detailed, affective, fleshly meditating of incorporeal things. Highly 'goostly' angels are thus repesented as if they were 'dissimilar', thoroughly bodily, humanity — happy faces and bending knees included — as with Gabriel:

> ❡ Now take hede, & ymagine of gostly þinge as it were bodily, & þenk in þi herte as þou were present in þe siȝt of þat blessed lord, with how benyng & glad semblant [*benign and glad countenance*] he spekeþ þees wordes. And on þat oþer side, how Gabriel with a likyng [*pleasant*] face & glad chere [*expression*] vpon his knen knelyng [*kneeling on his knees*] & with drede reuerently bowing receueþ [*receives*] þis message of his lord. (p. 23)

Love is keen to represent the formal correctness of the Archangel's address to the Almighty — a combination of blessed happiness and 'drede' decorous for the conduct of true reverence. The repeated mentioning of happy faces engages sentiments accessed through the interior meditating eye. Then, the reader/ hearer, having encountered an anthropomorphic Gabriel in heaven, is a little jarred by being told immediately after this that the Archangel shifted shape into 'mannus liknes' for the benefit of Mary:

> And so anone Gabriel risyng vp glad & iocunde [*cheerful*], toke his fliȝt fro the hye heuen to erþe, & in a moment he was in mannus [*human*] liknes before þe virgine Marie. (p. 23)

Gabriel has gone from being a non-manly *gostly substance* in heaven, whom we are permitted to imagine as a man, to an otherwise incorporeal substance assuming by its own powers the likeness of a man on earth. Love's meticulous 'frame-breaking' would remind the reader instinctively of the provisionality of imaginative meditation: it is as if devout imagination lays itself bare in good faith by reminding the reader of its artificiality. It does not, however, have to be assumed that affective engagement with the narrative would thereby be discontinued or inhibited by an awareness on the part of the reader of this artificiality. Such self-conscious frame-breaking is inevitable when things incorporeal, imag-

---

[40] Joannes Januensis, *Catholicon*, s.v. *de tropo* under *parabola*, unfol.

ined in bodily form, interact in the narrative with genuinely corporeal things. Love provides frequent reminders throughout his work of the inevitable artificiality of such *gostly* imagining. Indeed, it would appear that this ritualized foregrounding of the very process of imagining was conceivably part and parcel of habituated affectivity — a spur to go feelingly into devoutly imaginative mode.

To a willing and trainable mind, such instructions to imagine, and such reminders that the meditative narrative is indeed imaginative, would have functioned as emotionally charged cues to heightened feeling and to a more intent, vivid interiority. Contrary to one recent critical opinion, then, I would contend that Love's drawing of the reader's attention to the imaginative status of narrative events does not need to be seen as militating against the emotive impact or value of what is being meditated upon. In her recent book, Michelle Karnes complains that the *Mirror* is not as much like (her understanding of) the *Meditationes vitae Christi* as it should be, and that one of these alleged shortcomings is Love's habitual reminding of the reader that what is being narrated is a matter of devout imagination — as with this instance of Love's rendering of the Ascension:

> when Love narrates the ascension, he allows the meditant to witness it only indirectly. Compare the following accounts:
>
> > *MVC*: The Lord Jesus opened the gates of Paradise which up to that time had been closed to humanity, and entered in triumph and joy, with all that happy and magnificent multitude.
> >
> > Love's *Myrrour*: Nowe go we up by devout contemplacion to oure lorde Jesu[,] beholding in ymaginacion of hevenly þinges by likenes of erþely þinges, howe he with alle þat foreside worþi & blisfulle multitude of holi soules, oponyng heven ȝates þat were before sperede aȝeynus mankynde, [...] seide, Fader I þonke þe.
>
> The passage from the *MVC* occurs in the midst of a description of all the things one 'sees' when Christ ascends, and it thus permits the meditant to participate in the journey with Christ. As the gates to Paradise open, the meditant herself seems to gain access to the heavenly wonders, which the author evocatively describes in the chapter's continuation. Love's ascent entails no departure from earth. A 'devout contemplacion', it permits access to 'hevenly þinges' only by indirect analogy to 'erþely þinges.' Love's meditant witnesses Christ's return to heaven by comparing it to sensible things, beyond which he never ventures.[41]

---

[41] Karnes, *Imagination, Meditation, and Cognition in the Middle Ages*, p. 221. For further readings by Karnes of Love's revision of the Latin, see pp. 218–25.

This interpretation unnecessarily dismisses the possibility or likelihood that Love's readers or hearers could combine an awareness of the provisional status of physicalized heavenly imaginables with an affective appreciation of narrative content. Love's licence for his readers to engage in the *mise-en-scène*, however, can more credibly be seen as giving them responsibility and encouragement to observe feelingly, not only during reading/hearing but also in continued meditation thereafter. Such indirectness is not necessarily inhibiting: Love's approach provides an enablement of, and a cue to, affective performability. Moreover, when, in Karnes's analysis of the quotation from the original, it is held to be a good thing that the meditant is presented with a passage of unmediated third-person narrative, it could equally be said that this kind of narrative might make the meditant feel more detached as a witness than is the case in the Middle English version. Love's readers, unlike those of the original, are drawn into the action by going up to 'oure lorde', and are invited not just to see *that* the Lord is present but 'howe' he acts. This vernacular 'howe' requires active creative input — imaginative probing, exploration, conjecturing, and decision-making about unresolved possibilities within the *mise-en-scène*. Love's reader is thus required to make more through imagining than is the onlooker-reader of the more fixed third-person report of the Latin passage.

Nor is it adequate simply to declare that 'Love's ascent entails no departure from earth', because, as Love says straightforwardly enough, 'Nowe go we up by devout contemplacion to oure lorde Jesu'. This is *imaginative* ascent — the only sort available. It would be very wrong indeed to assume that Love's readers are somehow meant to forget that they are alive on earth reading or listening to the *Mirror* rather than being ravished into forgetfulness of their or their text's corporeal natures. Similarly problematic is Karnes's claim that 'Love's meditant witnesses Christ's return to heaven by comparing it to sensible things, beyond which he never ventures'. This misses the point that all imaginable things of heaven have to be described in corporeal discourse anyway: no one can venture beyond the fleshly imagination while engaging in a narrative of heavenly events (though in due course s/he might transcend both narrative and imagination — but that is another, higher, process).

So, in the exemplary cases of angels and the Council of Heaven, to say nothing of the opening of the gates of Paradise, Love is clear about what kinds of representation are provisionally enabled in the meditating imagination. The negative limitations, on the other hand, of the carnal mind are also made clear by Love when, reflecting the concern of theologians that the Trinity be not misrepresented by bodily thinking, he interpolates into his text an appropriate warning to his readers not only against over-credulously taking fleshly

(mis)representation of the mysteries of the Trinity too far but also against peril-
ous solo conjecture:

> Bot now beware here þat þou erre not in imaginacion of god & of þe holi Trinite,
> supposyng þat þees þre persones þe fadere þe son & þe holi gost bene [*are*] as þre
> erþly men, þat þou seest with þi bodily eye, þe whech ben þre [*the which are three*]
> diuerse substances, ech departed fro oþere, so þat none of hem [*them*] is oþer. Nay
> it is not so in þis gostly substance of þe holi trinyte, for þo þre [*those three*] persones
> ben on substance & on god [*are one substance and one God*], & 3it is þere none of
> þees persones oþer. Bot þis maiþ [*may*] þou not vndirstande by mannes reson ne
> conceyue with þi bodily wit, & þerfore take here a generale doctrine in þis mater
> now for algate [*now and forever*]. What tyme þou herest or þenkest of þe trinyte or
> of þe godhede or of gostly creatours as angeles & soules þe whech þou maist not se
> with þi bodily eye in hire propre kynde [*in their natural condition*], nor fele with
> þi bodily witteᵗ study not to fer in þat matere [*not too far in that matter/business*]
> occupy not þi wit þerwiþ [*with it*] als [*as*] þou woldest vndurstande it, by kindly
> reson [*natural/inborn reason*], for it wil not be while we ben in þis buystes [*coarse*]
> body lyuyng here in erþe. And þerfore when þou herest any sich þinge in byleue þat
> passeþ þi kindly reson [*natural/inborn reason*], trowe soþfastly [*believe truly*] þat it
> is soþ as holy chirch techeþ & go no ferþer. (p. 23)

Here, Love puts his ecclesiastically authoritative foot down, but it should not
be forgotten either at this point that most layfolk were not would-be academic theologians. The imagination is limited, then, not only in having to follow orthodox doctrine, but also in being conceptually unequal to the task of
replicating the incorporeal theological givens that it must nevertheless try to
accommodate. Although reason has a role in constructing 'imaginacion of god
& of þe holi Trinite', it should not investigate this too deeply on earthly terms,
because imagination provides only insufficient, albeit serviceable and affective,
notions of 'gostly' things:

> for as *Seynt Gregory* seiþ, þerfore is þe kyngdome of heuene likenet to erþly þingesᵗ
> þat by þo þinges þat bene visible & þat man kyndly knoweþ [*knows naturally*]ᵗ he
> be stirede & rauyshede [*ravished*] to loue & desire gostly inuisible þinges, þat he
> kyndly [*naturally*] knoweþ not. (p. 10)

Here, the relatively humble starting place for Love's readers is acknowledged,
beginning as it does with 'kynde' knowledge. However, the important point
is made that the 'gostly' invisible things in themselves remain unknown. Love
does not say here that love itself is a form of mystical knowledge. Devotional
desire here is not presented as equivalent to, or integrated with, knowledge
of the things desired. However, the imagination can and does direct the *affec-*

cioun towards these unknown things. This movement towards what is desired is consistent with the emphasis, in the opening part of the *proheme*, on hope, that theological virtue and human emotion which stirs the soul towards God from within, and for which the meditative matter of the life of Christ provides plenteous occasion and encouragement for Love's readers. This is not matter of trivial desire. Neither is Love's conception of his readers' affective and salvific use of his book by *devout imaginacioun* infantilizing or unduly restrictive. Indeed, we shall see next that the figure of St Cecilia, invoked by Love in his *proheme*, is a positive example of what may be achieved by meditating on the life and Passion of Christ. Moreover, we shall also see that Love does not forbid spiritual ambition in his readers; for he is ready to encourage them, by sending them onward to Walter Hilton, to venture upon contemplative ascent itself.

Cecile, Hilton, and the 'Oppression' of Love's Readership

In *devout imaginacioun*, it would appear, Love deploys a fruitful and versatile model for the users of his book. Not so, according to Nicholas Watson (and others): Love oversimplifies, and infantilizes his intended readership: '[Love's] readers are [unlike lettered clerics] specifically instructed *not* to ascend', being fobbed off with having to imitate St Cecilia, 'who "set her meditacion and her thouht night and day" in the "most devoute" sections of the gospels, and, "when she hade so fully alle the manere of his life over gon [*gone over*], she began agayne"'.[42] The questionable method of Watson's analysis of St Cecilia has already been raised in Chapter 1. This is the place, however, for an assessment of how Love translates and represents the saint — with some suggestions as to why.

Cecilia, by the example of her conduct in her marriage ceremony, illustrates the power that the life of Christ has to stabilize the soul and to stop all other spiritual threats from entering it (hardly an infantilizing phenomenon). Love's treatment of the source with his own telling configuration of English doublets reinforces and develops the Cecilian norm positively and suggestively:

> ut patet in praedicta beata Caecilia, quae ita cor suum repleverat de vita Christi, quod in ipsam vana intrare non poterant: unde in pompa nuptiarum existens, ubi tot vana geruntur, cantantibus organis, ipsa stabili corde soli Deo vacabat, dicens: 'Fiat, Domine, cor meum, et corpus meum immaculatum, ut non confundar'. (*Meditationes vitae Christi*, ed. by Peltier, p. 510)

[42] Watson, 'Conceptions of the Word', p. 98.

as is evident in the aforementioned blessed Cecilia, who had so filled her heart with
the life of Christ that nothing vain could enter her consciousness. Thus, even as a
guest amid the pomp of wedding celebrations where so much vanity was on display
and the blaring music played on, she prayed with unshaken heart, and sang to her
God alone, '*Keep my heart clean, O Lord, that I not be confounded*'.[43]

þis is opunly shewede in þe blessed virgine *Cecile* before nemede, when she fillede
so fully her herte of þe life of cristˈ þat vanytees of þe worlde miȝt not entre in to
her. For in alle þe grete pompe of weddyngis, where so many vanytees bene usede,
whene þe organes blewene & songene, she set hir herte stably in god, seying &
praying. *Lord be my herte & my body clene, & not defiledeˈ so þat I be not confondet.*
(p. 12)

'Vana' is clarified by Love as 'vanytees of þe worlde'. Love is also more particular
than the original about the mode of operation of organs. 'Organis' in Latin and
'organes' in Middle English can refer more generally to many musical instruments and even melodies (that is, musical noise),[44] but Love seems perhaps
to have in mind a wind instrument, for 'cantantibus' becomes the doublet
'*blewene* and songene'. The literal sense of the Latin, that of 'organes' singing,
is more moralizingly represented in the vernacular by a fuller picture of organs
(or musical noise) as blowing ('blewene'), doubtless puffing with 'vanytees of
þe worlde' and pride.

A second doublet is worthy of comment. Love adds the idea of praying
(which is implicit in the original) to 'dicens' by translating this Latin word
as 'seying & *praying*'. The Middle English thereby reinforces the essential idea
of the personal prayerfulness and devotion in Cecile's address to God amidst
the noisy useless anonymous public vanities and wasted *voces* of the wedding.
The rhyme makes for ornamental effect, but it does more because its palpable artificiality draws attention to the deliberately well-prepared sententious-
ness and spiritual decorum of the saint's own words. Delivered out loud rather
than just being privately thought, and standing out amidst and above the rest
of the prose, just as it and Cecilia herself stand out from the imagined scene,
the words of the saint are shifted into an elevated prayerful key. This is signally fitting, given that the exercise of meditating on the life of Christ leads on
frequently to prayer. Love therefore highlights an archetypal performance of
an imitable trajectory. But there is more to these doublets, 'blewene and son-

---

[43] John de Caulibus, *Meditations on the Life of Christ*, trans. by Taney, Miller, and Stallings-
Taney, pp. 1–2.

[44] I am grateful to John Burrow for this information.

gene' and 'seying & praying', than two separate ad hoc choices for Englishing two Latin words. The two doublets square up to each other: Cecile's doublet-dressed words of prayer, delivered in a speaking voice, fittingly answer and oppose the other foregrounded doublet describing the vain puffing and singing of the 'orgenes'. Love's final doubleting — of 'immaculatum' as 'clene, & not defilede' — not only assumes and advertises the desirability of cleanness/chastity, but also opens up a suggestion of the dire possibilities of unwilled privation of virginity by defilement.

Taken as a whole, the doublets in this passage build up an impression of St Cecilia's well-rehearsed poise and controlled resistance. This is something for the reader to rehearse in turn. Cecile's moral and spiritual courage, moreover, is at once public and private — just as the *Mirror* itself was the most public and private of books. All in all in this passage, Love can take credit for his choices as a translator, for they make the Middle English text more vivid for his readers and listeners, and remind them that the imagining of the life of Christ is not merely *matere* to be read and left, but a living and enduring *manere* to be carried in the heart for ever and enacted as a discipline.

Despite Love's ambitions for the spiritual welfare of his readers, however, Karnes laments that Love's readers are put into an 'unending novitiate'.[45] This complaint, however, is not supported by the textual evidence. The implication that medieval English Christians should all have been, or really wanted to be (or would have really wanted to be had they not been obstructed by the likes of Love) professed religious with contemplative bents is not a promising assumption when it comes to the bulk of the users of the *Mirror*. Granted, the *Mirror* does not itself directly teach advanced contemplation of the Divinity (why should it have to?), but its great benefits are available to all. When Love recommends the life of Christ, 'þe whiche byholdeþ inwardly & loueþ and foloweþ þe wordes & þe dedis of that man in whome goddes sone ȝaff [*gave*] himself to vs in to ensaumple of gode leuyng [*good living*]' (pp. 9–10), its efficacy is unpatronizingly declared to be socially universal: it would therefore include the social equals of the Prior of Mount Grace and his superiors (and it would also number those who commissioned or were early presentees of the original work — folk not to be looked down on — like Joan de Holland and other socially lofty types: 'Wherfore nowe boþe men & women & euery Age & euery dignite of this worlde is stirid to hope of euery lastyng [*everlasting*] lyfe' (p. 10). Devotion for *simple soules* is not here devotion for simpletons, nor does it make simpletons of the intelligent or spiritually adept.

---

[45] Karnes, *Imagination, Meditation, and Cognition in the Middle Ages*, p. 216.

Those 'men & women and euery Age and euery dignite of this worlde' (p. 10), then, must number all clerics, all nobility, even royalty (is Love really looking down his devotional nose at them?); and, if any of Love's not-so-simple *simple soules* think that they can 'move on' from the *Mirror* to progress further in the contemplative life or the mixed life, they are referred, at the end of this very chapter, to the next logical step in vernacular devotion, Hilton's *Epistle on the Mixed Life*:[46]

> Whereof & oþer vertuese [*virtuous*] exercise þat longeþ to contemplatif lyuyng, & specialy to a recluse, & also of medelet [*mixed*] life, þat is to sey sumtyme actife & sumtyme contemplatif, as it longeþ to diuerse persones þat in worldly astate hauen grace of gostly loueꞇ who so wole [*wishes*] more pleynly be enformed & tauht in english tongeꞇ let him loke þe tretees þat þe worþi clerk & holi lyuere Maister Walter Hilton þe Chanon of Thurgarton wrote in english by grete grace & hye discrecionꞇ & he shal fynde þere as I leue [*believe*] a sufficient scole [*school/schooling*] & a trew of alle þees. (pp. 122–23)

Hilton can provide Love's readers with a rule, a discipline for a profitable spiritual life, even though they will still have cares and responsibilities in the everyday world. Love, who turns out to be a truly Hiltonian 'Beginner's Friend', evidently conceives of devotional works as being harmonized and graded into a hierarchy, though they all partake of the same ultimate scriptural *sentence* and draw on the same doctrinal truths.

In choosing a specific audience, source, and reworking of it, Love does so from an awareness of a range of other accessible works and audience possibilities. He sees his non-monolithic *Mirror* as co-operatively complementing other works. So, not only does he shape the works of others for his own variegated audience, he also shapes audiences for other works: *translatio lectoris* (to coin a term). Nor, therefore, does he insist, as Watson maintains, 'on treating as permanent a state of soul [i.e. meditating on the Passion] [that] Rolle and Hilton think of as a beginning'.[47] Neither is it true that 'in the theological model Love assumes in offering this account of lay devotion to Christ's life and passion, Christ sheds most of his divinity on the way to becoming human',[48] for in instructions prefacing the Passion Love's readers are told in no uncertain terms, as we have already seen, that they should never believe the Manhood to be in

---

[46] For a modern edition, see Walter Hilton, *The Mixed Life*, ed. by Ogilvie-Thomson. See also *Yorkshire Writers*, ed. by Horstmann, I, pp. 262–92.

[47] Watson, 'Conceptions of the Word', p. 97.

[48] Watson, 'Conceptions of the Word', p. 97.

reality sundered from the Godhead, but only departed 'in manere' for the provisional purposes of devout imagination (p. 159). Contrary too to the notion
that Love excludes the possibility of higher spiritual experience, we can see that
he is all too aware of the possibility that a reader or hearer of the *Mirror* might
feel grace or even a certain mystical sweetness: 'who so rediþ or heriþ þis boke
felyng any gostly swetnes or grace þereþorth [*through it*]' (p. 13). It is scarcely
fair to say, then, that Love is set on pulling back to earth those with *gostly* pre-
dilections or experiences. On the contrary, he sees spiritual experience beyond
the carnal as a credible eventual outcome of the *Mirror*, and he is happy for
readers to ascend to other texts and spiritual ventures.

In the best tradition of medieval religious translation (and nearly all medieval religious texts are translations of one sort or another), Love regards his activity as a complementary act of co-operation with other Latin and vernacular
works, each having its functionally diverse role in a living tradition, determined
by the perceived desires and needs of an intended audience and the restricted
justice that any single text can do to the superabundant *sentence* of the Bible
and the life of Christ. This means that Love, like all devotional and academic
writers, is both permitted and obliged to exclude materials not pertaining to his
audience. This might even extend to whole individual meditations of the Latin
original; for, once a *simple soule* is reasonably well acquainted with the meditative technique, s/he does not need to have narrated to her/him a specific meditation on each separate episode of the *vita*. Love accordingly tells his readership
that he has cut several of them out (p. 76), because they may be tedious. Instead,
he presents his readers with a general re-usable meditation to be applied to subsequent portions of narrative — a *manere* fitting for a variety of *matere*:

> ¶ Wherefore as þe same Bonauenture biddeþ þou þat wolt [*you who would*] fele þe
> swetnesse & þe fruyt of þees meditaciones take hede algate [*always*], & in alle places
> deuoutly in þi mynde beholdyng þe persone of oure lorde Jesu in alle hese dedes,
> as when he stant with hees disciples, & when with oþer sinfulmen. And when he
> precheþ to þe peple, & how he spekeþ to hem, & also when he eteþ oþere bodily sus-
> tenaunce & also when he worcheþ myracles, & so forþ takyng hede of alle hese dedes
> & hees maneres, & principaly beholdyng his blessede face, if þou kynne [*can*] ymag-
> ine it, þat semeþ to me most harde of alle oþere, bot as I trowe it is most lykyng [*pleas-
> ant*], to him þat haþ grace þerof [*grace thereof*]. And so what tyme þat singulere [*indi-
> vidual*] meditaciones bene not specifiede‡ þis generale shale suffice. Amen. (p. 76)

Here Love trusts his readers as adults capable of applying a method independently and with discretion to holy materials and to a narrative in which their
imaginations have a degree of autonomy and responsibility: this is scarcely
infantilizing or authoritarian.

Likewise, Love's exclusion of higher contemplative matter does not have to be seen as restrictive but simply as the targeted tailoring of matter for his lay audience, as he explains clearly enough with regard to his abbreviation of the exposition of Mary and Martha and the active and contemplative lives:

Of Actife Life and Contemplatife Life.

By þees tweyn [*two*] sisteres before seide, Martha & Marie, as holy men & doctours writen⸵ ben vndurstande tweyn maner lifes of cristen men [*two manners of life of Christian men*], þat is to sey actif lif & contemplatif lyfe. Of þe whech þere beþ many tretees, & gret processe made of diuerse doctours. And specialy þe forseid Bonauenture in þis boke of cristes life makeþ a longe processe aleggyng [*discourse citing*] many auctoritees of seynt *Bernard*, þe whiche processe þouh [*though*] it so be þat it is ful gude & fructuouse as to many gostly lyueres⸵ neuerles for it semeþ as inpertynent [*unsuitable*] in gret party to many comune persones & symple soules, þat þis boke in english is writen to, as it is seid oft before, þerefore we passen ouere shortly takyng þereof þat semeþ profitable & edificatife to oure purpose at þis tyme (p. 118)

Here Love is not responding to his source alone, but to the accessible textual tradition of representing Mary and Martha as the active and contemplative lives, '[o]f þe whech þere beþ many tretees, & gret processe made of diuerse doctours'. One aim of such a remark is to let the reader know that there is somewhere to go textually for further advice and information on this subject, if he or she wishes. Though he cuts this matter from the original, he still, in a manner, translates a significant sense of what is excised, because he delineates its context, availability and function by cutting out its characteristic shape and faithfully marking its accessibility in other works (in other words, those other writings identified in his *proheme* as written in Holy Church for stirring to hope and salvation (p. 10)).

At the same time as remodulating his source by excision of the Mary and Martha materials, Love recycles the language and imagery of taste and nourishment traditionally associated with meditative *ruminatio*. He does so, however, at a level appropriate to his readership, stressing that his work is not 'sadde mete of grete clargye [*learning*] & of hye contemplacion' but the 'mylke of lyȝte doctryne [*instruction*]' (p. 10), which does not need to be chewed, only to be swallowed. Doctrine, by its very nature, is authoritative and has to be believed in an immediate, passive, and transparent way. The same milk/meat image is traditional in Latin commentators and is also to be found in the English near-contemporary Love admired and recommended, Walter Hilton. In *The Scale of Perfection*, ii. 31, Hilton compares this lower sort of meditative knowledge to the milk which nourishes children, and the higher sort of contemplative knowledge to the solid food given to the weaned soul's intellect. According to Hilton, there are two ways of knowing God, one principally in imagination, the other principally in understanding, for 'chosen soulis bigynnynge and profitynge in grace, that knowen God and loven Hym al manli not goostli', are 'tendirli norischid as children, til thei ben able for to come to the fadris boord [*Father's table*] and taken of his hande hool breed'.[49]

Love's choice of milk does not mean that he is dismissing the benefits of higher contemplation, nor should his choice be despised by modern scholars, for the 'pleyn sentence' (p. 10) of the text, its clarity of moralizing, and its accessible affectivity help to make its meditative elements all the more profitable to 'symple soules' (p. 10). It should be no surprise, then, that the need for plain doctrine and teaching influences the treatment of the source in the main body of the work. We have already seen that this involves the exclusion of advanced contemplative materials. Alongside such cutting, Love has concomitant priority for moralization, which is sometimes amplified from, or even added to, the *Meditationes*. For example, in the *Die Lune* section, in Chapter 5, 'How Joseph þouht to leue priuely [*secretly to leave*] oure lady seynt Marie' (pp. 34–37), Love turns the narrative into more of a moral exemplum than in the original, emphasizing the profitable doctrine of a variety of virtues that are individually exemplified by the three protagonists:

> And so in þis forseid processe we haue profitable doctrine & gude ensaumple first in oure blessed lord Jesuᵗ of penance suffrynge of perfite Charite & trew compassion. Also in his modere Marieᵗ of profonde mekenes & pacience in tribulacion, & in hire hosbande Josephᵗ of vertuese ristwisnes aȝeynus fals suspicion [*virtuous righteousness against false suspicion*]. (p. 37)

Not only put by Love in an emphatic position at the end of the chapter for moralization, but also signposted by a marginal annotation drawing on the notion of *utilitas* from the academic literary theory ('Nota vtilitatem precedenciam' ('Note the profit from the preceding')), this statement does not exist in the Latin text.

Such highlighting of exemplary virtues is in accord with how Love's *proheme* prioritizes them more than the *Meditationes*. This issue of virtues and moral conduct must not be thought of in isolation, however. It is utterly inseparable from the other devotional *fruytes* and *profite* of the *Mirror*; for the point of good conduct before God is to exercise obedient loving faith, and through

---

[49] Walter Hilton, *The Scale of Perfection*, ed. by Bestul, ɪɪ. 31.

such faith to gain access to heaven by salvation, towards which all humans are stirred by the theological virtue and human emotion of hope. Virtues, good living, and hope of salvation are all folded by Love into the project of the *Mirror*, and these priorities are eloquently evidenced in the precise decisions he takes in his minutely attentive translating not only of the *Meditationes* but also of other vital and authoritative textual matter. It is to such priorities and translating that we turn next.

Love's Translation of Pauline Hope and Augustinian Virtues

So far, we have taken note of how Love distinctively situates and performs his work within a tradition of imaginative devotional writing without infantilizing or hamstringing the ambitions of his readers, and without degrading the literary or spiritual merits of the Latin source. It is now time to take our analysis deeper into the fabric and workings of Love's *Mirror*, into the revealing details of language, sentiment, devotion, theology, and cultural strategy that speak when we observe how and why Love translated as he did.

Without doubt, there is one profound theme and desiderative force that defines and animates Love's translating and crucially differentiates the *Mirror* from the *Meditationes vitae Christi*: hope. With great significance of intent and planning, Love gives pride of place in his proem and throughout his work to the Theological Virtue of hope as a benefit and motivation for his readers. This highly efficacious motion of the human will towards God has a distinguished pedigree in a triad with faith and charity. It is also the prime emotion that joins each Christian on earth to heaven. As 'the firm expectation of future beatitude arising from God's grace and our own merits', hope moves the earthly towards the heavenly, the human towards the divine, and is a foretaste of the beatitude to come.[50] A good idea of the power and dignity enjoyed by hope at this time may be seen in another didactic religious work of the fifteenth century, *The Court of Sapience*, which blazons it as 'the pollisshide myrrour of hevenlynes'.[51] Much the same could be said of the *Mirror* Love made. To be in a state of hope,

---

[50] Such is the standard definition in authorities such as Nicholas of Lyra, *Postilla literalis*, ed. by Leontorius, fol. 30ᵛ; see also Peter Lombard, *Sententiae*, bk III, dist. XXVI, cap. I (91), p. 159, and Joannes Januensis, *Catholicon*, s.v. 'spes'.

[51] *The Court of Sapience*, ed. by Harvey, l. 2334. Some of the following discussion revises materials from Johnson, 'The Non-Dissenting Vernacular and the Middle English Life of Christ', pp. 230–32.

then, is to reflect the genuinely heavenly — something even the athletic mystic would respect and cherish unquestioningly.

The *Mirror* accordingly opens with the famous and oft-exploited dictum of St Paul in Romans 15. 4, that all that is written is written for our doctrine, so that by patience and consolation of the Scriptures we have hope:

> Quecumque scripta sunt ad nostram doctrinam scripta sunt vt per pacienciam & consolacionem scripturarum spem habeamus, ad Romanos xv° capitulo. [*Whatever is written is written for our doctrine/instruction, so that by pacience and consolation of the Scriptures we may have hope. Romans, chapter 15.*]

> Þese ben þe wordes of the gret doctour and holy apostle *Powle*. (p. 9)

So often in international medieval literary culture, this verse of the Bible — or rather this first portion of it with the rest of the verse lopped off — 'Quecumque scripta sunt ad nostram doctrinam scripta sunt' — was used as a *carte blanche* for reading or writing what one liked, and its message about hope was de-emphasized, to say the least.[52] A notable and relevant exception to this, however, is Walter Hilton's *Scale of Perfection*:

> Seynt Poul seith thus: *Quecumque scripta sunt, ad nostram doctrinam scripta sunt, ut per consolacionem scripturarum, spem habeamus.* Al that is writen, to oure techynge it is writen, that bi confort of writynge we mai have hope of savacioun. [...] For the eende of this knowynge is savacion of a soule in ai lastynge liyf [*everlasting life*]; and the ende of othere as for hemself is but vanité and a passynge delite, but yif thei be [*unless they are*] turned thorugh grace to this eende.[53]

It is telling that Hilton glosses 'scripturarum' as 'writynge'. Evidently, like Love in his exposition, as we shall see below, he has in mind here the activity of the making of holy books as well as the 'goosteli' seeing of Jesus in the Scriptures. He is also extremely clear that no spiritual 'knowynge' or experiences are of more importance than the business of 'savacioun', and that the purpose of such 'writynge' is to fortify hope thereof.

Citing chapter and the verse in full with comparable propriety, Love attributes the Latin to Paul, an *auctor* who was both Doctor and Apostle; there is a marginal annotation 'Poule' to this effect. He proceeds to expound the *sentence* as it suits his *entent* for his chosen audience. Having benefited rhetorically from opening with a Latin scriptural text, Love goes on to expound it in English with one single, enormously long sentence, which consists of a build-up of

---

[52] Gillespie, 'From the Twelfth Century to *c.* 1450', p. 200.

[53] Walter Hilton, *The Scale of Perfection*, ed. by Bestul, II. 43.

unresolved clauses which are only dialectically and syntactically completed by a vernacular repetition of St Paul's words 'in-eched' with matter recommending *vitae Christi*;

> consideryng þat the gostly leuyng of all trewe crysten creatures in þis world stant [*stands*] specialy in *hope* of þe blisse & the lyfe þat is to come in another worlde.
>
> ¶ Ande for also mich as tweyne þinges pryncipaly noryschen & strenkþen þis *hope* in man þat is *pacience* in herte & ensaumple of vertues and gude liuyng of holy men *writen* in bokes꞉ Ande souereynly þe wordes and þe dedis *writen* of oure lord Jesu criste verrei god and man for þe tyme of his bodily liuyng here in erthe꞉ þerfore to strenkeþ vs & *comfort* vs in þis *hope* spekeþ the Apostle þe wordes aforseid to this entent seying þat all thynges þat ben written generaly in holi chirche ande specialy of oure lorde Jesu cryste þei bene wryten to oure lore that by pacience and conforte of holi scriptures we haue hope that is to say of the Life & Blysse that is to come in anothere worlde. (p. 9)

Sheer length of sentence is not often a significant critical category, but here the series of expository points creates a cumulative effect climaxing in a *conclusio* echoing and appropriating the Vulgate text, and finally returning triumphantly to the same *textuel* starting point. The first part of this sentence, up to the word 'entent', consists of a sequence of otherwise-independent commonplaces which interweave with and interpret Paul's words. Love's approach in this passage is quite adroit: he does not closely expound the original word-for-word or sense-for-sense so much as develop an argument constructed from points in the vernacular arranged in harmony with the Latin text, echoing key words (which I have italicized), such as 'hope' ('spem'), 'pacience' ('patientiam'), 'writen' ('scripta'), and 'conforte' ('consolacionem'). All these points, each of which leads logically to the next, would be self-justifying without recourse to an *auctoritas* like Romans, but the biblical text encapsulates and valorizes them all.

Firstly, the spiritual life of all true Christians is rooted in the hope of the life to come: this hope is strengthened by two things, patience and the virtuous examples of men written in books, and, in particular, Christ; this inevitably strengthens and comforts us in hope, in which spiritual life is rooted; thus St Paul said what he did. Though the first part of the sentence is at a somewhat elliptical distance from Romans it still draws authority from the Apostle. The second part translates Paul's words more closely but glosses them with the key points made in the first part of the sentence:

> to this entent seying þat all thynges þat ben written generaly in holi chirche ande specialy of oure lorde Jesu cryste þei bene wryten to oure lore that by pacience and

conforte of holi scriptures we haue hope that is to say of the Life & Blysse that is to
come in anothere worlde. (p. 9)

Thus, as a faithful translator, Love can be seen to be preserving in the vernacular not only the literal sense, but also the Englished *ipsissima verba* of Paul.
His exposition and rhetorical dressing of Romans very much suit his purposes,
in-eching (that is, by inserting expository words) a twofold *sentence* about the
nature, authority, and pertinence of the work to follow—that is, the supremacy,
under Holy Church, of the genre of the life of Christ, and its utility in providing example of virtues and of good living and, of course, hope for the afterlife.
Like many a biblical glossator and translator, Love inserts his own choice of
words amongst scriptural words. Unlike other writers, however, he does not use
Romans for the sole purpose of serving as a warrant for his own literary freedom. Instead, he deploys the second half of the original verse that deals with
hope, which is normally omitted by fellow-authors — the most famous example
being Geoffrey Chaucer in the *Retracciouns* to the *Canterbury Tales*.[54] Love's
reverential recuperating of the whole of Romans 15. 4 befits, then, the sacred
high seriousness of his decision to translate the *Meditationes vitae Christi* as a
book among those books that serve heaven, and as a book that moves readers
and hearers by hope towards salvation: these are scarcely oppressive intentions.

That Love writes of the 'thynges þat ben written generaly in holy chirche
ande specialy of oure lorde Jesu cryst' is not, however, only a reminder of the
ecclesiastical authority invested in the genre. It is also a reminder of the variegated collectivity of holy books sanctioned under the Church. In 'the vast
majority' of cases, Romans 15. 4, as Alastair Minnis points out, applies to 'a
grouping together or collection of diverse materials'.[55] Love's *Mirror* may well
be a rendering of a single source, but what he relates this citation to is no ordi-
nary compilation but the over-arching tradition or meta-*compilatio* of actual
and possible texts consisting of Holy Writ plus all writing thereon: 'scripture
ande wrytyng' (p. 10). (This collocation is intriguingly reminiscent of Hilton's
choice of the word 'writynge' in his exposition of this verse.) The *Mirror* is portrayed as scion of this, an option that is part of the diversity of which Love says
(after St Gregory), that 'holi writte may be expownet & vndurstande in diuerse

---

[54] See the *Canterbury Tales*, in *The Riverside Chaucer*, gen. ed. by Benson, x. 1081–92.
For critical discussion of the *Retractions* in the light of *compilatio*, see Minnis, *Translations of
Authority in Medieval English Literature*, pp. 206–10, and Johnson, 'The Ascending Soul and
the Virtue of Hope', pp. 254–60.

[55] Minnis, *Medieval Theory of Authorship*, p. 207.

maneres, & to diuerse purposes' (p. 11). The universal common denominator of all such diverse discourses is to move souls to salvific hope. The *Meditationes* is one such Latin book, and his *Mirror* will be realized as another. The *Mirror*, however, transcended its local connexions and became a special book for the English Church, licensed and commended universally to edify the faithful and confound all false Lollards and heretics, as the *memorandum* of the licensing by Arundel attests (p. 7). As an obedient and ordained instrument of Holy Church, Love was a literary preacher-translator expounding his texts in the vernacular as part of his *officium praedicatoris* for the benefit of his chosen audience, and as a Carthusian he was of course obliged to teach from the virtual pulpit of edifying textuality by making holy books as a form of 'preaching with the hands'. The famous words of Trevisa, that 'prechyng ys verrey Englysch translacion' applies *par excellence* to the *Mirror*.[56]

Love's vernacular theology exists in, and proceeds by, details of translation, and it is to translation that the rest of this chapter must therefore pay attention. So far, we have seen how Love's Englishing of Romans reflects and textually enforces his own priorities for his *Mirror*. Virtues (and in particular the Theological Virtue of hope), good living, and the life of Christ are thus from the outset bound up together inextricably as the parameters, grounding, *fruyte*, and *sentence* of Love's whole project. This is evident, for example, at the beginning of this passage when the Carthusian adds to Paul's words 'ensaumple of vertues and gude liuyng'. Even though neither the example of good virtues nor the topic of good living is mentioned in Romans 15. 4 itself, both are held here to be the business of this text in particular, as it is of holy books in general. Both are, moreover, accorded considerable priority in his general approach to how he recasts the *Meditationes* — as we shall see later in instances of Love the translator at work.

Love completes his exposition of Paul by (re)confirming that such fortifying and ecclesiastically sanctioned writings are, of course, produced in order to stir consolation and hope. That he chose Romans 15. 4 here means much: the deployment of this *auctoritas* is vital for orientating both source and readership and for situating the *Mirror* amidst other holy books. It is similarly telling, then, that this translator carefully chooses and strategically expounds a second clinching *auctoritas* in his paratext in order to frame, characterize, and valorize his project, this time from the greatest non-biblical *auctor* and Doctor of the Church, St Augustine.

---

[56] Waldron, 'Trevisa's Original Prefaces on Translation', p. 293.

This second decisive Englishing of an *auctor* specifies the unimaginable greatness and spiritually curative efficacy of the Incarnation as a universal spur to hope. It does not, as previously thought, consist of the Carthusian quoting and then elaborating in his own words a brief citation from St Augustine's *De agone christiano*; it is, in fact, a longer passage, consisting entirely of attentive translating from *De agone*, that embodies a theologically sensitive strategy revealing much about Love's conception of his enterprise.

At this early stage of his prologue Love has not yet declared that he is translating an authoritative work, let alone identified it as the mighty *Meditationes vitae Christi* written by so famous a holy clerk as Bonaventure. He has not yet readied his audience fully for contact with his treatment of the source. So, moving on from the universal theme of hope and exemplary holy lives, he prepares the way by alighting on, and reworking, the words of St Augustine's *De agone christiano*, a short treatise on Christian doctrine and morals for the relatively unlearned.

In his monumental edition of the *Mirror*, Michael Sargent describes Love's use of *De agone christiano* as 'a brief citation' (Introduction, p. 48), identifying it in his Explanatory Notes (p. 352) as a passage of some three lines: 'Goddes son toke man & in hym he soffred that longeþ to man & was made medicyne of manꝭ & this medicyne is so mykell þat it may nouȝt be þouȝt' (p. 9).[57] Further comparison, however, of Love's text with *De agone* reveals that Love continues his translation-stint from the end of the passage identified by Professor Sargent by simply following what is next in the source. He then takes two further sentences from two other separate places in Augustine's treatise. The end result is a passage of fluent Middle English prose disguising the fact that it is a series of pastings-in closely rendered straight from the Latin source, as can be seen below:[58]

> Here to accordyng spekeþ *Seynt Austyn* þus, Goddes son toke man & in hym he soffred that longeþ to man & was made medicyne of manꝭ & this medicyne is so mykell [*great*] þat it may nouȝt be þouȝt. For þer is no pryde bot þat it may be heled þruȝe þe mekenes of goddis sone. Þer is no Couetyse bot þat it may be heled throw is [*His*] pouerteꝭ No Wrath bot þat it may be heled throw his pacience. No Malice bot þat it may be heled þrowȝe his charitie.

[57] Augustine, *De agone christiano*, in *Patrologia latina*, XL (1845), cols 289–310 (col. 297). References to this work will be cited in abbreviated form in the text of this chapter. For an up-to-date and wide-ranging account of this work and its reception, see Verschoren, '*De agone christiano*'.

[58] The following discussion of Love's use of *De agone* revises materials from Johnson, 'What Nicholas Love Did in his *Proheme*'.

❡ Ande more ouer þer is no synne or wickednesse, bot that he schal want it and be kept fro it þe whiche byholdeth inwardly & loueþ & foloweþ þe wordes & þe dedis of that man in whome goddes sone ʒaff [*gave*] himself to vs in to ensaumple of gode leuyng [*good living*]. Wherfore nowe boþe men & women and euery Age and euery dignite of this worlde is stirid [*stirred*] to hope of euery lastyng [*everlasting*] lyfe. (pp. 9–10)

Itaque Filius Dei hominem assumpsit, et in illo humana perpessus est. Haec medicina hominum tanta est, quanta non potest cogitari. Nam quae superbia sanari potest, si humilitate Filii Dei non sanatur? Quae avaritia sanari potest, si paupertate Filii Dei non sanatur? Quae iracundia sanari potest, si patientia Filii Dei non sanatur? Quae impietas sanari potest, si charitate Filii Dei non sanatur?[59]

Accordingly the Son of God took on the form of Man, and in him suffered unto the very end that which was Man's. This medicine of Men is so great that it may not be thought. For what pride can be cured if it is not cured by/through the humility of the Son of God? What avarice can/may/is to be cured if it is not cured by/through the poverty of the Son of God? What anger/irascibility can be cured if it is not cured by/through the patience of the Son of God? What impiety can be cured if it is not cured by/through the charity of the Son of God?[60]

Qua perversitate non careat, qui facta et dicta intuetur et diligit et sectatur illius hominis, in quo se nobis ad exemplum vitae praebuit Filius Dei?[61]

From what perversity is he not kept, who contemplates and loves and follows the deeds and words of that man in whom the Son of God gave/offered up Himself as an example for life.

Itaque jam et masculi et feminae, et omnis aetas, et omnis hujus saeculi dignitas ad spem vitae aeternae commota est.[62]

Accordingly, both men and women and those of every age and of every rank in this world are now stirred to hope of life eternal.

The *conclusioun* to this passage looks for all the world like it could be Love's own statement in his own words about the universality of his *Mirror* for that national audience of the faithful famously proclaimed in the Memorandum of Arundel's commending of the book (p. 7). But it is close translation of

[59] Augustine, *De agone christiano*, Caput XI, col. 297.

[60] Translations of *De agone christiano* are mine, unless otherwise indicated.

[61] Augustine, *De agone christiano*, col. 298.

[62] Augustine, *De agone christiano*, col. 298.

Augustine, and it chimes with Love's earlier exposition of Romans ('consideryng þat the gostly leuyng of all trewe crysten creatures in þis world stant specialy in hope of þe blysse & the lyfe þat is to come in another worlde'; and 'we haue hope that is to say of the Life & Blysse that is to come in anothere worlde' (Love, p. 9)). Evidently, Love carries Augustine into his exposition of Romans; both authoritative passages are made, by deft exposition, to echo and confirm each other in setting the terms on which the Pseudo-Bonaventuran tradition is being renegotiated here by Nicholas Love for his own ends and for his own audience. He renders *De agone christiano* with his own strategic slant and applies it to his work as a whole in a carefully crafted theological trajectory that, like the immediately-preceding Pauline exposition to which it is joined and with which it is made to agree, returns harmoniously at its conclusion to Romans' desideratum of stirring all Christians to hope of everlasting life: 'Wherfore nowe boþe men & women and euery Age and euery dignite of this worlde is stirid to hope of euery lastyng lyfe'.

The basic thrust of the Augustinian exposition is that, although the nature and scale of Christ's incarnational and redemptive healing are too great to be thought, nevertheless the human imagining of the Incarnation, in the form of the virtues, words, and deeds of Christ, provides example to all Christian souls of how to handle sin in this earthly life, and moves them to hope of the next. A parallel and a connexion are thus drawn between, on the one hand, Christ's redemptive healing of Man's sin and, on the other, the exemplary power and moral utility of His life on earth. It is also vital to Love's presentation to his audience of this meditative life of Christ that this parallel and connexion should be expressed so authoritatively and so clearly with particular reference to the capacities of the human mind, and in particular the imagination, wherein each reader of the *Mirror* 'byholdeth inwardly' such a life and may, through following it, accordingly reap the benefit of being able to overpower sin and thereby cultivate ample cause for hope of future beatitude.

Love's translational approach to Augustine reveals the strategic-mindedness of a canny vernacular pastoral theologian setting up the advisory parameters for his readership and working with telling cultural and linguistic tact on an audience he both knows and constructs. His rhetorically foregrounded and patristically validated broaching of the cognitive challenge of comprehending the Incarnation enables him, at this point of the *proheme*, to prepare his readership/audience for the difficult but desirable task of meditating on a curative *vita* at once human and divine, and for understanding how 'this medicyne' may and may not be thought. His handling and conveyance of translational nuance reveal his delicate but apprehensible redrawing of the lineaments of doctrinal

sense and sentiment for the guidance of the vernacular meditant in accommodating the working of incarnational medicine in the penitent soul. This medicine of Christ is of such a nature, and of such a greatness, that it may not be
conceived by humanity as it really is, for 'this medicyne is so mykell þat it may
nouȝt be þouȝt'. Its effects, impacts, and operation, however, may be 'þouȝt',
because they are observable and imaginable in His virtues — virtues that are
also part and parcel of the terms and conditions of penitential routine that
would be familiar to Love's audience.

In penitential theory and practice, as found in the 'Vices and Virtues' tradition, specific virtues were remedies for specific sins, as is the case here. The
virtue of humility/meekness, for example, does away with pride as a standard
remedium contra peccatum. Normally in this tradition, remedies were characterized as something to be exercised by penitents themselves. This is not quite
so here, where each remedy is Christ's — 'his'. With a theological discrimina-
tion that aims to remodulate the penitential *habitus* of the user of the *Mirror*,
Nicholas Love compiles into his *proheme* a line of argument from Augustine
that proclaims the Son of God, in Whom all salvific virtue originates, as the
overarching and empowering fount, exemplar, and agent of individual penitential virtues and as the healer of original human sin. Whereas, in the common
run of penitential discourse, our own meekness, for instance, may routinely
be portrayed as being able to chase out pride through our own contrite free
choice, Love picks this moment of entry into his *vita Christi* to proclaim to the
frail and sinful Christian that the *fons et origo* of this process and the sovereign
example of the operation of virtues are to be found in Christ's life — which it is
the task of the meditating soul devoutly to imagine and imitate.

Each of the quartet of remedial virtues is emphatically catalogued as being
in the Son's possession ('þe mekenes of goddis sone', 'is [*His*] pouerte', 'his pacience', and 'his charitie'). As instances of an exemplary theological process, they
all partake of the same 'mykell' nature, a single 'medicyne'. Just as the Manhood
is possessed by God's Son and is thus *His*, so too these virtues are *His*. Even
more significantly, it is important to note the subtle but transparent decisive-
ness of Love's translating when he treats each remedy as something *through*
('þruȝe [...] thorgh [...] throw [...] þrowȝe') which, not *by* which, healing is
effected. The Latin would permit the latter translation but the ablative end-
ings of each preposition-free virtue — 'humilitate', 'paupertate', 'patientia', and
'charitate' — are in themselves semantically indecisive as to which sense might
apply. Were 'by' to have been used by Love, there might have been an implication that each virtue possessed in itself the potency to effect a cure, whereas it
would be more theologically correct to say, as does Love, that the exercise of

virtues is a matter of the human soul cooperating in free will with God's grace *through* those virtues. Love's modulation of his source here shows a theological delicacy and accuracy not articulated so finely by the ablative ambivalence of the prepositionless Saint or by Love's fellow-translators.

This is but one instance among many of Love's great gifts as a translator of pellucid, self-aware subtlety. It is also a particularly revealing instance of vernacular theology in minute practice in the form of highly discriminating, context-specific rendering designed by Love to valorize and modulate the utility and the authority of his work. Its relevance to Love's conception of his project is underlined all the more a little later in the *proheme* when he translates from the *Meditationes* a passage advertising the profitability of the Pseudo-Bonaventuran work as a repository of typically Franciscan virtues. The Franciscan virtues of the *Meditationes* are, however, overgone in translation when Love exchanges them for his Augustinian quartet from *De agone christiano*. In the original, prayer, and wisdom, and obedience ('sapientiae, orationis, [...] obedientiae') are itemized, but the translator cuts them, adding the all-important Augustinian virtue of charity:

> Ubi enim virtutes excelsae paupertatis, eximiae humilitatis, profundae sapientiae, orationis, mansuetudinis, obedientiae, patientiae, caeterarumque virtutum exempla et doctrinam sic invenies, sicut in vita Domini virtutum? (*Meditationes vitae Christi*, ed. by Peltier, p. 510)

> Where else will you find such virtues of lofty poverty, extraordinary humility, profound wisdom, prayer, mildness, obedience, patience, such examples of other virtues and doctrine as in the life of the Lord of virtues?[63]

> For where salt þou fynde so opun ensaumple & doctrine, of souereyn charite, of perfite pouerte, of profonde mekenes of pacience & oþer vertues, as in þe blessed lif of Jesu crist. (p. 12)

Does this reorientation of the *Meditationes* represent a kind of translational displacement by which Love uses the Bishop of Hippo to repurpose the source? The original presents a series of virtues more or less associated with the Franciscan or monastic life: poverty, humility, wisdom, prayer, meekness. obedience, patience, plus other non-specified virtues.[64] Love excludes profound

---

[63] Translation mine.

[64] The first virtue mentioned by Love, 'charite', as well as being in the Augustinian text, might have been in his Pseudo-Bonaventuran source already, for the Italian version of the *Meditationes vitae Christi*, as represented in Paris, BnF, MS ital. 115, includes at this point 'exam-

wisdom ('profundae sapientiae'), presumably because he thinks it to be beyond the capacity of simple souls (and nearly all the rest of humanity, to be fair), and also because he cares more about getting his readers saved. Prayer ('orationis') is more for the professed religious. Obedience smacks of monastic vows ('obedientiae'), but may be held to be preserved in a more general sense in 'mekenes', as would be mildness and humility ('mansuetudinis'; 'humilitatis'). Indeed, Love's newly imposed quartet of virtues is appropriate to his vernacular audience, be they Carthusian lay brothers or layfolk more generally; the omitted virtues are better suited to those in the religious life.[65] In any case, each virtue cut from the Latin would fall into the compensatory safety-net of 'other vertues'. Love's 're-keying' of virtues here is, clearly, conditioned by his choice of 'Augustinian' *auctoritas* to define his whole project. Evidently, he chose material from *De agone christiano* because it suited his conception not only of his prefatory re-characterizing of the *Meditationes* but also of his re-orientation of the Pseudo-Bonaventuran tradition — and this was largely accomplished through details of translation.

A concomitant 'retuning' is visible in other translation choices Love makes in the same thematic zone. These may be details, but they are telling in that they seem to constitute an important cluster of four features, central to Love's agenda, that appear to entail each other, even to the point of being, on occasion, mutually interchangeable. They are: firstly, virtues and the acquisition thereof; second, good living; third, the life of Christ as the source and exemplar of such virtues and good living, and fourth, in connexion with the third feature, Love's own work, the *Mirror of the Blessed Life of Jesus Christ* itself. This cluster harks back to the *in-echings* of Love's exposition of Romans and his nuancing of material from Augustine. So, when, for example, perhaps self-aggrandizingly echoing the title he has devised for his work (to be discussed in Chapter 4 of this book), he translates 'vita Domini virtutum' ('life of the Lord of virtues'; *Meditationes vitae Christi*, ed. by Peltier, p. 510) as 'the blessed lif of Jesu Crist' (p. 12), he thereby somewhat subsumes Christ's virtues into something resembling and evoking the title he has chosen for his work (a *nomen libri* signally different from 'Meditationes vitae Christi'). For Love, his own new

---

ples and teachings of charity', though it does not declare charity to be 'souereyn'. See *Meditations on the Life of Christ: An Illustrated Manuscript*, trans. by Ragusa and Green, p. 3. See also John de Caulibus, *Meditaciones vitae Christi*, ed. by Stallings-Taney, p. 8, which also includes charity.

[65] For discussion of Love's possible intentions towards Carthusian lay brothers as an audience for the *Mirror*, see Falls, 'The Carthusian Milieu of Nicholas Love's *Mirror*'.

title is becoming something of a portmanteau for the virtues that originate in Christ for humanity's benefit.[66]

A similar thing happens when, not for the last time, Love pointedly inserts into the *Meditationes* the idea that the life of Christ has utility for the acquisition of virtues. In translating the declaration that 'nec hostes nec vitia irruere vel fallere possint' ('neither enemies nor vices can make inroads or deceive you'; *Meditationes vitae Christi*, ed. by Peltier, p. 510); 'neither enemies nor vices can make inroads or deceive you')[67] as 'that hit kepeþ fro vices and disposeþ souereynly to getyng of vertues' (p. 12), Love adds virtues to the Pseudo-Bonaventuran mention of vices alone. In an earlier passage, in similar vein, Love adds to the *Meditationes* a claim that one benefit of meditating, as with St Cecilia, is the 'encrese & getyng of vertues' (p. 11). The very next sentence is then completed with a proclamation that the life of Christ not only teaches one how to counter vices but, once more in addition to the source, how to acquire virtues:

> Nusquam enim invenies, ubi sic doceri possis [...] contra hostium tentamenta et vitia, sicut in vita Domini Jesu. (*Meditationes vitae Christi*, ed. by Peltier, p. 510)

> Indeed, you will find no place else where you can become so schooled against [...] the temptations and vices of your enemies and vices, as in the life of the Lord Jesus.[68]

> For soþely [*truly*] þou shalt neuer finde, where man may so perfitely be taght [...] & forþermore to be kept fro vices and to getyng [*the acquisition*] of vertues¦ as in þe blissede life of oure lorde Jesu. (pp. 11–12)

The 'fro [...] to' vice-to-virtue curative trajectory, reminiscent of the process of virtuous cure as seized on by Love from *De agone*, is not in the original either, and further accentuates his 'Augustinian' approach to his main source. In the same passage, the words 'vita Domini Jesu', noticeably expanded to 'þe blissede life of oure lorde Jesu', likewise echo and valorize the new title constructed by the Carthusian for his own and his readers' work. It is also significant that this *in-eching* of title goes hand-in-hand with the *in-eching* of 'getyng of vertues' into this passage. Clearly, one entails the other, just as Love's translational stressing

---

[66] A little later Love uses the term 'lord of vertues' (p. 12), rendering 'Domino virtutum', so the concept as expressed in the original is by no means lost to the *Mirror*.

[67] John de Caulibus, *Meditations on the Life of Christ*, trans. by Taney, Miller, and Stallings-Taney, p. 2.

[68] John de Caulibus, *Meditations on the Life of Christ*, trans. by Taney, Miller, and Stallings-Taney, p. 1

of virtues and the getting thereof are concomitant with his emphasis on Christ's example of good living as elements to go into the mix of the devout reader's interior fleshly imaginings of the *gostly*. It is to a closer examination of the translator's linguistic making of the topography of imaginable *gostly* interiority in this passage that we turn next for further revealing evidence concerning Love's orientation of source, readership, and the 'psycho-logistics' of affective theology.[69]

Translational Topographies of Language and Imagination

Middle English devotional translators like Love knew that it was their duty to think and work well *gostly* by thinking and working *bodely* language and imagination well. A good translator of *devout imaginaciouns* will know how to represent ideas, emotions, and experience linguistically in order not only to communicate nuances of meaning to his readers, but also to move and set their souls into the precise configurations in which they need to arrange themselves for the exercises intended for them; for the logistics of language and the imagination converge in mechanisms that articulate the sensible. Nicholas Love is such a translator.

In order to do this we will continue to examine the same short passage just discussed. In this passage the spatially and dynamically re-imaginable interrelations of key theological and psychic concepts are reconstructed translationally through Love's subtle addition and modulation of unglamorous but vital verbs and prepositions. It should be noted first, however, that shortly before this passage the *Meditationes vitae Christi* declares that having Christ's *vita* in the heart can lead 'to a higher level' of meditation — 'ad celsiorem gradum' (*Meditationes vitae Christi*, ed. by Peltier, p. 510). Unlike his source, as we know already, Love is not interested in turning his readers into contemplatives, but he is happy to appropriate contemplative literary style to help blazon his ambition of inculcating in his readership not only the cultivation of virtues and good living but also the avoidance and rejection of vices. So, imitating the language of Middle English contemplative texts, he alters his source, upgrading its comparative adjective ('celsiorem') grammatically to a superlative at the same time as downgrading (or recycling) its spiritual ambition: he does not wish to bring his readers to a *higher* degree of contemplation; instead he prefers, for them, 'þe *hyest* degre of gude liuyng', adding also to the Latin the specification that such a 'degre' is 'in encrese and in getyng of vertues' (p. 11). This re-slanting of the

---

[69] This analysis will revise some materials from Johnson, 'Translational Topographies of Language and Imagination'.

original towards good living and virtues prepares the ground for the passage in question, in which Love deals with the morally and spiritually transformative power of the life of Christ, but adds to, and sophisticates, the theological and psychological logistics of what is in the source:

> Nusquam enim invenies, ubi sic doceri possis contra vana blandimenta et caduca, contra tribulationes et adversa, contra hostium tentamenta et vitia, sicut in vita Domini Jesu, quae fuit absque omni defectu perfectissima. (*Meditationes vitae Christi*, ed. by Peltier, p. 510)

> Indeed, you will find no place else where you can become so schooled against vain and passing enticements, trials and adversities, and the temptations and vices of your enemies, as in the life of the Lord Jesus, a life that was absolutely perfect and without any defect.[70]

> For soþely [*truly*] þou shalt neuer finde, where man may so perfitely be taght, first for to stable his herte aȝeynus vanitees & deceyuable likynges of þe worlde, also to strengh him amongis tribulacions & aduersitees, & forþermore to be kept fro vices and to getyng of vertues፡ as in þe blissede life of oure lorde Jesu, þe which was euere withoute defaut most perfite. (pp. 11–12)

The first noticeable change is that the second-person singular implied recipient of the Latin original (as evidenced by the second-person verbs 'invenies' and 'possis') undergoes a subtle shift and multiplication. Love commences by addressing, as in the Latin, a second-person singular 'þou', but discontinues this by introducing the generalizing noun 'man' and then the third-person pronouns 'his' and 'hym'. In other words, the original's 'you will find no place else where you can become so schooled' becomes, for Love, something more like 'you will find no place else where Man can become so schooled'. These shifts do not necessarily mean that the reader is no longer being tackled: s/he will always be one human amongst all humanity, but such generalizing suits Love's conception of his audience as a community of individual souls, a conception broader than that initially targeted by the Latin *Meditationes*, written ostensibly for one Poor Clare. However, a new sense is added here by Love to the original: not only will *you* ('þou') find such incomparable perfect experience of teaching, *you* will also find and witness others' experience of this perfect teaching too. Love conceived of his audience as a collectivity, universal but varied, drawing from 'boþe men & women & euery Age & euery dignite of this worlde' (p. 10). After all, the *Mirror* was endorsed for the widest possible circulation by Archbishop

---

[70] John de Caulibus, *Meditations on the Life of Christ*, trans. by Taney, Miller, and Stallings-Taney, p. 1

Arundel himself, as attested in the memorandum affixed to many manuscripts of the work (p. 7).

Whereas the Latin itemizes a trio of undesirable things against which the life of Christ teaches, the *Mirror*, also acknowledging this didactic function, makes more of this threefold division by adding the ordinating adverbs 'first [...], also [...], & forþermore'. The triple sequence is highlighted all the more by the *ordinatio* of the ensuing discussion being marginally glossed with 'Primum', 'Secundum', and 'Tercium' (p. 12).[71] Each element of the threefold division is also accorded its own verb, not present in the original, designating discrete but overlapping virtuous actions of, respectively, stabilizing ('to stable his herte'), self-fortifying ('to strengh him'), and protection/keeping/preventing ('to be kept fro vices and to getyng of vertues'). The first English infinitive, 'to stable', is collocated with the preposition 'aӡeynus', a close translation of the Latin 'contra', but the second verb, 'to strengh hym', is attached to a different preposition, 'amongis'. The third added verb, 'to be kept', is put with two prepositions expressing linear movement and process: 'fro' and 'to'. More analytically detailed than the source, the new vernacular disposition of verbs, adverbs, and prepositions supports a finer-grained articulation of the variously adaptable powers of the life of Christ in aiding the beleaguered soul. How His powers work is represented here with greater logistical complexity than in the source, and with a directionally more varied distribution of resolving dynamic concepts. In particular, newly added collocations of verbs-plus-prepositions open out a more inter-relationally complex psychomachic space, animated by vices/adversity and virtues pertinent to the mechanically imagined shifting vulnerabilities and situations of the individual Christian reader.

The way Love deploys verbs and prepositions cognitively enriches the semantic, theological, and psychic space, actions, and phenomena of his text. Thus, 'to stable' signals an action of fixity and enduringness fit for the addressing and sorting out of undesirable spiritual and moral weakness or slippage. As a teleological process, it positively intensifies its own proper qualities of strength, befitting a solving action. It is collocated with 'aӡeynus', which reproduces the Latin preposition of opposition or contrariety repeated unvaryingly throughout the original passage. The second verb, 'to strengh hym', is also an intensifying verb, fulfilling the end proper to its agency, but, unlike 'stable', it places the individual yet generalized Christian soul ('hym') not dualistically

---

[71] It is conceivable that these marginal glosses are authorial, or at the very least that they were authorized early in the tradition of transmission, for, as Sargent points out, 'the marginal notes to texts of the *Mirror* are [...] relatively stable, and must be treated as part of the text itself, for all textual-critical purposes' (introduction to Nicholas Love, *Mirror*, ed. by Sargent, p. 102).

against ('aȝeynus') some things, but 'amongis' a multiplicity of them, exposing 'hym' spatially *amidst*, not *against*, hostile forces that could come at 'hym' from any direction. A soul 'amongis' things is always surrounded and outnumbered. Unlike 'aȝeynus', 'amongis' does not signify any capacity within the Christian soul for resistance or opposition to tribulations and adversities, but points to an inert situatedness rather than a directional agency contrary to these. To be 'amongis' such things also brings temporality into play, because the plurality of 'tribulacions & aduersitees' will not assail the vice-threatened soul only once; rather, they will attack severally in time. The effect of this is to suggest time itself as an extensible medium of vulnerability.

The third collocation of verbs and prepositions produces an even greater logistical complexity of psychomachic space and conceptual action: 'to be kept fro', indicating protection, suggests at the same time the creation and/or maintenance of a secure distance from vices (a spatializing effect). The preposition 'fro' is to do with being away from, or parted from, vices: a directional separateness. The preposition 'to', on the other hand, may be the opposite of 'fro', but it moves in the same direction as 'fro', that is, towards the positive action of 'getyng of vertues'. The action of 'getyng of vertues' that 'to' points to is performed by 'man': none of these is, however, in the original. This added action of getting is one of moral aggrandizement, and not just about staving off tribulations and vices, which is the concern of the original at this point. As antitheses in rhetorical equilibrium, 'to' and 'fro' are in concert in a causal and temporal sequence signalling the beginning and end of a trajectory of moral transformation from the vicious to the virtuous, even though the two processes they designate may be performed in a single moral action in the Christian soul. The totalizing 'fro'/'to' antithesis, not in the original either, further enhances not only the sense of the comprehensive power of the life of Christ, but also its moral transformativeness. This is important to note, because in general the *Mirror* programmatically gives a higher profile to moral transformation, good living, and the getting of virtues than the *Meditationes vitae Christi*. Here, Love's translating combines oppositionality, directionality, and change in an acute conceptually and grammatically realised reworking, articulated in discriminating, fine-grained prose.

Finally, the word 'vita', rendered 'blissede life', reveals Love alluding to his chosen English title from within his translating, and thereby suggestively valorizing his literary work with the power of Christ's life and with all that it means. Indeed, it seems that some scribes perhaps heard the echo of Love's title so loudly here that they added at this point in the text the word 'crist' to 'þe blissede life of oure lorde Jesu'.[72] It would appear then, that they were, even to the detriment of performing their professional duties accurately, properly sensitized to Love's overall strategy with his work: they were picking up on something that was meant to be there and meant to be noticed.

So, when Nicholas Love does something grammatical he does something imaginative and something theological that follows through to other places in the text and to other sites and occasions of reader-experience — all for the purposes of educating the spiritual *habitus* of the reader. Indeed, at the high point of the Last Supper, which we discuss next, the same *modus agendi*, with the same thematic preoccupations, can be seen to be at work.

A Last Supper of Hope: Translating an Earnest of Heaven

Love's treatment of the Last Supper, like his *proheme* and his Treatise on the Sacrament, engages in the business of adding to the *Meditationes vitae Christi* in order to change it. It is one of those key orientation points of the *Mirror* which is vital in (re)defining the theological and affective function of the work for its intended readership.[73] But before discussing how and why Love's Last Supper departs from the original it would be a good idea to look at part of the text from the beginning of the Passion section, just after the Supper. Here is a profoundly important passage in which the benefits and the enormous transformative power of meditating on the Passion are described. This passage has a theme and trajectory of hope — that experience and virtue of grace, as flagged up in the *proheme*, which is an individual foretaste of heaven:

> Forþermore after þe processe of Bonauenture, whoso desireþ with þe apostle Poule to be be ioyful in þe crosse of oure lorde Jesu criste, & in his blessede passion‡ he moste with bisy meditacion abide þereinne. For þe grete misteries & alle þe pro-

---

[72] See the critical apparatus in Nicholas Love, *Mirror*, ed. by Sargent, p. 246, where Sargent cites two manuscripts: London, British Library, MS Additional 19901 and MS Arundel 364, and also New York, Pierpont Morgan Library, MS 226, as sharing this feature. In another scribal/editorial variation recorded by Sargent (p. 246) as occurring in the α3 branch of the Table of Affiliations, 'amongis tribulacions and aduersitees' becomes 'ayenst tribulacions and aduersitees': perhaps someone knew the Latin and preserved the 'contra'; or perhaps 'ayenst' was the more expected and natural preposition after the infinitive 'to strengh him'. That Love himself does otherwise by opting for 'amongis' is part and parcel of his theologically conscious *mouvance* of his source in his translating of it.

[73] This discussion of the Last Supper revises a passage in Johnson, 'The Non-Dissenting Vernacular and the Middle English Life of Christ', pp. 232–34.

cesse þerof, if þei were inwardly consideret with all þe inwarde mynde & beholdyng of mannus [*Man's*] soule: as I fully trowe, þei sholde bringe þat beholdere in to a newe state of grace. For to him þat wolde serche þe passion of oure lorde with alle his herte & alle his inwarde affeccione: þere shuld come many deuout felynges & stirynges þat he neuer supposede before. Of þe whech he shuld fele a newe compassion & a newe loue, & haue newe gostly confortes, þorh þe whech he shold perceyue him self turnede as it were in to a newe astate [*state*] of soule, in þe which astate þoo forseide gostly felynges, shold seme to him as a nerneste & partie [*an earnest/pledge and a part*] of þe blisse & ioy to come. (p. 160)

To encounter a new state of grace, spiritual consolation, and a pledge and foretaste of the transcendent beatitude of the life to come constitutes no mean experience, and would indicate that Love's *Mirror* does not deny heavenly 'process' to the yearning soul, which is portrayed as having the independence, free will, and capacity to 'serche þe passion of oure lorde with alle his herte & alle his inwarde affeccione'. This is scarcely a dumbing down of the capacities of the vernacular soul.

A little earlier, in the Last Supper chapter, the same virtue and emotion of hope is highlighted at the climax of Jesus's sermon to His disciples. This is not so in the *Meditationes vitae Christi*. By deft reworking of the source and its scriptural quotations and by some new cutting and pasting directly from John's Gospel, Love turns up the *auctoritas* level and somewhat overgoes the original. This Carthusian conservative is perfectly prepared to feed his audience vernacular Scripture, either from Pseudo-Bonaventure or direct from the Bible, as and when it suits. Love introduces the theological virtues at the head of this passage in the usual order of faith, hope, charity, but in a fascinating move he ensures that Christ's actual sermon treats of charity, then faith, and finally, at the high point and *conclusio*, hope. Let us look at what Love's affective hermeneutics of hope does with Gospel quotations:

In hope also he conforted hem in many maneres, & first touching þe effecte of praiere, seyinge to hem in þees wordes, *If ȝe duelle in me & my wordes abyden stedfastly in ȝow: what so euer ȝe wole aske: it sal be ȝiuen ȝow.* (p. 155)

None of this is in the *Meditationes*. The message to the reader in this addition, which renders John 15. 7, is that if s/he engages with Christ's life and subsequently dwells therein (like Cecilia, no infantilizing exemplar), all that is asked will be granted. Note the use of 'what so euer' and 'it': their open indefiniteness, an accurate translation of the Vulgate Latin, befits the reader's free will and also the unknown-ness of what s/he might ask for. Hope has the property of 'kindly inclining' towards what is yet unknown: heaven. It brings the reader to the threshold of the divine in the firm but not presumptuous expectation of affective fruit and salvific success, that is, of getting what is asked for. The reader's 'wole', a verb of mere human will, is translated here not so much as influencing the divine will as in effect compelling it ('sal').

A few lines later and in similar vein, the same sermon ends with the triumph of hope translated from Christ to the reader via a gloss of Love's on the biblical text (John 16. 33):

> And þen he concludet in þees wordes, *Alle þese forseid wordes I haue spoken to 30w vnto þat ende, þat 3e haue þese in me. In þe world 3e shole haue sorow & anguysh, bot trusteth wele by sadde* [steadfast] *hope, for I haue ouercome þe world,* as who seiþ & so sal 3e. (p. 155)

As Christ overcame the world, so will the reader who hopes overcome the world. It is particularly suitable that the word *sadde* is deployed as a qualifier for hope, because in being able to mean 'sad/sorrowful' as well as 'steadfast' it simultaneously contains both problem and solution. Selectively highlighting hope once more, Love renders the Latin word 'confidite' (translated as 'have faith' in Taney, Miller, and Stallings-Taney's Modern English version of the Latin)[74] as 'trusteth wele by sadde hope', thereby proclaiming the instrumentality and efficacy of this virtue for overcoming the world. Love's gloss, 'as who seiþ & so sal 3e', elucidates what is left unsaid but is clearly intended in the *sensus literalis* of the divine utterer, Christ. In emerging from *narratio* into gloss Love's voice transmutes from that of a reporter/rehearser into that of a confidant and preacher directly addressing the reader with the personal import of Christ's words. The key message is this: you, the reader, can rely on steadfast hope because Christ overcame the world in which you, the reader, suffer sorrow and anguish. At one and the same time the text traces a movement across two important boundaries: firstly, from biblical text to vernacular gloss; second, from meditative *narratio* to the application of a *sententia* in the 'real world' of Love and his reader. Love's gloss turns the words of Christ reporting the past yet also future fact of His overcoming of the world into an explicit future fact for the reader who hopes, and who, by simply knowing and following these words, shall therefore have the power and grace to overcome the world in his/her turn.

---

[74] John de Caulibus, *Meditations on the Life of Christ*, trans. by Taney, Miller, and Stallings-Taney, p. 234.

Prayers and Heavenly Translation

This chapter has concentrated on passages of translating from places like the Last Supper and the *proheme* because of the nature of the evidence they provide for Love's take on hope, virtues, the fruitfulness of the life of Christ and its blessedness — and for his overall strategy and ambition for the whole enterprise. If further support for the findings of these analyses of Love at work were needed from elsewhere in the *Mirror*, it should be sought in those other parts of the text where he makes deliberate changes or additions to the *Meditationes* for the purposes of orientating the work for his chosen audience: this is where changes count most. It is therefore pertinent to conclude with two further passages that Love adds to the *Meditationes* in order to re-orientate it to see how far they tally with or develop the findings that so far seem to have been emerging in this chapter. Both passages, intriguingly, are prayers.

Why choose prayers? Prayers present an unusual and revealing species of textual evidence because, as a personal yet shareable textual form, they have to be as performable and as answerable before an omniscient God for their writer as they have to be for the readers for whom they are intended. In articulating a prayer, Love is obliged to be honest and specific before God: this is a much more pressured and exposed transaction than presenting words only to humans. We shall discuss Love's intralingual translating in the prayer appended to the 'Treatise on the Sacrament'; but first we shall look at the versified prayer that he puts at the end of the prose exposition (pp. 29–30) of the *Ave Maria* (pp. 30–31) that he adds to the *Meditationes*:

> *Heil Marie*⋮ maiden mekest.
> Gret of [*Greeted by*] þe angel gabriel in Jesu graciouse conceyuyng.
> *Ful of grace*⋮ as modere chast [*mother chaste*]
> without sorow or peyne þi son, Jesu blessed beryng.
> *Oure lord is & was with þe*
> by trew feiþ & byleue at Jesu ioyful vprysyng.
> *Blessed be þou souereynly in women,*
> by sadde [*steadfast*] hope seying þi sone Jesu to heuen mihtily vpsteyng
>   [*arising/ascending*].
> *And blessed be þe fruyt of þi wombe Jesus,*
> in euerlastyng blisse þorh [*through*] perfite charite þe quene of heuen
>   gloriously cronyng [*crowning*].
> Be þou oure help in al oure nede, & socour at our last endynge. *Amen.*
>
>   (pp. 30–31)

At this point it is important to note that in the β1 group of manuscripts there is, according to Sargent, 'a Latin version' (Introduction, p. 145) of Love's poem:

Ave Maria virgo mitissima
digna angelica salutacione
Gracia plena Mater castissima
in tui prolis iocunda generacione
Dominus tecum, fide firmissima
in tui filij gloriosa resurreccione
Benedicta tu in mulieribus spe certissima
in eius admiranda assencione
Et benedictus fructus ventris tui Jesus
Caratitate plenissima te coronans in celesti habitacione
Esto nobis auxiliatrix
in omni angustia et temptacione Amen.

Hail Mary, mildest virgin,
Worthy of angelic greeting,
Full of grace, Mother most chaste,
Joyful in the generation of your offspring,
The Lord is [or be] with you, most steadfast of faith.
In your son's glorious resurrection
Blessed are you amongst women, most steadfast of hope
In His wondrous Ascension.
And blessed is the fruit of your womb, Jesus,
Crowning you, brim-full of love, in your heavenly dwelling place.
Be our help
In all perplexity and temptation. Amen.

This rhyming Latin poem is tight and formal in its structure. It is, surely, more likely that Love's lines are a loosened versified unpacking of the Latin than that the Latin is a freshly patterned streamlining of the English. This would mean, then, that in all probability the English poem (with the Latin looming usably behind it) is in fact an immediate source of the prose exposition that Love also includes in this chapter (pp. 29–30). Both of the above prayer-poems clearly possess artfulness, despite the irregular line lengths and prosodic haphazardness of Love's effort. The important 'virtuous' terms 'mekest' and 'chast', for instance, are adjectives representing two of the key virtues identified in the prose exposition and in the Latin poem. In the latter, these opening two Marian virtues, 'mitissima' and 'castissima', rhyme. In Love's verses 'mekest' and 'chast' are paired as half-rhymes: he takes care not to lose emphasis on them by misplacing them in an unstressed place earlier within the line.

Bearing in mind Love's valorizing of hope elsewhere in the *Mirror*, the following is also significant:

> *Blessed be þou souereynly in women,*
> by sadde hope seying þi sone Jesu to heuen mihtily vpsteyng.

It has already been observed that, in his radical adaptation of the chapter on the Last Supper (see above), Love deliberately introduces the collocation 'sadde hope' as a special term steering the *ipsissima verba* of the Vulgate towards this theological virtue. Here, 'sadde' ('firm' or 'steadfast') renders 'certissima' ('most certain'). Love could have been more verbally accurate by, say, using 'moost certeyne' or something similar, but he did not do this: instead he opted for a link with a pressure point in his own highly particular rendition of the Last Supper; or, if he wrote the Last Supper section after he made this poem — and this is not impossible inasmuch as the Last Supper happens well after the Annunciation — then his version of the poem would have fed into his transformation of the word 'confidite' ('have faith') in the later episode.

Love elucidates the theological and devotional *sentence* of this verse in *prose pleyne*:

> ¶ In þe ferþe [*fourth*] parte þat is in þes wordes, *Iblessed be þou in women or elles aboue al women* may be vndirstonde þe ferþ ioy þat she hade, in þe siht of hire sone Jesu miȝteli to heuen vp steing [*ascending*]. In þe which siȝt [*sight*] þe hope þat sche hadde in his godhede was fullich strengþede & confermede seying þat oþer women neuer dide þat was þat part þat he toke of hire in fleisch & blode bodily þoruȝ þe miȝt [*through the might*] of þe godhed boren vp to heuen & so hoping withoute drede þat she sholde folow aftere. Wele þan miht it be seid þat tyme & now may to hire [*Well then may this be said to her at that time to her and also now*]. *Blessed be þou souereynly in women*, seing þi son Jesu mihtily to heuen vpsteynge. (p. 30)

Mary provides a model for the meditating reader, 'hoping withoute drede þat she sholde folow aftere' to heaven (unlike common humanity, she is innocent and therefore has nothing to dread). Indeed, the sight of Jesus's Ascension is so powerfully cheering for her that her fourth virtue, hope, seems itself to be tinged with her 'joy':'þe ferþ ioy þat she hade, in þe siht of hire sone Jesu miȝteli to heuen vp steing. In þe which siȝt þe hope þat sche hadde in his godhede was fullich strengþede & confermede'. Mary, her heart set on Jesus and heaven, clearly provides an analogue and exemplar of human hope for Love's readers, who would be accustomed, in the tradition of *compassio Mariae*, to sharing imaginatively in her woes as a model beholder of the Passion rather than in her feelings in the more positive episode of the Ascension. It could also be said that

Mary here complements and augments the figure of St Cecilia as a model user of, and respondent to, the life of Christ.

With regard to how its structure is waymarked by strategically situated words, Love's prayer-poem accosts consciousness from out of nowhere with the performative 'hail', as any greeting interruptively does — especially the greeting of an angel appearing from out of the blue. Unlike the Latin poem, it completes itself with a device to counterbalance the opening: a self-announcing death-closure, 'endynge'. In between these, the linear process of ascent is tracked by lingeringly active present-participial rhyme-words at the end of the long glossatory lines of the English verses. These trace, in the here and now of the reader, an upwardly promissory trajectory of hope that is finally redeemed celestially at the 'endynge' of the foregrounded *gradatio* 'conceyuyng [...] beryng [...] vprysyng [...] vpsteyng [...] cronyng [...] endynge'. Though Love's poem is looser than the Latin one, its calculated suggestive artifice and its theological function are very much in harmony with what he we have seen elsewhere in the *Mirror*.

The same is true of the second, partnering, exposition of prayer, this time an addition to the *Meditationes* at the very end of the work, featuring in the so-called 'Treatise of the Sacrament'. The 'Treatise', of course, has its own fascinating textual history. At a late stage in the genesis of the *Mirror*, Love, possibly at Arundel's behest, or at least with the intent of pleasing the Archbishop, added to his text the 'Treatise'.[75] Clearly, its function is to expound the orthodox doctrine of transsubstantation and so to fortify and scare the faithful with stories of eucharistic miracles advantageous to the Church's position and perceived interests. (The *Mirror*, of course, is shot through with well-attested eucharistic piety, as is the *Meditationes*.)

The 'Treatise' incorporates an interesting and important prayer, drawn from *The Seven Poyntes of Love*, a Middle English part-translation of Henry Suso's *Horologium sapientiae*. *The Seven Poyntes* was probably another Mount Grace production, and Love made good use of it for his prayer (pp. 238–39).[76] As with the treatment of the *Ave*, Love's modification of his source (this time intralingual rather than interlingual) is marked by the same thematic and terminological concerns that characterize the other translating that this chapter has discussed. Accordingly, we find that 'hele in body and sowle by þy gracious

---

[75] See the introduction to Nicholas Love, *Mirror*, ed. by Sargent, pp. 66–74, 150–53; also Sargent, 'Nicholas Love's *Mirror of the Blessed Life of Jesus Christ* and the Politics of Vernacular Translation', p. 218.

[76] For parallel presentation of this part of *The Seven Poyntes* and the prayer in 'Treatise', see the introduction to Nicholas Love, *Mirror*, ed. by Sargent, pp. 71–72.

presence' becomes 'medicine and hele in body & soule, be vertue of þi blessede presence' (p. 238): clearly, 'medicine' is reminiscent of Love's exposition of *De agone* in his *proheme*, and 'blessede' chimes with his earlier enthusiastic insertions of this word into his source to valorize the power of the life of Christ and of his own work. Likewise, 'my hope be strengthed' becomes 'myne hope confortede & strengþede with þis blessede sacrament' (p. 238), in which 'blessede' is additional, and 'confortede' echoes the consolatory strengthening of which Love made much in his exposition of Romans 15. 4 at the very start of his *proheme*.

The climax of Love's rendering of this prayer sees him adding yet more *Mirror*-referencing, self-valorizing verbal tokens, for 'and atte laste I mowe haue a blessed hennes-passynge to lyfe euer-lastynge' becomes 'þat I may come wiþ þe to life euerlastyng, Jesu lorde by vertue and grace of þi life blessede wiþ out endynge' (p. 239). Love's supplicant-reader is, suitably, made to voice herself/himself as bound up with the *vita Christi*, endeavouring by His life to be in the company of Jesus in his/her ascent to heavenly salvation. In line with the exposition of *De agone*, s/he is enabled to be saved 'generically' by the life of Christ: here Love both makes a fideistic assumption and stakes a claim for the efficacy of his text and everything that it entails. At the same time, he also has the confidence (and indeed the hope) to address and solicit the Almighty on his *Mirror*'s terms, 'by vertue and grace of þi life blessede'. This is rhetorically reinforced by the fact that 'life euerlastyng' (intralingually rendered from *The Seven Poyntes*) parallels his own addition to the source, 'þi life blessede'. The object of hope — salvation — is thus partnered with the means of achieving it, the *vita Christi*, or, perhaps to put it more accurately, it is partnered by *The Mirror of the Blessed Life of Jesus Christ*. Again, as with his translating of the *Ave Maria*, Love ends self-reflexively with 'endynge', which gives both expositions a similar flavour of decorously fulfilled spiritual completion and achievement.

To sum up, the rendering of these two prayers does show important links with how and why Love translates elsewhere as he does. For example, his *Ave* connects profoundly with his treatment of the Last Supper, and his Susonian adaptation petitionarily invokes the title of his own work as a distillate of Christ's saving life. It could also be said that the Marian voice of the *Ave* overlays and harmonically enhances the Cecilian voice of the *proheme*. Indeed, Love's Susonian prayer, pitched, as are all prayers, on the edge of heaven, encapsulates, uses, and offers the whole *sentence* of the *Mirror*. Voiceable by Love and his readers alike, it assumes *lectio*, *meditatio*, and *oratio* in brief compass, and does so with a promise of being endlessly repeatable for those who need or want it. Love's sacred work, in the final act of translation, becomes the reader's sacred work.

Conclusion: The Translation of Hope in Love and in his Readers

In endeavouring to evaluate Love as a translator of *devout imaginacioun*, this chapter started off by looking at how he and his *Mirror* related to a mainstream learned Latin and vernacular literary understanding of imagining the Sacred Humanity. It then moved on to observe how his valorizing of hope, virtues, and the profitability of life of Christ itself were articulated in his vernacular exposition of his sources. Along the way the discussion has tried to give Love and his work rather more sympathetic critical attention than has too often been the case from the mid-1990s up until the present. By looking in some detail at some under-discussed aspects of what the Prior of Mount Grace apparently wished to do, and what he actually did, this chapter has challenged some of the assumptions that have driven recent expressions of disapproval of Love.

In conclusion, it would be difficult to deny, even for those modern scholars for whom Love is a political or spiritual allergen, that he is a remarkable translator and maker of prose. Despite this, he is still going to be disliked for his conservatism and authoritarianism, which were all too real. After all, he did 'collaborate' with Arundel, and he certainly agreed with his politics, even though his prime motivation in getting the *Mirror* publicly licensed was in all probability to secure his priory's future by shifting Mount Grace from the doomed Ricardian camp to Lancastrian patronage.[77] Despite this, it is a safe bet that he will continue forever to disappoint those who think he should have made more of the morally and socially reformative potential of, say, the Sermon on the Mount, and that he will vex unceasingly those who would disallow his approach by contrasting it with the fecund sublimity of Julian of Norwich or even the (allegedly) pre-democratic individualism of *Book to a Mother*.[78] For all this, however, it should not be forgotten that for huge numbers of people who wanted, used, and adapted it throughout the fifteenth century and beyond, Love's *Mirror* did meet a genuine taste for the kind of work that it was, and for the kind of work that it could be made to be.

It would appear, then, within the details and across the generality of Nicholas Love's project of rewriting the *Meditationes vitae Christi* for a vernacular audience, that there is a remarkably high level of inventive nuanced consistency in

[77] Sargent, 'Nicholas Love's *Mirror of the Blessed Life of Jesus Christ* and the Politics of Vernacular Translation', pp. 215–18. See also the introduction to Nicholas Love, *Mirror*, ed. by Sargent, pp. 23–37, esp. pp. 26–30.

[78] Watson, 'Conceptions of the Word', pp. 111–14; Karnes, *Imagination, Meditation, and Cognition in the Middle Ages*, p. 217.

the application of translational strategy and performance — whether we are talking about the reworking of the norms of meditative *imaginatio*, or of the topography of interiority, or of theologically vital terms and sentiments. The Prior of Mount Grace does not dumb down the *Meditationes* or infantilize his readers, but offers them spiritual versatility, moral *fruyte*, a gateway to salvation, and respectful encouragement to proceed further in contemplation, if they are so inclined. He also has the theological, psychological, and theological tact to put at the live centre of his work (which is also his readers' work) the transcendent pragmatics of hope, serviced by deftly vernacularized *imaginatio*. In the translational economy of Love's work, the hope that readers bring to, and take from, the *Mirror* joins earth and heaven in mutual process, at the same time enacting — with spiritual profit (not detriment) — the *sententia* of the work in all manner of souls, simple or not.

Love was not the first or last English translator to take on the *Meditationes vitae Christi*. A few years later at Sheen another Carthusian monk set about the same task, but when he found out that Love had been there before him he threw up his hands in exasperation and, apparently, would have abandoned his effort altogether, had not his prior stiffened his resolve to carry on making a (Pseudo-)Bonaventuran-style life of Christ for a Birgittine sister of Syon, as he had originally promised. It is odd, though, that this (Pseudo-)Bonaventuran translator fulfilled his promise not by providing a new English version of the *Meditationes vitae Christi*, but by compiling and reshaping a whole panoply of *matere*, from the Vulgate and Nicholas of Lyra's *Postillae* to Walter Hilton's *Scale of Perfection* and *Mandeville's Travels*. The 'Pseudo'-Bonaventuran *Meditationes vitae Christi* is one thing, but a Middle English *'Pseudo'-Meditationes vitae Christi* would be something else — something else, in fact, for the next chapter on the *Mirror*'s thoughtfully self-conscious younger sibling, the extraordinary *Mirror to Devout People* or *Speculum devotorum*.

Chapter 4

'INCREASING OF LOVE' IN THE *SPECULUM DEVOTORUM*: THE 'GROUNDE AND THE WEYE TO ALLE TREWE DEUOCYON'

This chapter has as its object of discussion the text of a life of Christ that has had very little critical attention to date, though it has enjoyed fine contextual and editorial work in recent years.[1] This text is particularly rich from a literary-theoretical point of view. Many of the places in the work where its maker is most revealing and eloquent about the business of compiling, translating, and meditating in the vernacular have not yet been brought to light in their complexity and distinctiveness. A good many features of literary interest in this work have connective tissue with each other: they need to be seen together, and this chapter attempts to give them some critical space. This text responds fascinatingly to themes and issues that this book has been

---

[1] For excellent contextual consideration and a rich bibliography, see Gillespie, 'The Haunted Text'. See also Edwards, 'The Contents of Notre Dame 67', pp. 107–28, and Brantley, 'The Visual Environment of Carthusian Texts', pp. 173–216. See, for further contextual information and an edited text based on the Notre Dame manuscript, '*Myrror to Devout People (Speculum Devotorum)*', ed. by Patterson. Professor Patterson is currently preparing a critical edition of this work for the Early English Text Society based on the Cambridge manuscript, which has been preferred for the purposes of producing a full critical edition. This is the manuscript used by James Hogg in his incomplete edition, *The 'Speculum devotorum' of an Anonymous Carthusian of Sheen*. I use Hogg's edition pending the appearance of Patterson's EETS edition, citing by page number in the main body of the text. This chapter revises materials passim from Johnson, 'Vernacular Valorizing: Functions and Fashionings of Literary Theory', pp. 240–50.

addressing: hence the sustained attention of this chapter to the testimony of a single but highly significant primary text, and its engagingly self-conscious compiler-translator.

A Carthusian prose compilation by an unknown monk of Sheen, probably composed before the middle of the fifteenth century and no earlier than 1410, the meditative *Speculum devotorum*, or *A Mirror to Devout People*, was intended for a religious woman, a 'gostly syster', most probably a Birgittine of Syon Abbey.[2] It is narrative, imaginative, exegetical, moralizing, and prayerful. Extant in two manuscripts of the fifteenth century, it consists of a series of meditations on the life of Christ, arranged in thirty-three chapters, after which is a panegyric on St John the Evangelist, a Latin colophon, and the Latin prayer *O Intemerata* together with an English rendering of it. The most important sources of the *Speculum devotorum* are the Gospels together with the *Postilla litteralis* of Nicholas of Lyra and the *Historia scholastica* of Peter Comestor.

With only five chapters devoted to the Ministry of Christ, the *Speculum devotorum*, like the *Legenda aurea* and the *Stanzaic Life of Christ*, concentrates on the parts of the *vita* which reflect the main feasts of the Church year, the book being able to be used accordingly if desired. Sources are excerpted and combined in order to render a moralizing, meditative, and at times prayerful *expositio sententiae* not only for the *gostly syster* but conceivably also for the ears or eyes of other devout souls who might come by the work. One of the most notable features of the text is its *prefacyon* — a remarkably fluent scholastic-type prologue, in which all the major traditional categories are accommodated with facility, even though the writer of this work has not found the actual task of making the life easy (pp. 1–11). This merits some critical discussion.

From Passion to Vita: Promise and Performance

Having announced the beginning of the *prefacyon*, the writer of the *Speculum devotorum* addresses the 'gostly syster' in epistolary tone, reminding her of an earlier promise to write her a Passion meditation:

> Here begynnyth a prefacyon to the boke folowynge. Gostly syster in Ihesu Cryste
> I trowe hyt [*trust it*] be not 3ytt fro 3oure mynde that whenne we spake laste togy-

---

[2] See generally the typescript introduction in the *Speculum devotorum*, ed. by Hogg, esp. pp. vi–xli, and Patterson's introduction. Hogg's edition, as published, covers only the first twenty-nine chapters. For the remainder of the work, see Patterson's edition and also Wilsher, 'An Edition of "Speculum Devotorum"'.

derys I behette ȝow [*promised you*] a medytacyon of the passyon of oure lorde, the
whyche promysse I haue not putte fro my mynde but be dyuerse tymys be the grace
of god I haue parformyd hyt as I mygthte; oure lorde graunte þat hyt be to hym
pleseable & to ȝow profytable or to eny othyr deuot seruant of god. (p. 1)

As with the makers of the *Mirror*, the *Ormulum*, and the *Stanzaic Life of Christ*,
the compiler of this work is under an obligation ('promysse') to someone to
whom he 'behette' his work. Though the tone is personal, as one would expect
in an address to a *gostly syster*, the work is declared (as in the *Meditationes vitae
Christi* and Love's *Mirror*) to be applicable 'to eny othyr deuot seruant of god'.
A use of the polite second person plural here is not just a mark of civility; it
suits the potential plural audience of 'othyr' souls. This suggests that the writer,
in his own quiet way, is conscious that he could be preaching to a wider audience and not just to a *gostly syster* (Carthusian texts were often copied and
circulated well beyond their initial or intended readership, and it was often
institutions outside the order, such as the house at Syon, that disseminated
Carthusian texts).[3] The making of devotional books, of course, was an integral
part of Carthusian life, and was defined officially as a form of preaching by the
enclosed for the benefit of the Christian souls who might come by such texts.
In his *Consuetudines*, Guigo, the fifth prior of the Grande Chartreuse, wrote
that monks of the order must make books, because, although they cannot
preach by mouth, they can do so by using their hands: 'quia ore non possumus,
Dei verbum manibus praedicemus'.[4] This attitude keeps company with Trevisa's
equation of preaching with translation.

This writer, like any translator-preacher such as Orm or the maker of the
Stanzaic Life, sees himself as having 'parformyd' his work 'be the grace of god'.
His role is somewhat instrumental — permitted and guided by divine grace, yet
at the same time delimited by his personal human capacities ('as I mygthte').
His performance, however, has been more extensive than was originally prom-
ised, for he has not written a Passion meditation but a larger life of Christ:

---

[3] See Gillespie, 'The Haunted Text': 'I suspect that in London the main such conduit, and a
notably leaky one, was in fact Syon. I also suspect that, with or without the conscious consent or
permission of the Carthusians over the river, the special circumstances of the Syon Brethren and
the special configuration of the double convent at Syon led to books originating at Sheen being
propelled into much wider circulation' (p. 136).

[4] *Speculum devotorum*, ed. by Hogg, introduction, p. xlviii, for the citation of this quotation. For Guigo, see *Guigonis Carthusiae Maioris Prioris Quinti Consuetudines*, in *Patrologia
latina*, CLIII (1854), cols 631–758 (XXVIII. 3, cols 693–94); also Guigues I, *Coutumes de
Chartreuse*, XXVIII. 3.

But I do ȝow to wyte that be conseyle I haue put to myche more thanne I behette ȝow [*promised you*] to more encresynge of ȝoure loue to god & of vertuys or of eny othyr that mygth be þe grace of god profyte be the same. (p. 1)

He has over-'parformyd' his 'promysse' not from his own authority, but 'be conseyle', such advice being taken from other suitable persons, 'gostly fadrys' (p. 3) like his Prior. Not content to limit himself to the Passion, he has added considerably more *materia*, for he has 'put to myche more', thereby increasing the devotional and moral *utilitas* of the work, that is, 'encresynge of [...] loue to god & of vertuys'. This positive decision to go beyond a Passion meditation conceivably reflects a notable fifteenth-century development in the tradition of meditative literary treatment of the Sacred Humanity — that of rendering not just the Passion but the whole of the life of Christ. From the fourteenth century several separate treatments of the Passion section of the *Meditationes vitae Christi* survive, but no versions of the work in its entirety are extant.[5] Conversely, there would appear to be a complementary paucity in the production of Pseudo-Bonaventuran Passion texts in the 1400s, which witnessed such comprehensive renditions of the whole life as Love's *Mirror*, the anonymous translation of Pseudo-Bonaventure, and the Englishing of Ludolphus the Carthusian's mighty work.

It is not unthinkable, then, that the compiler of the *Speculum devotorum* felt pressured to respond to a shift in tradition, doubtless made all the more manifest in the vernacular by the precedent of the *Mirror* — to say nothing of its excellence and fame. The 'conseyle' that the monk of Sheen followed may also have reflected this wider shift. Clearly, the plenitude of the Sacred Humanity and its manifold *utilitas* are articulated better through the Englishing of the whole *vita* than through the Passion alone. The addition too of moralizing materials reflects the spiritual temper of the Birgittines, and would also suit 'eny othyr' souls — the kind of devout laity for which Syon Abbey might find itself catering.

'That one leuyth anothyr supplyeth': Gospel Harmony, Other Clerks, and 'Simple' Retranslating

Lives of Christ may usefully be seen as knowing retranslations, either of the Vulgate (itself a translation) or of other lives of Christ. The *materia* which a translator reworks has invariably been reworked by someone else before. The

---

[5] Salter, *Nicholas Love's 'Myrrour of the Blessed Lyf of Jesu Christ'*, pp. 102–03.

vita Christi is therefore an example *par excellence* of what medieval rhetoricians labelled *materia exsecuta*, that is, well-known and authoritative material that has already been accorded repeated literary treatment because it is prestigious — and is prestigious because it has been accorded repeated literary treatment.[6] The maker of the *Speculum devotorum* is all too aware of this, and claims to have been discouraged to the point of repeatedly considering abandonment of the whole project, not only on account of his own 'vnworthynesse' but also because the great clerk Bonaventure himself had written a Life of Christ:

> Also I haue be steryd ofte tymys to haue lefte thys bysynesse bothe for my vn-worthynesse & also for Bonauenture a cardynal & a worthy clerke made a boke of the same matere the whyche ys callyd Vita Christi. (p. 2)

The *Meditationes vitae Christi* is obviously an intimidating impediment to his work, as well as a precedent to be emulated. The self-label of 'vnworthynesse' refers not only to literary deficiencies but also to his unworthiness as a morally fallible man; he certainly cannot hope to match up to the 'cardynal and worthy clerke', who is not only scholastically but also spiritually superior, with a holy *vita auctoris* to buttress his works. Note here the use of the term 'matere' from the scholastic prologue, referring here to the biblical and meditative *matere* of the *vita* rather than to a specific textual source or sources.

The maker of the *Speculum devotorum* has often been 'steryd' to give up. This word normally signals the devout 'stirrings' of heavenly influence, affective piety, or moral goodness. Here, however, this oft-holy term denotes abandon-ment of a devout labour. As such, it may be taken as a sign of humility, or at the very least a topos of humility, modesty, and inability.

Worse than having to compete with Bonaventure is having to reckon with vernacular English Carthusian competition, for the monk of Sheen was stirred to give up 'most of alle whenne I herde telle that a man of oure ordyr of char-turhowse had I turnyd [*translated*] the same boke into englyische' (p. 2). This 'boke' is most likely Nicholas Love's *Mirror*. He does not say outright that he has read the *Mirror*, only that he has 'herde telle' of it. It sounds as if the news came to him as a nasty shock after he had started his project. Whether or not after this news he managed to see or read the *Mirror* before completing the *Speculum devotorum* is not certain. It would, though, be a little strange if this famous and much-circulated Carthusian vernacular work, licensed and man-

---

[6] See Copeland, 'Rhetoric and Vernacular Translation in the Middle Ages', pp. 63–64, for discussion of *materia exsecuta* in the context of vernacular translation.

dated by Archbishop Arundel himself, was completely unseen by the monk of Sheen — but then again, as a Carthusian living the eremitic life he would have missed out on all kinds of things that would have been well known enough to most other folk. Perhaps the *Mirror* was the last thing he wanted to see. Or, perhaps, it was the very thing he wanted to see and to do something about, or even something with. Later in the chapter we will entertain the possibility that the compiler's advertisement of his self-made new Middle English title for his work is in some way a response to the performance Nicholas Love makes in his proem of his own vernacular *nomen libri*.

The translator tells us that before beginning the work, and also during his greatest doubts in the throes of performing it, he consulted suitable people, including, most importantly, his Prior, who had a personal spiritual responsibility for him, and, by extension, for all his work, including this text. To follow such advice lends a form of *auctoritas* to the text different from and beyond the authority to be gained from the sources alone. It also takes some of the responsibility for the work from the shoulders of the writer:

> but er I began thys occupacyon I askede conseyil of spiritual and goode men and most in specyall leue of my pryoure. And ȝytt aftyrward whenne I was moste in dowte of alle & hadde purposyd to haue lefte alle togyderys [*altogether*] & no more vttyrly [*utterly*] to haue do therto, ȝytt I thowgth [*thought*] þat I wolde aske conseyil of my pryoure the whyche I specyally louyde & truste myche to, & I trowe I tolde hym what mevyde me. (pp. 2–3)

The advisors, it is pointed out, were 'spiritual and goode men', like 'the manie gode felawis and kunnynge' present at the translating of the second version of the Wycliffite Bible.[7] What did the Prior advise?

> And he ful charytably confortyde me to parforme hyt wyth sueche wordys as cam to hys mynde for the tyme. (p. 3)

The semi-autonomous instrumentality of the compiler is again highlighted by the use of the term 'parforme' to describe his literary role; the term carries a sense of fulfilling and carrying out to completion as well as one of performance. Care is taken to show the Prior's correct attitude to the production of devotional texts. The Prior does what he does 'ful charytably', with a loving intention, thus blessing the book with the purity and authority of his own *entent*, which, also by virtue of his office and his personal spirituality, raises the level of

---

[7] See 'Prologue to Wycliffite Bible, Chapter 15', ed. by Hudson, p. 68, where 'good lyuyng' (p. 72) is depicted as necessary to the enterprise of translating the Bible.

authority of the writer higher up the scale of efficient causality than otherwise. The word 'confortyde', with its connotations of consolation (as in the contemporary Boethian *Boke of Coumfort*),[8] is important. It means more than kindly emotional bolstering, for it is a palpably didactic and psychological process of managing a problem and a state of mind. Consolation is a trajectory of persuasion from an unenlightened state of woe to a fortified one of restored self-awareness and a resolve to follow virtue. We do not know, then, what the words of the Prior to our author actually were but we do know the type of discourse it was. Someone properly consoled is not someone ordered: the writer has to resume his work freely according to his refreshed understanding of the situation and a recommitment to doing what is for the best.

With regard to the idiomatic theoretical precision with which our monk refers to his literary role, it is revealing that he designates himself more than once as the 'fyrste wrytare' of the meditations (pp. 5, 11, 21), a mere scribe, or *scriptor*, as Bonaventure put it in his fourfold definition of the ways of making books (discussed at the opening of Chapter 2 of this book). The scribe occupied the humblest medieval literary role, with no significant input other than that of replicating the words of others. To call oneself no more than the first in a line of scribes, and not even a humble compiler, would be to invoke a humility topos indeed. But there is possibly more to this self-label than meets the eye. In two of the passages in which he calls himself 'the fyrste wrytare' (pp. 11, 21) he asks for the prayers of whosoever reads the book. By requiring that the prayers go in aid of the 'fyrste wrytare' he is ensuring that they benefit him and do not go astray to scribes who might copy his work in the future. It is also possible that the designation 'the fyrste wrytare' conceivably carries an aura of authorial responsibility and creditworthiness. It is not, however, a sign that he believes himself to be a fully-fledged *auctor*.

Being 'sumwhat bore vp' by the 'conseyil of gostly fadrys' and by the merits of those who are intended to profit from the work (a mix of institutional push and reader pull), the monk presses on to 'make an ende therof', but refuses to take credit for his text if readers find profit in it:

> In the whyche yf ȝe or eny othyr devout seruant of god fynde enythynge profytable or edificatyf [*edifying*] hyt ys to be redressyd to the mercy of god & the merytys of hem þat mowen be profytyd therby; & yf enythynge be founde the contrarye hyt ys to be redressyd fully to my vnabylnesse & vnkunnynge [*inability and lack of know-how*]. (p. 4)

---

[8] 'The Boke of Coumfort of Bois' ed. by Kaylor, Jr. and Phillips.

This refusal is not just pious rhetorical flannel. It is theologically precise and tactical. He does not attribute anything good or profitable merely to God but pointedly to God's mercy. God's mercy, as such, has already been applied to himself in the form of the divine grace that has assisted him in completing the work: the same grace is what he obligates his readers to recognize as being intrinsic to any of them deriving benefit from using the work.

Again (and not unlike Chaucer in the *Retracciouns* to the *Canterbury Tales*), the monk takes responsibility for any inability and lack of know-how on his own part — 'vnabylnesse & vnkunnynge'. He safeguards himself in advance against such personal ineptitude through his purity of *entent*. It is no sin to have a good intention, and diligent incompetence is no moral or spiritual vice. Sinless *entent* therefore empowers the translator's imperative to the readers to excuse him, although his humble-looking instruction somewhat hides its status as a command in representing his readers as *letting themselves* ('lete hym') excuse the translator's 'entent':

> for thowgth the werke be but symple 3ytt the entent of hym that dede hyt was ful goode, & therfore hoso cunne not escuse the werke lete hym escuse the entent. (p. 5)

There is a degree of self-interested rhetorical spin in attaching the word 'symple', which normally refers to people, to the literary work itself. In fifteenth-century religious discourse, simplicity, far from being morally reprehensible, can always be allowed for. By fixing this infinitely excusable quality to his work (with its devout connotations of self-meeking humility), our monk renders his whole project as excusable as himself. This little statement must rank as a classic instance of a policy of constructing security through purity of intention, but here it has a twist: the act, 'the werke', is formally divided from the 'entent' with the precision of a moralizing clerk — but it is simultaneously and slyly kept attached through shared simplicity.

There is a further dimension to our translator's overall strategy, drawn from learned tradition, to protect him in his work. The *matere* of the meditations, by its own inalienably evangelical merits, is intrinsically profitable, despite the shortcomings of the compiler. As we shall see, however, it is not only the *materia* of the Gospels, but also the principle of Gospel harmony itself, that is used to justify the making of the *Speculum devotorum*.

A writer excusing himself and his work through purity of *entent* is one thing; but excusing oneself and one's text through a *translatio* of the principle of Gospel harmony is another. The *Speculum devotorum* eloquently deploys, in its own distinctive way, the classic argument used a few years earlier by the pilgrim Chaucer in his *Prologue to Melibee*. Geoffrey justified his further retreatment of well-known *matere* with the following logic: that inasmuch as all four evangelists treated the same material diversely, yet truthfully and profitably — and without discord of *sentence* amongst them — then it must be the case that anyone should be allowed to provide a different version of any existing textual *matere*. In the *Speculum devotorum* this particular excuse is especially pertinent and urgent: for we are not talking about 'any other' text — we are talking about retreatment of the Gospels themselves:

> ¶ Ferthyrmore lest eny man that mygth aftyrwarde rede the boke folowynge schulde conseyue [*conceive*] temptacyon that I þat am bot a sympyl man schulde do sueche a werke aftyr so worthy a man as Bonauenture was sygth [*since*] he wrote of the same matere [*subject matter*], hyt mygth be ansueryd to þe satisfaccyon of hys conscyence thus: Ther ben foure euangelyst that wryten of the manhede of oure Lorde Ihesu Cryste, & ȝytt alle wryten wel & trewly, & that one leuyth anothyr supplyeth. Also the doctorys of holy chyrche exponen the same euangelyis þat they wrote diuerse wysys [*in diverse wises/ways*] to the conforte of crystyn peple & ȝytt alle ys good to crysten peple & necessarye & profytable. (pp. 4–5)

What Bonaventure (or even Love) 'leuyth', the *Speculum devotorum* 'supplyeth'. Gospel matter will always be necessary to know and edifying. Paradoxically, there is a double warrant to retranslate — on one hand, on the basis of the fertile difference and, on the other, of the replicatory truthfulness of the new version. It is possible to diverge in treatment from other versions of this material but still to be a faithful interpreter, for the *sentence* of the Gospels is greater than any one version of them can contain. Each life of Christ supplements and complements (and falls short of) others. Each varies, as we already have seen, according to form, subject matter, and audience, but each has its own valid place and role.

In reality, no single extant Middle English life of Christ merely replicated another, nor was it rendered irreversibly useless or mute by a successor, or even by a predecessor like Love's *Mirror*. The popularity and the authority of Nicholas Love's *Mirror* were likely to have been a factor in the modest circulation of the *Speculum devotorum*, but the later text still attracted readers and users, however few and however intermittent, who would nevertheless have gained from this work *profyte* that they could not have gained from the *Mirror* or any other work.[9] Indeed, as our compiler points out, 'the doctorys of holy chyrche' stated that the evangelists wrote diversely for the spiritual comfort

---

[9] The circumstances of the early ownership and use of MS Notre Dame 67 are a case in point. See '*Myrror to Devout People (Speculum Devotorum)*', ed. by Patterson, pp. 22–32.

of Christian people, so his own diversity has a precedent. This is reminiscent, perhaps, of Love's citation of a much-used *auctoritas* of Gregory the Great: 'as seynt Gregory & oþer doctours seyn, þat holi writte may be expownet & vndurstande in diuerse maneres, & to diuerse purposes, so þat it be not aȝeyns þe byleue or gude maneres' [*against the faith or good conduct*].[10] This tradition recognized the divinely intended advantages of the multiple exposition of the Bible — a tradition that applied in particular to the life of Christ which, articulated in four equal but not identical Gospels, could not be other than imperfectly embodied in one single linear discourse thereafter by lesser mortals for feeble human understanding. Retreatment is nevertheless 'profytable', 'confortable', and 'goode' (p. 5).

What better example, licence, and encouragement could there be for the compiler of 'anothyr' life of Christ than the harmony of the four evangelists themselves and their divinely sanctioned complementary differences? As Trevisa's Lord and the Wycliffite Bible translators argued,[11] there is always room for another biblical retranslation, because all frail humans will fall short in any one enterprise, and each effort will shed its own fresh light on the *matere*:

> no synfol man doþ so wel þat he ne myȝte do betre, noþer makeþ so good a translacyon þat he ne myȝte make a betre. Þarvore Orygenes [*Therefore Origen*] made twey [*two*] translacions and Ierom [*Jerome*] translatede þryes þe Sauter [*the Psalter thrice*]. Y [*I*] desire no translacion of þeus bokes [*these books*], þe beste þat myȝte be, for þat were an ydel desyre vor eny [*for any*] man þat ys now here alyue, bote Ich wolde haue a skylfol translacion þat myȝt be knowe and vnderstonde.[12]

Trevisa's Lord settles for the achievably useful: 'a skylfol translacion þat myȝt be knowe and vnderstonde'. Such a translation will always have a utility, whatever its differences may be from, or with, other possible renderings. In the same spirit, the maker of the *Speculum devotorum* knows full well that his version shares significant features with, but is profoundly different in form, content, and flavour from the *Meditationes vitae Christi* (and even from Love). He also knows that, at the very least, it too is something profitable 'þat myȝt be knowe and vnderstonde'.

---

[10] Nicholas Love, *Mirror*, ed. by Sargent, p. 11.

[11] 'Prologue to Wycliffite Bible, Chapter 15', ed. by Hudson, p. 71.

[12] Waldron, 'Trevisa's Original Prefaces on Translation', p. 293.

Making a Name: The Rhetoric of Entitlement in Love and the Speculum devotorum

The *Speculum devotorum*'s highly fluent academic prologue takes care, in a single long sentence — and in a manner similar to Nicholas Love — to assemble and gloss its vernacular *titulus/nomen libri* bit by bit until the full name is revealed in an announcement that resolves the sentence both syntactically and thematically. The structural and thematic similarities of the two Carthusian expositions of title are immediately striking:

Love's *Mirror*

And so for als miche as in þis boke bene conteynede diuerse ymaginacions of cristes life, þe which life fro þe bygynnyng in to þe endyng euer blessede & withoute synne, passyng alle þe lifes of alle oþer seyntes, as for a singulere prerogatife, may worþily be clepede þe blessede life of Jesu crist, þe which also because it may not be fully discruede [*described*] as þe lifes of oþer seyntes, bot in a maner of liknes as þe ymage of mans face is schewed in the mirroure: þerfore as for a pertynent name to this boke, it may skilfully [*reasonably*] be cleped [*called*] the *Mirrour of þe blessed life of Jesu criste*.[13]

Speculum devotorum

❡ And for the entent of hym that dede hyt was to sympyl, & deuout soulys þat cunne not or lytyl vndyrstonde latyn [*know no Latin or little understand it*], & also for the deuout thynkynge of oure lordys passyon & manhede ys the grounde & the weye to alle trewe deuocyon, thys boke may be callyd a Myrowre to deuout peple. (p. 5)

The sentence in which Love discloses his *nomen libri* is a *gradatio* that employs sustained logical sequencing to justify and to uncover the finally assembled title, which represents a deliberate shift of denotation from the literal meaning of 'meditationes vitae Christi'. At the same time, it is a distillate of the original's and of Love's *modus agendi* and also a declaration of the generic supremacy of the work amidst all other mere hagiography. The *Speculum devotorum*, in its own way, also edges towards naming the title via unresolved clauses, but, in so doing, unlike Love's *Mirror*, it succinctly indexes a range of prologue categories: its *materia* ('of oure lordys passyon & manhede'), its meditative *modus agendi* ('deuout thynkynge'), and its *utilitas* ('the grounde & the weye to alle

---

[13] Nicholas Love, *Mirror*, ed. by Sargent, p. 11.

trewe deuocyon'), with its 'entent' being to deliver the *utilitas* to 'sympyl, & deuout soulys þat cunne not or lytyl vndyrstonde latyn'.

The compiler of the *Speculum devotorum* uses the indefinite article for his title ('*a* Myrowre'): this may be a sign or topos of humility; his is just another 'Mirror'-book among many. Love's use of the definite article implies that his work, rather more assertively, is the one place where the benefits of the Sacred Humanity are to be found.

Whereas *The Mirror of the Blessed Life of Jesus Christ* has an exposition of title centring on *manere*, *A Myrowre to Deuout Peple* refers, unlike Love, to the audience. This does not mean that the works are at odds, for Love had a very strong and strategic sense of different audiences as he revised his work.[14] Indeed, the titles of these two lives of Christ could be switched round without harm. It is significant, nevertheless, that the compiler of the *Speculum devotorum* made a choice recognizing and defining an audience.

As with Love, the translator of the *Speculum devotorum* argues his *nomen libri* into being by building up the elements that go to make the new title. The similarity of method used by both writers in their title-making raises the question of whether the writer of the later work had access to the *Mirror*, and whether he wanted to follow or even emulate the precedent of arguing for a title.

The first half of the argument, up to 'latyn', justifies the inclusion of the words 'deuout peple', and the rest of the passage explains why the book is worthy of the name 'a Myrowre'. The *Speculum devotorum* refers not to a 'gostly syster' at this point but to a wider audience of 'deuout peple'. The *entent* is to write for simple and devout souls with little or no Latin, and hence no access to the devotional literature inscribed in that tongue. Syon was not just a place for enclosed nuns: there were plenty of novices, socially elevated pious guests, vowesses, and other sponsors and associates attached to the place.[15]

The term 'thynkynge' chosen by the *Speculum devotorum* is synonymous with meditation and the devout use of the imagination — so there is further good reason for giving the book the kind of mirror-title that this imaginative genre of holy interiority tended to attract. The declaration that the meditation of the Sacred Humanity is the ground and way to all true devotion recalls the attitudes of Love, Hilton, the *Cloud*-author, and, indeed, much ortho-

[14] See in general the introduction to Nicholas Love, *Mirror*, ed. by Sargent, which is fascinating in its discussion of Love's strategic aiming of his work at changing audiences and political circumstances.

[15] Gillespie, 'The Haunted Text', points out, for example, that 'a number of high-born vowesses were associated with Syon in the fifteenth century' (p. 144).

dox Pseudo-Dionysian theory of imagination, which (as we saw in chapter 3) regarded such 'thynkynge' as good in its own right, as well as being the starting-point and the way to higher contemplation.

Here we should also recall that the term 'ground', at this time, was commonly used to refer to the literal-historical sense of the Bible (the Lollards particularly like the term).[16] It was at this 'grounde'-level, consisting of narrative events and inspired human words, that the devoutly meditating imagination took its expository and experiential 'weye'. It is intriguing that the translator metaphorically sees the pragmatics of his text as being constituted by a fixed foundational 'grounde' and a teleologically directional route (and means) — a 'weye' thereon. Such a 'weye' is necessarily dynamic and requires the action of movement.

Intriguingly, this 'weye' of thinking ('the deuout thynkynge of oure lordys passyon & manhede') is also, according to the formula of the translator, a 'grounde'. Accordingly, 'alle trewe deuocyon' is undetached from that 'grounde' and from the 'weye' too. The word 'alle' declares that nothing falling outside that ground or outside that way of thinking on Christ's Passion and Manhood counts as true devotion. This definition looks rather exclusionary of other potential textual claimants to devotional validity, but inasmuch as many if not most religious works would accept these premises (even though they may not be lives of Christ) it would probably be safe enough to take this as meaning in effect that all other devotion is dependently contained and validated by such premises.

The title, 'a Myrowre to deuout peple', consists of two elements, 'a Myrowre' and 'to deuout peple'. Each of the two clauses that precede the announcement of the name links to one of these two elements. The latter, 'to deuout peple', emerges from 'for the entent of hym that dede hyt was to sympyl, & deuout soulys þat cunne not or lytyl vndyrstonde latyn': it is straightforward enough to see a transparent connexion here. The former, 'a Myrowre', valorizing the tradition of Gospel meditation, is paired with 'for the deuout thynkynge of oure lordys passyon & manhede ys the grounde & the weye to alle trewe deuocyon'. In its choice of title and in its display of reasons for this choice, the *Speculum devotorum* firmly positions itself at the epicentre of human life, arriving in vernacular textuality spiritually and culturally self-canonized.

---

[16] For instance, the translators of the Wycliffite Bible appropriate the term. See 'Prologue to Wycliffite Bible, Chapter 15', ed. by Hudson, p. 69. Throughout his works Reginald Pecock makes extensive use of the term — something that is presumably meant to impress the laity he is trying to win over for orthodoxy.

Nicholas Love's announcement of his *nomen libri* is the rhetorical climax of his *proheme* — or at least the climax of that part of his *proheme* that he wrote himself under his own steam and appended to the beginning of his source's proem. The Latin *prohemium* of the original, as translated by Love, spends much of its length discoursing on the many benefits of the *Meditationes* (as we know from discussing Love's rendering of such material in Chapter 3 of this book). The *Speculum devotorum*, in similar vein, after announcing its title, also turns to translating Latin material that proclaims a repertoire of *utilitates* gained from meditating on the life of Christ. This repertoire is not taken from 'Bonauenture' but from Henry Suso, another authoritative pillar of contemporary international Christocentric piety. Substantial Susonian passages authoritatively declare the supreme position and manifold profitability of the genre of the meditative life of Christ. By moving and instructing the pious, the act of thinking on the Sacred Humanity leads infallibly to virtues, spiritual knowledge, true loving of God, and the contemplative sweetness of grace:

> ¶ Ferthyrmore ȝe schal vndyrstande þat the dylygent thynkynge of oure lordys manhede ys a trewe weye wythoute dysseyte [*deceit*] to vertuys, & to the gostly knowynge, & trewe louynge of god, & suetnesse [*sweetness*] in grace to a deuot soule that canne deuoutly & dylygently occupye hym therinne. (p. 6)

Quotation then follows from the 'Orlege of Wysedom', that is Henry Suso's *Orologium sapientiae* which, like the works of Hilton and the *Cloud*-author, declares that no one can approach the 'hynesse of the godhede' without first meditating on the 'manhede', for 'thys ys the gate (that is, the manner of proceeding) be the whyche an entrynge ys grauntyd to the desyryd ende' (p. 6). Like Nicholas Love, this translator sees Passion meditation as a step on the way to higher things for those who are able — and this first step is not to be despised but loved and praised.

There is another point of comparison with Love's *Mirror*, albeit entirely conventional: Love in his *proheme* declares that the life of Christ is beyond comparison with mere saints' lives and sovereignly edifying.[17] The compiler of the *Speculum devotorum* says something similar:

> for whatsumeuere parfeccyon maye be founde in seyintys & holy fadrys lyuynge ther maye none be lykned to that, that oure lorde dede in hys owen person, ne so edyfycatyf schulde be to a trewe crystyn soule. (pp. 7–8)

---

[17] Nicholas Love, *Mirror*, ed. by Sargent, p. 11.

When it comes to the *vita Christi* as against other holy lives, there is simply no comparison: 'ther maye none be lykned'. However, even though Love's *Mirror* and the *Speculum devotorum* are rather different from each other, they share this core belief that the genre of the life of Christ is in a class of its own.

The Gospel, the Doctorys, *and* Drawyng ful loonge

This chapter is, in effect, an inaugural conspectus of a remarkable but critically overlooked work. It does not, however, provide occasion or space for a thorough and sustained examination of the repertoire of the translator at work with his many sources. This has to be accomplished elsewhere.[18] In Englishing its materials, the *Speculum devotorum* is a refined *compilatio*, remarkable for the range and generic mix of sources it deploys. The *prefacyon*, in good compiling fashion, names the main sources in descending order of *auctoritas*, starting with the Gospels (pp. 9–10). The most important works actually drawn on include the Vulgate, Lyra's *Postilla literalis*, Peter Comestor's *Historia scholastica*, Church Fathers like St Augustine and Gregory the Great, the *Legenda aurea* of Jacobus a Voragine, Walter Hilton's *Scale of Perfection*, Henry Suso's *Orologium sapientiae*, and a wealth of 'licensed' mainstream female visionary and devotional writers ('sum reuelacyonys of approuyd wymmen' (pp. 9–10)) such as Catherine of Siena, Mechthild of Hackeborn-Wippra, and, of course, St Birgitta of Sweden. Even *Mandeville's Travels* gets a look-in. Whereas Nicholas Love focuses on one work by one named *auctor*, the later work refracts itself through an extraordinary range of *materiae*: this is wide-ranging and enterprising *compilatio* indeed.

The most important sources, tellingly advertised for their centrality to the translator's project, are the 'gospel & the doctorys goynge thervpon':

> ¶ Ferthyrmore gostly syster ʒe schal vndyrstande that þe grounde of the boke folowynge ys þe gospel & þe doctorys goynge thervpon, & specyally I haue folowyd in þys werke tueyne [*two*] doctorys of the whyche at one ys comunely called the Maystyr of storyis [*Master of Histories*] & hys boke in englyisch the scole storye that othyr Maystyr Nycholas of Lyre þe whyche was a worthy doctur of dyuynytee & glosyde alle the byble as to the letturul vndyrstandynge [*literal sense*], & therfore I take these tueyne doctorys most specyally as to thys werke for they goo neryste to the storye [*history/historical events*] & to the letturul vndyrstandynge of eny doctorys that I haue red. (p. 9)

---

[18] To this end, see Ian Johnson, '(Not) Translating the *Meditationes vitae Christi*: The Repertoire of the *Speculum devotorum* in Handling its Sources' (in preparation).

The Gospel, then, is the 'grounde' of the book, and the 'doctorys' are in active mobile contact with it. The Bible is the unmoving ground, and the 'doctorys', in 'goynge thervpon', provide explicatory purchase on that 'grounde'. Paradoxically, however, for all their 'goynge thervpon', the 'doctorys' are also at the same time 'grounde' themselves, for the 'grounde' of the book *is* the gospel *and* the 'doctorys goynge thervpon'. The 'doctorys' may operate at one remove from the Bible but as institutionalized commentators valorized by tradition they are also inextricably foundational: they are 'groundly', as the Lollards would say.

To obtain the most authoritative version of the life of Christ, the two most-used and highly valued medieval 'doctorys', Peter Comestor, the sacred historian, and Nicholas of Lyra, the great literal-sense commentator, have been used. The *entent* in using them is to get as close as possible to the physical, historical events, as expressed by the literal sense of the text of the evangelists. Comestor, the Master of Histories, explains these events in their historical, geographical, and political context. Lyra elucidates the literal-historical sense — the whole intention of the inspired human authors in expressing their Gospels. It is easy to see why Lyra in particular is so valuable to the compiler of the *Speculum devotorum*.

One example of how useful Lyra could be: on one occasion, his sympathetic and intelligent theological psychologizing of the Sacred Humanity is cited from his *Postilla* with regard to the episode of Jesus praying on His own in the Garden. Just as the Passion is about to begin, Christ is thrown into a 'stryfe'. Lyra explains that this strife was caused by a clash between His acceptance of providence through His divinely informed reason and His perfectly human dread of death:

> but att þys tyme he was putt in a stryfe; & thys stryfe as Lyre seyth was betuene the senseualyte dredynge deth & resun acceptynge hyt; for be the vertu of god he seyth euyryche [*every*] parte was suffryd to doo & to suffre þat that was propyr [*proper/ natural*] to hym. (p. 227)

Lyra's compact analysis of Christ's inner strife and its acutely and uniquely incarnational nature makes excellent theological and psychological sense: this is an exposition to spur greater perceptiveness and understanding in someone engaging in sympathetic meditation. In this way Lyra is at one and the same time invaluable to the hermeneutic and affective project of the *Speculum devotorum*.

In contradiction of a modern view that post-Arundelian vernacular literary culture (especially in the mainstream) was timid when it came to working with the literal sense of Holy Writ, the invincibly orthodox commentator-translator of the *Speculum devotorum* taps straight into Scripture and its literal sense, as found in highbrow mainstream biblical exegesis — and, ironically enough, as prized by the Lollards, who had a huge respect for Lyra and turned to him readily. In the *Speculum devotorum*, *devout imaginacioun*, the Bible text, and the Lyrean *sententia litterae* were all pious bedfellows.[19]

That this translator uses the great literal-sense commentator to advance his meditative project goes to show that both meditation and translation were understood as forms of exposition. We have already discussed at some length how translation was thought of as a form of commentary. Meditation's role within the practice of religious reading gave it too a hermeneutic character. In the tradition of devotional reading originating in, and sustained by, the monasteries, rumination of a text, *meditatio*, which was necessarily interpretative, followed on from an initial stage of reading, *lectio*. Meditation was regarded, like translation, as a mode of expounding the sense and *sentence* of a text.[20] It is telling then, that the maker of the *Speculum devotorum* should use the same term — 'drawe' — to refer to both translation and meditation.

This twofold usage occurs in the discussion of a passage that the compiler has 'drawe' into English in 'schort' manner, almost word-for-word, from St Birgitta. Inasmuch as these are understood as the revealed *ipsissima verba* of the Virgin Mary to the Swedish saint, it is important to that they are rendered as closely as possible. Meditation on these words, however, allows and encourages the reader to draw them out at great length by devout thinking and diligent beholding within the imagination, 'drawe ful loonge in a soule':

> ¶ These be the wordys þat oure lady hadde to seyint Brygytt [...] the whyche I haue drawe here into englyische tonge almoste worde for worde for the more conuenyent forme and ordyr of these sympyl medytacyonys & to ȝoure edyfycacyon or eny othyr deuout creature þat can not vndyrstande latyn; the whyche ȝe maye thynke vndyr forme of medytacyon as I haue tolde ȝow of othyre afore; for thowgth hyt be schortly seyde here vndyr a compendyus manyr, ȝytt hyt maye be drawe ful loonge in a soule þat can deuoutly thynke & dylygently beholde the werkys of oure lorde that be conteynyd therinne & in sueche manyr thynkynge beholde inwardly & wysely. (pp. 145–46)

---

[19] For an example of a translator productively using Lyra in an expository and meditative text, see the discussion in Chapter 2 of Love's use of this commentator. For further discussion of this work's use of Lyra and commentary tradition, see Johnson, 'Prologue and Practice: Middle English lives of Christ', pp. 76–80.

[20] For a magisterial account of this tradition, see Leclerq, 'Monastic Commentary on Biblical and Ecclesiastical Literature'.

The Carthusian instructs the *gostly syster* to 'drawe' the imaginations 'ful loonge' *in herself.* The two meanings in the wordplay on 'drawe', however, also represent the two poles of the translator's activity: the *Speculum devotorum* exemplifies a range of translation procedures, not only close, word-for-word translating, but also more expansive vernacular commentary-methods for expounding Gospel *matere* for the purposes of meditation, as we saw in Chapter 2. The maker of the book (like the ideal reader) is encouraged to 'drawe' the Gospel 'ful loonge' in order to make the imaginative English text-as-work meditatively profitable. Whether this *drawyng* takes the form of close translation of a revelation of St Birgitta or a more periphrastic *in-eched* exposition of Biblical *materiae* and commentary-tradition, it is still important to note that a copiously imagined realization of events, arising from the historical-literal sense of the Gospels, constitutes the common *matere* for both reader and translator to 'drawe' variously and at greater length. Without being identical, translation and meditative exposition conceptually and pragmatically overlap and sustain each other. Note that the process of *drawyng ful loonge*, ideally, can and should continue long after reading when, in the imagination and memory, the soul draws out profit at spiritual length again and again, even though the written text may be physically absent from the reader.

Translation and meditative exposition, then, meet and co-operate in the same activity.[21] A variation on this pairing, albeit with specific reference to the meditative process of beholding, complicates things yet more productively when the monk of Sheen says to his reader that she may and should 'in sueche manyr thynkynge beholde inwardly & wysely the gret mekenesse charytee & obedyence of that worschypful lorde, & also þe pacyence and pouertee of oure lady and Ioseph' (p. 146). Here, beholding (seeing) becomes more than the visual imagining of narrated events. Beholding — normally a perceiving of events or an attentive watching within the soul — is now classed as the hermeneutic and ethical act of inferring from the narrative (in other words interpreting) the virtues of Christ and His parents. The compiler thereby subsumes the process of inward moral and spiritual exposition under the term 'beholde', as if it were as natural, as spontaneous, and as primary as (imaginative) seeing. To behold is to expound, and to expound is to behold — and both are *drawyng*. The lesson of these convergences is that, for the well-disciplined soul, moral and spiritual exposition should be as immediate and as intuitive as seeing: hence the instruc-

---

[21] This paragraph revises material from Johnson, 'Translational Topographies of Language and Imagination'.

tion to behold not just inwardly but 'wysely', in which *sapientia*, normally the hallmark and outcome of a hard journey of mental exertion properly applied, is attached to an intuitively habituated discretion now translated to the occasion of the inner vision of the imagining mind. In the previous chapter we saw how in his *proheme* Nicholas Love translated with acute 'psycho-logistical' awareness and concretely linguistic imaginativeness. His fellow-Carthusian, in equating the imaginative thinking of meditation with translating, invites us to think of translating, by return, as a form of imaginative thinking and not just a linguistic operation.

Carnal Souls and a Compiler's Conscience

Early in the *prefacyon* the Carthusian of Sheen asks for his pure *entent* to be 'escused' (p. 5). This advertisement of good conscience secures his activity and himself as ethically sound. A little later, the same theme of security through good conscience takes an interesting turn, reflecting a significant policy decision by the compiler about the nature of the work he is making.

Towards the end of the *prefacyon* he tells us that he might have included meditations more 'delectable to carnal soulys, [...] more confortable to some carnal folke', but by 'conscyence', which 'ys sykerest' (p. 10), he has excluded such imaginings. This is a clear example of a compiler exercising his prerogative to include or exclude material as part and parcel of his collecting activity. What, however, is the significance of this decision? Perhaps he is worried that his meditative life, slowly paced in prose, and laden with thorough explication, moralization, reflection, and exhortation, lacks in imaginative vivacity and dramatic spectacle when compared with other visionary works (which is of course true). One might also wonder whether the Carthusian of Sheen was concerned to avoid, and implicitly to discourage a taste for, the emotionally charged fantastical excursions and the kinds of self-dramatizing excitements and carnal sensationalism to be found in the more enthusiastic continental visionaries, or even, more locally, the self-comforting, wish-fulfilling fancies of the likes of Margery Kempe.

In any case, the word 'carnal', referring as it does to the potential experiences of those who may have been hoping for more 'delectable' imaginations, bears negative undertones in contradistinction with the other adjective used to classify 'soulys' — 'deuout'. Presumably, this word choice is a ruse to bolster the staying power of the *Speculum devotorum*'s potentially wavering readers, and to trigger feelings of guilt in them the moment that they flag, so that they would blame not the text but their own evidently 'carnal' dispositions for any spiritual listlessness. This tactical nudging of potentially 'undelighted' members of the readership towards self-blame is given further impetus by the writer's trumpeting of the crucial role of his own conscience as the 'sykerest' guarantor of the *auctoritas* and/or integrity of himself and his text. Here is a hefty hint that to flag or become inattentive is to be morally or spiritually defective, especially in comparison with the 'fyrste wrytare'. For a well-mannered religious lady in the politest of nunneries, who knows our first writer (who is doing her a spiritual favour) on an individual basis and is in the habit of speaking with him, this would also be a personal insult — terrifically bad social as well as spiritual form.

Holy Name and Holy Person

The monk of Sheen is a conscientious literal-sense *expositor* typical of his time, and aware of the relevant niceties of theory — not just for their own sake, but as they pertain to the pragmatics of textual production and, of course, reader response. This is well illustrated in his discussion of the onto-theology, affective semantics, and *utilitas* of the name of Jesus, in which he acknowledges the devotional significance and function of the Holy Name:

> Thys ys the name that ys so suete & confortable to the louyers of god; for as seyint Bernarde seyth hyt ys hony in the mowthe, melody in the ere & in the herte a suetnesse þat maye not be tolde. (pp. 88–89)

This closely renders the Latin of Bernard, as quoted in the *Legenda aurea*.[22] The passage continues until the yet higher authority of the Apostle Paul is reached:

> And in the name of Ihesu euyry kne be bowed of heuenely thyngys, erthely, & helly [*infernal*], as seynt Poule seyt: & ther ys no name vndyr heuene vntake thys [*except for this*] that we maye be sauyd by, as the same apostyl seyt. (pp. 89–90)

The writer, at first sight, appears to be discoursing on the power of the name per se, but he then makes a most important theoretical distinction between the nominal *signans* and its referent. Dismissing onomastic mysticism, he warns his reader not to invest belief in the power of the name *qua nomine*, but rather to be in mind of what that name refers to:

---

[22] Jacobus a Voragine, *Legenda Aurea*, ed. by Graesse, p. 80. The typescript introduction to *Speculum devotorum*, ed. by Hogg, pp. cl–cli, cites this as a particular example of the translator's ability to reproduce both the clausal and phrasal structures of the Latin whilst at the same time doing aesthetic justice to it.

> alle thys commendacyon of the name of Ihesu & myche othyr that ys seyde &
> maye be seyde therof vndyrstandyth yt not symply and barely for thys name Ihesu
> cryste I wryte or spoke [*written or spoken*], but for hym that þys worschypful name
> betokenyth the whyche ys oure blysful lorde Ihesu cryste god and man the sauyoure
> of mankynde to whom thys suete name ys specyally & trewly apropryed [*befitting*], &
> therfore hyt ys so suete to the louyers of god & of so gret vertu as ys forseyde. (p. 90)

Clearly, he looks sternly on the superstitious and magical thinking that tainted
the cult of the Holy Name by attributing power to the name itself rather than
using it as a affective and mnemonic aid to thinking about Christ and His life,
and accessing His person through mainstream devotional routines. In this life
of Christ, meditation, to be sure, is generated, like translation, from the literal
sense that expresses the biblical events to be imagined. The most important
thing to be understood, loved, and followed in the use of the Holy Name in this
text is therefore the person of the biblical Christ and all the meaning and grace
that flow therefrom.

This valuing of the Holy Name as a functional connexion with the lovable
and imaginable humanity of Christ and all it stands for has a counterpart in
the personal engagement with Christ encouraged in meditation. Chapter 5
contains instructions on how to translate the Gospel events into the imagination and how to translate the meditating subject into the imaginative *mise-en-
scène*. These proceed from the literal-historical sense, encouraging the reader to
observe and feel the events as if she were there, and even to imagine herself par-
ticipating in them, thereby becoming an agent in the narrative, and phenome-
nologically both subject and object. There is more to this instruction, however,
than a command merely to imagine oneself *there*. In keeping with the association of 'beholding' with exposition discussed earlier in this chapter, the reader
must, on the basis of a well-understood literal-historical narrative, behold the
meditation of the Nativity and then follow through with an appropriate moral
understanding and affective response:

> In alle these thyngys kepyth ȝowself present as thowgth ȝe seygth al thys done afore
> ȝow; & ymagynyth also what reuerence worschype & seruyse ȝe wolde haue doo
> there to oure lorde, to oure lady, & to Ioseph, & how hertyly haue thankyth oure
> lorde for thys gret benefeet I doo [*done*] to mankynde & also how gladly ȝe cowthe
> [*could*] suffre pouertee & penaunce for hys loue þat thus myche toke & suffrede for
> ȝow, for sueche affeccyonys [*sentiments/feelings*] ben rygth profytable & merytorye
> [*meritorious*]; & thys maye be the medytacyon of oure lordys byrthe. (p. 83)

The reader is to play a reverently helpful role in her imagination, paying 'reuer-
ence worschype & seruyse' to the holy family. Note that the transition from

meditatio to *oratio* within the dramatic frame, commencing with the exhortation '& how hertyly haue thankyth oure lorde', follows on immediately from
the narrative instructions in such a way as to impel the reader to thank the
imagined Christ as He is currently realized, in her mind, as a child, with herself
still a dramatic character embedded in the narrative rather than being just a
nun on her own in a cell fourteen hundred years after the event. In this passage,
there is no transcendent leaving behind of the meditation in the movement
to prayerfulness. The emotions generated by this dramatic transaction possess
utilitas in their own right, for they are 'rygth profytable & merytorye'. These
merits and fruits owe themselves indubitably to an understanding of the literal-
historical sense of the Gospel as expounded in the imagination by conscious
thinking and through well-directed 'affeccyonys'.

Meditating within and beyond the Bible

A compiler has the right to cut material that might usually or often be a can-
didate for inclusion in a *vita Christi*, and this compiler is no exception. In an
interesting case, the maker of the *Speculum devotorum* is open about cutting
out the bulk of a certain category of narrative matter, but he compensates for
this by providing his readers with a transferrable meditative *modus agendi* that
will enable them to treat the kind of matter he has cut in the event of them
finding themselves encountering the cut matter — in this case miracles of Jesus
— elsewhere.

Not all of the miracles of Jesus are narrated in this life of Christ, and even
then, apart from a cursory treatment of the changing of the water into wine,
they tend to be mentioned summarily (p. 176), or, if narrated at any length,
they are expounded allegorically, the water's transformation to wine being, for
instance, paralleled with the soul's turning 'fro þe suetnesse of deuocyon into
brennynge [*burning*] loue and affeccyon' (pp. 175–76), and the three dead
people raised by Jesus corresponding to degrees of sinners (pp. 190–04). Care
is accordingly taken by the compiler to justify his exclusion of such materials.
Firstly, he argues that it is not necessary, in an imaginative life of Christ, to
report all of the Lord's miracles because one exemplary meditation on a mira-
cle provides the formal wherewithal to meditate on the others. Thus, as with
the instructions concerning the 'drawing long in a soul' of the revelation of
St Birgitta, the brief rendering of the evangelical *matere* that the compiler has
selected for incorporation is to be met in the reader's imagination by a long
meditative drawing out:

manye othyre myraclys he wrowthte to schewe [*wrought to show*] hys godhede &
to brynge men to þe rygth feythe of þe whyche summe I haue tolde ʒow in general
wordys for hyt were to loonge to make a medytacyon of euyryche werke þat the
euangelystys telle of oure lorde & also I trowe hyt nede not for a deuout soule maye
be þe grace of god draue thys þat ys schortly seyde into loonge medytacyon yf he
wole & be dysposyd þerto be grace; but ʒytt not wythstandynge I wole telle ʒow
some werkys þat oure lorde dede in specyal to ʒoure more conforte in hym & that
ʒe maye the bettyr thynke othyre. (p. 177)

There is enough in the meditations on the relatively few miracles of Jesus included
in the English work to establish an all-important appreciation that Jesus has
fully demonstrated 'hys godhede' by those miracles. The 'general wordys', which
cursorily expound the value of the unmentioned miracles, point towards the
same *sentence* as do the miracles that *are* included for meditation. The compiler's
cutting has occurred at the level of *verba* and *narratio* but not at an overarching
level of *sentence*, which concerns Christ's showing of His divinity.

Why, then, does the compiler say that he will narrate some works so 'that
ʒe maye the bettyr thynke othyre'? This decision reflects an understanding of
the profitable re-applicability of meditative form and practice beyond the textual confines of the *Speculum devotorum*. The reader, having learnt the proper
form of meditation for the miracles mentioned in the text, can then proceed to
meditate on 'othyre' deeds of Jesus consciously omitted or simply absent from
the *Speculum devotorum*. Paradoxically, then, even though in such a case the
reader would be dealing with *matere* untreated by the *verba* and *narratio* of the
Speculum devotorum, she would still be guided and governed by the *sentence*
and *manere* of the work beyond its narrative boundaries.

This move by the compiler represents further *utilitas* or *profyte* in this work:
that it is as re-useable in its meditative *manere* as in its sententious *matere*. Its
manere or 'forme', being exemplary and disciplinary formats of conduct and
attitude, can be applied beyond the *Speculum devotorum* to textual or memorial
matere outside the English work. In a way the work is self-transcending, and
can generate, through the re-use of its *manere*, further *translationes* of the substance, doctrine, and emotions of the faith. This is hardly evidence for passive,
timid, and unengaging 'Age of Brass' piety.

The next issue concerning the translator's tactical awareness of the opportunities and variants of biblical meditation are to do with adjudicating the correct
ways of imagining the logistics of the Crucifixion.[23] The problem of whether

---

[23] This short discussion of variant Crucifixions revises Johnson, ''*Auctricitas*? Holy Women
and their Middle English Texts', p. 181.

and how to imagine events not explicit in the evangelists, and also the question of how to imagine one's way through any apparently contradictory accounts amongst them, throws up a number of age-old difficulties. A case in point occurs when the compiler presents a version of the Crucifixion attributed to the evangelists and another based on the revelations of St Birgitta.

The difference between them, however, is not seen as embarrassing, for Syon was a Birgittine house, and the revelations of the saint would have carried an authority of their own in one of her own nunneries. Other lives of Christ, including the *Meditationes vitae Christi*, present alternative versions too: here in the *Speculum devotorum*, the first version tells how Christ was nailed to the cross lying on the ground; the second, Birgittine, version, has Christ ascending the cross and stretching out His arm willingly to be nailed. In the ostensibly non-interventionist manner of medieval compilation both versions are separately rehearsed, under the following rubric:

> How & in what wyse oure lorde was crucyfyed the euangelystys make no mencyon in specyal but in general. Wherefore I wole telle ȝow too manyrys, whyche of hem maye beste styre ȝow to deuocyon that takyth [*which of them may best stir you to devotion, take that*]. (p. 266)

Both versions are fruitful, but the choice between them is left to *lectoris arbitrium*. Though the Carthusian of Sheen admits that the first meditation on the manner of crucifixion 'ys oo wyse [*is in one manner*] as I trowe some deuout men haue ymagynyd' (p. 267), he loyally recommends the Birgittine version in preference to the other: '¶ Anothyr wyse ȝe maye thynke hyt aftyr seyint Brygyttys reuelacyon & þat I holde sykyrer to lene to, & þat ȝe maye thynke thus' (p. 267). The perhaps manipulative use of the word 'sykyrer' ('more secure') undermines the trustworthiness of the first, evangelical, version. Perhaps the belief that in her holy vision St Birgitta must have seen the Crucifixion 'live', just as it must have happened, is doubtless influencing the Brother of Sheen here. It would, in any case, be difficult to undermine a key familiar revelation of St Birgitta in her own house with one of her own nuns.

In his intrusions, the maker of the *Speculum devotorum*, like Nicholas Love, is very much concerned to appear to wear his heart on his sleeve with the utmost spiritual decorum, especially with regard to the allowability of meditation in such 'awkward' or 'uncertain' cases as the Crucifixion. The problem of what and how to meditate, however, can also pose a question of what and how to translate. For example, when the angel greets Mary, what is (so the translator argues) meant but not said in the text of the Bible comes to be expressed plainly in his text in the angel's address to the Virgin:

> ¶ Now thanne beholdyth deuoutly how the angil entryth in the forseyde cytee of Nazareth [...] he salutyth as seyint Ierom seyth. And thanne he seyith thys fayre salutacyon to here: Hayle Marye ful of grace (thys worde Marye thowth ys not there in the texte but hyt ys vndyrstonde & sone aftyr expressyd). (p. 40)

The Middle English word 'there' is more emphatically locative than its modern English counterpart, and means something like 'at this particular point', and not just 'present'. The translator is anxious to point out that the name 'Marye' is expressed elsewhere in this passage, and, in terms of literal-sense intentionalism, is 'vndyrstonde' and therefore transferrable within the angel's address. Of course, the really decisive pressure forcing this rendering is intertextually liturgical: the familiar and traditional authority of the formula *Ave Maria* (we saw how Love took inventive expository care of this prayer in the previous chapter). Here the translator of the later work is thinking, to use his own words, 'ordynatly aftyr the forme of holy chyrche' (p. 91).

At other times, however, a complementary, but nevertheless pious and theoretically respectable indefiniteness as to the exact form of words in the sources feeds through to an imprecision concerning the particular words to be used by the reader in the process of vernacular meditation. For example, the grief of Mary for her crucified son is described as being uttered in *such manner of words or the like*: 'wyth myche lamentacyon sche lyftyth vp here handys seyinge sueche manyr wordys or lyke' (p. 284). Again a little later, we read 'sueche manyr wordys or lyke' (p. 285), and once more:

> And in seyinge of sueche manyr wordys as beforseyde or lyke þat mowen mekely be conseyuyd in a deuout soule aftyr the forme of medytacyon ȝe maye thynke sche fylle downe. (p. 286)

Affeccioun and devotion are trusted, it would seem, to generate permissible *verba*, which are nevertheless responsibly acknowledged in diligent clerkly fashion as not being provably known or present in the text. But this, apparently, does not matter. What does matter is the disposition of Mary's will and the fact of her grief: these are accorded the status of knowable and affectively compelling truth. Even though the words of the Virgin may need to be invented in the imagination, they should reflect the right sentiment with discretion: in the sentiment is the *sentence*. The self-conscious indefiniteness of this passage is a sign of theoretical conscientiousness and decorum, for no words are presented as authoritative or authentic even though the sentiments are. The compiler is not so always so overtly cautious, it must be said, about evidently nonauthentic *matere*, nor has he always the need to be, because he can often rely on the authority of familiar pious tradition concerning features absent from the evangelists. For example, the non-biblical Longinus is included in the *narratio* as if he were evangelically factual (p. 288).

There is an important difference, however, between narrative that, on the one hand, is positively untrue, and therefore not to be allowed, and narrative which, on the other hand, is unverifiable, but which may be true. Such narratives may be imagined for the purposes of devout meditation only. The maker of the book, however, is firm in his rejection of positively inauthentic *matere* from 'Nychodemys euangelye':

> ¶ What oure lorde dede there or what wordys he hadde to hem or they to hym or what songys of preysynge there were seyde or songe in hys presence hyt maye not sykyrly [*securely*] be seyde but yf a man hadde hyt be specyal reuelacyon; but ȝytt Nychodemys euangelye makyth mencyon what he dede there but for hyt ys not autentyke & also for the forseyde doctur Lyre prouyth hyt euydently false be autoryte of holy wryt & seyingys of othyre doctorys I ouyrpasse hyt & wole not pote sueche thynge here þat ys so vnsykyr [*insecure*] & mygthte be cause of erroure to sympyl creaturys. But thys ȝe maye thynke for certayne þat they were in parfyth ioye [*perfect joy*] in hys presence as ys forseyde, & in more ioye þan eny deedly man [*mortal man*] maye seye. (pp. 312–13)

Having deprived his audience of such detailed meditative narrative on the authority of Nicholas of Lyra, the maker of the work nevertheless gives his readership something else instead in the same narrative zone for their *affecciouns* to latch onto: the credible statement that the long-waiting souls trapped in Hell were in a state of perfect joy inexpressible in mortal discourse. There is no bar to imaginatively producing *sentence* from a credible narrative situation even though the best-known text narrating that situation is to be dismissed.

The translator's judgement that the souls in Hell 'were in parfyth ioye in hys presence as ys forseyde, & in more ioye þan eny deedly man maye seye' is a good example of a self-consciously correct use of orthodox medieval theory of imagination, because no corporeal discourse or fleshly imaginations can do justice to the reality of substances in Heaven or, as here, to the reality of those happily harrowable souls in Hell. The joy of such souls really is inexpressible: this is no mere topos; this is good theory.

A different approach, however, is taken to the same 'gospel of nychodeme' in the case of the 'non-authentic' appearance of Christ to Joseph of Arimathea:

> This apperynge is redde in þe gospell of Nichodeme, as it is aforseide. Bot for it is not autentyke, as I haue tolde yowe before in þe xxviiithe chapitle, I commytte it to þe dome of þe reder whether he woll [*will*] admytte it or none.[24]

---

[24] '*Myrror to Devout People (Speculum Devotorum)*', ed. by Patterson, p. 217.

This *matere* is passed on to the judgement of the reader; responsibility is disa-
vowed. All that is offered is a compiler's *recitatio*. This appearance is something
that is not known definitively to have happened, or not to have happened:
hence the referral 'to þe dome of þe reder whether he woll admytte it or none'.
It is not clear here whether the doom of the reader is meant to be a judgement
concerning whether the appearance happened or not, or whether the reader is
being left to judge, somewhat differently, whether the appearance (authentic or
not) is admissible for the purposes of meditation or not. The *Speculum devotorum* is genuinely ambiguous at this point.

　　This brings us to the famously non-biblical appearances of Christ to His
mother. That Jesus's first appearance after the Resurrection was to His mother
cannot be substantiated from the text of the Gospels. A somewhat touching
but hardly scholarly orthodox belief in the significance of evangelical silence
motivates the compiler to advertise as 'stabyl & serteyne' that Christ appeared
first of all to His mother. This has been made canonical through the practice
of Holy Church, as expressed in the Stations of the Cross, and as cited in the
Legenda aurea:[25]

> Othyre thre apparycyonys ther be [*There are three other appearances*] the whyche
> be tolde to haue falle also the same daye of þe resurreccyon but they be not in the
> texste of the gospellys. Of the whyche one ys þat oure lorde schulde haue apperyd
> fyrste to hys modyr oure lady seyint Marye; & þat ys rygth resunnably seyde to my
> vndyrstondynge. And þat as hyt semyth the chyrche of Rome approuyth þe whyche
> the same daye of the ressurreccyon halowyth a stacyon att a chyrche of oure lady
> in Rome as Ianuense [*Januensis*] seyth in the legende þat ys callyd aurea. (p. 318)

Even though a Station of the Cross in Rome is mentioned, it is a theological
and exegetical argument, rather than a Roman ecclesiastical tradition, that is
used to show why Christ appeared to Mary first. The argument goes like this:
it would be inconsistent of God to break His own commandment to honour
one's parents, and God can never be inconsistent, therefore He kept this com-
mandement 'in hys owen persone' (p. 319), and appeared to His mother before
anyone else. A theological logic is drawn on to argue this point, as is an accompanying devotional logic, which has implications for the meditative behaviour
of the reader. Not only is there authority in the evangelists' silence, there is
also a productive metatextual authority in the exemplary quality of the Blessed
Virgin's devotional need for consolation as well as in her supreme worthiness
as a human being:

[25] Jacobus a Voragine, *Legenda Aurea*, ed. by Graesse, p. 241.

⁋ And for oure lady ys the wordyest [*worthiest*] persone of alle othyre, & also for oure lorde apperyde fyrste to here as ȝe maye mekely beleue [*meekly believe*] wythoute eny dowte thowght the euangelystys make no mencyon therof; for Ianuense [*Januensis*] seyth þat the euangelistys wolde not wryte hyt, but they lefte hyt as for stabyl & sertayne. As ho seyth, they knewe hyt so opyn þat hyt nedyde not to wryte hyt, for they wyste wele inowf [*knew well enough*] that eny man or woman þat hadde resunnable wytt mygthte wel wyte þat he apperyde fyrste to here, for hyt ys no doute þat sche was moste sory for hys deth, & therfore sche nedyde moste the conforte of hys gloryus resurreccyon. (pp. 318–19)

It is intriguing here that the word 'opyn' is used here — a word so commonly used in the Middle Ages about translation itself, which is often depicted as having the intent and function of making its sources 'opyn'. An unambiguous text, like that of the Gospel in its literal-historical sense, was also commonly referred to in medieval learned discourse as being 'open' (whereas the Old Testament was 'dark' and needed efforts of typological, allegorical, and historical interpretation to make it open to Christian understanding). Here, however, we have an open sense emerging in and from evangelical textual silence. Mary's devotion, love, and need for the Sacred Humanity earn her the first appearance of the resurrected Son. The same efficaciously Christ-accessing devotional attitude is recommended for the enclosed female reader who would and should behold the risen Christ through her own reading experience. Mary, a role-model for the female reader, sits 'in mount Syon for there ȝe maye thynke sche abode stylle' (p. 319), waiting for Jesus, and so too in turn abides the *gostly syster* herself at meditation in the English Syon. Both the Blessed Virgin and the *gostly syster* would gain the company of the Lord by virtue of their love, compassion, and presence to Christ — the former in an assertively supposed history, and the latter through meditating on that history.

Not only is Mary accorded an exemplary meditative role — a role to be imitated by the reader — she also has an authorial role as an 'auctrix' behind the evangelical *auctores*, for it was she, it is claimed, who told them the details of the Nativity and Infancy. Instead of going straight to Heaven with her risen son, she stayed on earth and fulfilled her authorial role, 'to þe enfourmynge of þe euangelistes of þe Incarnacioun and þe youthe of our Lorde, for she knewe þat beste of all other'.[26]

---

[26] '*Myrror to Devout People (Speculum Devotorum)*', ed. by Patterson, p. 224. This discussion of Mary's authorial roles revises Johnson, '*Auctricitas*? Holy Women and their Middle English Texts', p. 179.

And so, the Virgin has, for our translator, a genuine efficient causality in this work, not only via the revelations to 'approved women' like St Birgitta but also in the fabric of the chief source of the work, the Gospels themselves.

Conclusion

Whether it was in his dealings with the Gospels, or with Nicholas of Lyra, or with the Mother of God, or with his Prior, or with his own conscience, the maker of the *Speculum devotorum* did his modest best to get the right forces on his side. One hopes that the *gostly syster* was duly appreciative, for his labour was truly impressive and cost him some pains.

Combining many different sources whereas the *Mirror* relies for the most part on one, the translator of the *Speculum devotorum* certainly complements Love's approach and is not at theological or artistic odds with his illustrious predecessor; for both works deploy and value the same kind of meditative materials and processes. Even more than is the case with Love's theory-rich *proheme*, the *prefacyon* of the later work contains a highly fluent and multiply functional academic prologue, performing a full sweep of literary self-appraisal and, more importantly, making a fascinating and very human attempt to assure the project of success. In Englishing its materials, the *Speculum devotorum* is a refined *compilatio* of great reach and riches. It is agile and meditatively aware in the way it uses commentary-tradition, and is not afraid to have the Vulgate and Lyra at its meditative heart. That Lyra and devout imagination could 'go' together on the *grounde* of the harmonized Gospel in the *Speculum devotorum* should make us look again at what was conceivable and possible 'after Arundel'. That the quiet mainstream had such depth and breadth should invite modern scholarship to think again, and to *drawe* a reconsideration *ful loonge* through the modern narratives of late medieval religious literary culture.

CONCLUSION

Being culturally compulsory in late medieval England, *vitae Christi* are clearly of value historically and critically in their own right, and their variety and resourcefulness attest to this. Their status makes them invaluable as windows onto the ideology of making and reading works of authority in vernacular literary culture, especially when it comes to translation. In articulating their aims in their paratexts, and in their ways of trying to manage their sources and the piety (and immortal souls) of those in their care, Middle English lives of Christ have more to tell us than has been able to be said here. This book has attempted to make a range of observations and to use those observations to prompt some new thinking and some rethinking about the ways in which medieval translation and vernacular theology are portrayed and understood.

Works like the *Ormulum*, the *Passion of Our Lord* in Jesus College MS 29, and the *Stanzaic Life of Christ* represent some of the notably diverse approaches and energies that the genre was able to sustain. The first two of these remind us that there was much that was intriguing and significant in vernacular religious textuality a long time before the Lollards and their opponents (so often the focus of attention for modern literary scholars) occupied centre-stage as the seemingly defining forces (and defining modern topic) in late medieval English religious textual culture.

Two Carthusian *vitae* were given particular room in this study because they seem to express the possibilities of the tradition more (and more fascinatingly) than most other works would or could. As meditative prose lives in the Pseudo-Bonaventuran mode, the *Speculum devotorum* and Love's *Mirror* share much. Each, nevertheless, on closer examination, strikes out in its own way in its practice of theory, meditative imagination, interpretative commentary, compilation, and translation, illustrating again the subtle twists of vitality, range, and adaptability that characterize the vernacular genre of the life of Christ.

Vernacular literary theory and its translated idioms were, then, a thing of prestige and decorum, because they featured in texts that were *a priori* of value — texts like lives of Christ. Moreover, as has been seen throughout this book, late medieval English mainstream culture did not in general conceive of translation or theology in the native tongue as primarily a matter of antagonism and struggle between vernacular and Latin, or between the Church and the laity. Lives of Christ accordingly engaged the far reaches of English medieval culture in its mutuality with Latin and French languages, texts, and culture, and they did so with a generic scope and authority with few parallels in subsequent literary history. The securely canonical works of figures like Chaucer and Gower should therefore be read with the commanding status and cultural range of Middle English lives of Christ in mind, and due weight should be given to their theoretically inflected translating and their imagining of the Sacred Humanity as a sovereign exercise and hallmark of vernacular literary authority and cultural force. Moreover, the not-so-monolithic mainstream of religious literary culture, especially in the 1400s, should be allowed to be as complex, flexible, vivid, and as rich as it undoubtedly was.

BIBLIOGRAPHY

Manuscripts and Archival Documents

London, British Library, MS Additional 19901
London, British Library, MS Arundel 364
New York, Pierpont Morgan Library, MS 226
Notre Dame, Indiana, University of Notre Dame, MS 67
Oxford, Jesus College, MS 29
Paris, Bibliothèque nationale de France, MS ital. 115
Warminster, Longleat House Archives, MS 14

Primary Sources

Alan of Lille [Alanus ab Insulis], 'Compendium on the Art of Preaching', ed. by Joseph M. Miller, Michael H. Prosser, and Thomas W. Benson, in *Readings in Medieval Rhetoric*, ed. by Joseph M. Miller, Michael H. Prosser, and Thomas W. Benson (Bloomington: Indiana University Press, 1973), pp. 228–39

Augustine of Hippo, *De agone christiano*, in *Patrologiae cursus completus: series latina*, ed. by Jacques-Paul Migne, 221 vols (Paris: Migne, 1844–64), XL (1845), cols 284–310

——, *De consensu evangelistarum*, in *Patrologiae cursus completus: series latina*, ed. by Jacques-Paul Migne, 221 vols (Paris: Migne, 1844–64), XXXIV (1841), cols 1041–1230

——, *The Works of Aurelius Augustine, Bishop of Hippo*, ed. by Marcus Dods, 15 vols (Edinburgh: Clark, 1871–76), VIII: *The Sermon on the Mount; The Harmony of the Evangelists*, trans. by William Findlay and S. D. F. Salmond (1873), pp. 133–504

'The Boke of Coumfort of Bois [Bodleian Library, Oxford Manuscript AUCT.F.3.5]: A Transcription with an Introduction', ed. by Noel Harold Kaylor, Jr. and Philip Edward Phillips, in *New Directions in Boethian Studies*, ed. Noel Harold Kaylor, Jr. and Philip Edward Phillips, Studies in Medieval Culture, 45 (Kalamazoo: Medieval Institute, 2007), pp. 223–79

Bonaventura, *Opera omnia sancti Bonaventurae*, ed. by A. C. Peltier, 15 vols (Paris: Vives, 1864–71)

The Cloud of Unknowing, ed. by Patrick J. Gallacher <http://www.lib.rochester.edu/camelot/teams/cloufrm.htm> [accessed 23 March 2013]

The Cloud of Unknowing and Related Treatises, ed. by Phyllis Hodgson, Analecta Cartusiana, 3 (Salzburg: Institut für Anglistik und Amerikanistik, 1982)

The Cloud of Unknowing and The Book of Privy Counselling, ed. by Phyllis Hodgson, Early English Text Society, Original Series, 218 (London: Oxford University Press, 1944)

The Court of Sapience, ed. by Ruth E. Harvey (Toronto: University of Toronto Press, 1984)

Deonise Hid Diuinite and Other Treatises on Contemplative Prayer Related to the Cloud of Unknowing: A Tretyse of þe Stodye of Wysdome þat Men Clepen Beniamyn, A Pistle of Preier, A Pistle of Discrescyon of Stirings, A Tretis of Spirites, ed. by Phyllis Hodgson, Early English Text Society, Original Series, 231 (London: Oxford University Press, 1955)

Douglas, Gavin, *Virgil's 'Aeneid' Translated into Scottish Verse*, ed. by D. F. C. Coldwell, Scottish Text Society, 25, 27, 28, 30, 4 vols (1957–64)

Enarrationes in Matthei Evangelium (misattributed under the name of Anselm of Laon), in *Patrologiae cursus completus: series latina*, ed. by Jacques-Paul Migne, 221 vols (Paris: Migne, 1844–64), CLXII (1854), cols 1227–1500

English Metrical Homilies from Manuscripts of the Fourteenth Century, ed. by John Small (Edinburgh, William Paterson, 1862)

Guigonis Carthusiae Maioris Prioris Quinti Consuetudines, in *Patrologiae cursus completus: series latina*, ed. by Jacques-Paul Migne, 221 vols (Paris: Migne, 1844–64), CLIII (1854), cols 631–757

Guigues I, *Coutumes de Chartreuse*, Sources chrètiennes, 313 (Paris: Cerf, 1984)

Hilton, Walter, *The Mixed Life*, ed. by S. J. Ogilvie-Thomson, Salzburg Studies in English Literature, Elizabethan and Renaissance Studies, 92.15 (Salzburg: Institut für Anglistik und Amerikanistik, 1986)

——, *The Scale of Perfection*, ed. by Thomas H. Bestul <http://www.lib.rochester.edu/camelot/teams/hilintro.htm> [accessed 23 March 2013]

Hugh of St Victor, *De claustro animae*, in *Patrologiae cursus completus: series latina*, ed. by Jacques-Paul Migne, 221 vols (Paris: Migne, 1844–64), CLXXVI (1854), cols 1017–1182

——, *Eruditionis didascalicae libri VII*, in *Patrologiae cursus completus: series latina*, ed. by Jacques-Paul Migne, 221 vols (Paris: Migne, 1844–64), CLXXVI (1854), cols 739–838

Humbert of Romans, 'Treatise on Preaching', in *Readings in Medieval Rhetoric*, ed. by Joseph M. Miller, Michael H. Prosser, and Thomas W. Benson (Bloomington: Indiana University Press, 1973) pp. 245–50

Jacobus a Voragine, *Legenda Aurea: Vulgo historia Lombardica dicta*, ed. by Th. Graesse (Leipzig, 1890; repr. Osnabrück: Zeller, 1965)

Joannes Januensis, *Catholicon* (Mainz: [printer uncertain], 1460; repr. Westmead: Gregg, 1971)

Joannes Scotus, *Glossa on De mystica theologia*, in *Patrologiae cursus completus: series latina*, ed. by Jacques-Paul Migne, 221 vols (Paris: Migne, 1844–64), CXXII (1853), cols 267–84A

John de Caulibus, *Iohannis de Caulibus, Meditaciones vite Christi, olim S. Bonauenturo attributae*, Corpus Christianorum Continuatio Mediaevalis, 153, ed. by Mary Stallings-Taney (Turnhout: Brepols, 1997)

——, *Meditations on the Life of Christ*, trans. by Francis X. Taney, Anne Miller, and C. Mary Stallings-Taney (Asheville: Pegasus, 1999)

Langland, William, *The Vision of Piers Plowman: A Critical Edition of the B-Text*, ed. by A.V.C. Schmidt (London: Dent, 1978)

The Lay Folks' Catechism, ed. by Thomas Frederick Simmons and Henry Edward Nolloth, Early English Text Society, Original Series, 118 (London: Kegan Paul, Trench, Trübner, 1901)

Love, Nicholas, *The Mirror of the Blessed Life of Jesus Christ: A Full Critical Edition Based on Cambridge University Library Additional MSS 6578 and 6686*, ed. by Michael G. Sargent (Exeter: University of Exeter Press, 2005)

Ludolph of Saxony, *Vita Jesu Christi e quatuor evangeliis et scriptoribus orthodoxis concinnata*, ed. by A. C. Bolard, L. M. Rigollot, and J. Carnandet (Paris: Palmé, 1865)

Meditaciones de passione Christi olim sancto Bonaventurae attributae, ed. by Sister M. Jordan Stallings, Studies in Medieval and Renaissance Latin Language and Literature, 25 (Washington, DC: Catholic University of America Press, 1965)

Meditationes vitae Christi, in *Opera omnia sancti Bonaventurae*, ed. by A. C. Peltier, 15 vols (Paris: Vives, 1864–71), XII (1868), pp. 509–630

Meditations on the Life and Passion of Christ, ed. by Charlotte D'Evelyn, Early English Text Society, Original Series, 158 (London: Oxford University Press, 1921)

Meditations on the Life of Christ: An Illustrated Manuscript of the Fourteenth Century, Paris, Bibliothèque Nationale, MS. Ital. 115, trans. by Isa Ragusa and Rosalie B. Green (Princeton: Princeton University Press, 1961)

Meditations on the Supper of Our Lord, and the Hours of the Passion, ed. by J. Meadows Cowper, Early English Text Society, Original Series, 60 (London: Trübner, 1875)

The Mirour of Mans Saluacioun[e]: A Middle English Translation of 'Speculum humanae salvationis'. A Critical Edition of the Fifteenth–Century Manuscript Illustrated from 'Der Spiegel der Menschen Behaltnis', Speyer, Drach, c. 1475, ed. by Avril Henry (Aldershot: Scolar, 1986)

Miroure of Mans Saluacionne, ed. by A. H. Huth (London: Roxburghe Club, 1888)

More, Thomas, *The Confutation of Tyndale's Answer*, ed. by Louis A. Schuster, Richard C. Marius, James P. Lusardi, and Richard P. Schoeck, in *The Complete Works of St. Thomas More*, 15 vols. (New Haven: Yale University Press, 1963–97), VIII, pt 1 (1973)

The Myroure of oure Ladye, ed. by John Henry Blunt, English Text Society, Extra Series, 19 (London: Trübner, 1873)

'*Myrror to Devout People (Speculum Devotorum)*: An Edition with Commentary', ed. by Paul J. Patterson (unpublished doctoral thesis, University of Notre Dame, 2006)

Nicholas of Lyra, *Postilla literalis*, in *Textus Biblie cum Glosa ordinaria Nicolai de lyra postilla moralitatibus eiusdem Pauli Burgensis additionibus Matthie Thoring replicis*, ed. by C. Leontorius, 6 vols (Lyon: Mareschal, 1520), VI

An Old English Miscellany, ed. by Richard Morris, Early English Text Society, Original Series, 49 (London: Oxford University Press, 1872)

Orm, *The Ormulum*, ed. by Robert Holt, 2 vols (Oxford: Clarendon Press, 1878)

'*Orologium Sapientiae* or the *Seven Poyntes of Trewe Wisdom*, aus MS Douce 114', ed. by Carl Horstmann, *Anglia*, 10 (1888), 323–89

Pepysian Gospel Harmony, ed. by Margery Goates, Early English Text Society, Original Series, 157 (London: Oxford University Press, 1923 [1922])

Peter Comestor, *Historia scholastica*, in *Patrologiae cursus completus: series latina*, ed. by Jacques-Paul Migne, 221 vols (Paris: Migne, 1844–64), cxcviii (1847), cols 1049–1722A

Peter Lombard, *Sententiae in iv libris distinctae*, 2 vols (Grottaferrata: Editiones Collegii. S. Bonaventurae ad Claras Aquas, 1971–81)

'Prologue to Wycliffite Bible, Chapter 15', in *Selections from English Wycliffite Writings*, ed. by Anne Hudson (Cambridge, Cambridge University Press, 1978), pp. 67–72

Rabanus Maurus, *Commentaria in libros Machabaeorum*, in *Patrologiae cursus completus: series latina*, ed. by Jacques-Paul Migne, 221 vols (Paris: Migne, 1844–64), cix (1852), cols 1125–1256

Readings in Medieval Rhetoric, ed. by Joseph M. Miller, Michael H. Prosser, and Thomas W. Benson (Bloomington: Indiana University Press, 1973)

Richard of St Victor, *Benjamin minor*, in *Patrologiae cursus completus: series latina*, ed. by Jacques-Paul Migne, 221 vols (Paris: Migne, 1844–64), cxcvi (1855), cols 1–64A

The Riverside Chaucer, gen. ed. by Larry Benson (Oxford: Oxford University Press, 1988)

Rolle, Richard, *English Writings of Richard Rolle, Hermit of Hampole*, ed. by Hope Emily Allen (Oxford: Clarendon Press, 1931)

Smaointe Beatha Chriost .i. Innsint Ghaelge a chuir Tomás Gruamdha ó Bruicháin (fl.1450) ar an Meditationes Vitae Christi, ed. by Cainneach ó Maonaigh, OFM (Dublin: Institúid Árd-Léighinn Bhaile Átha Cliath / Dublin Institute for Advanced Studies, 1944)

The 'Speculum devotorum' of an Anonymous Carthusian of Sheen, ed. by James Hogg, Analecta Cartusiana, 12–13 (Salzburg: Universität Salzburg, 1973–74)

Speculum humanae salvationis, ed. by Jules Lutz and Paul Perdrizet, 2 vols (Mulhouse: Meininger, 1907)

Speculum humanae salvationis: A Reproduction of an Italian Manuscript of the Fourteenth Century, ed. by M. R. James (Oxford: Oxford University Press, 1924)

A Stanzaic Life of Christ Compiled from Higden's 'Polychronicon' and the 'Legenda Aurea' Edited from MS. Harley 3909, ed. by Frances A. Foster, Early English Text Society, Original Series, 166 (London: Oxford University Press, 1926)

Tatiani Evangeliorum Harmonia Arabice, ed. and trans. by Augustinus Ciasca (Roma: Polyglotta, 1888)

Victor of Capua, *Amonii Alexandrini evangelicae harmoniae*, in *Patrologiae cursus completus: series latina*, ed. by Jacques-Paul Migne, 221 vols (Paris: Migne, 1844–64), lxviii (1847), cols 251–358

The Vulgate New Testament with the Douay Version of 1582 in Parallel Columns (London: Bagster and Sons, 1872)

Wilsher, Bridget Ann, 'An Edition of "Speculum Devotorum", a Fifteenth Century English Meditation on the Life and Passion of Jesus Christ, with an Introduction and Notes', 2 vols (unpublished M.A. dissertation, University of London, 1956)

Wycliffe, John, *De veritate sacrae scripturae*, ed. by Rudolf Buddensieg, 3 vols (London: Trübner, 1905–07)

Yorkshire Writers: Richard Rolle of Hampole, An English Father of the Church, and his Followers, ed. by Carl Horstmann, 2 vols (London: Swann Sonnenschein, 1895–96)

Secondary Studies

Aers, David, *Sanctifying Signs; Making Christian Tradition in Late Medieval England* (Notre Dame: University of Notre Dame Press, 2004)

Aers, David, and Lynn Staley, *The Powers of the Holy: Religion, Politics, and Gender in Late Medieval English Culture* (University Park: Pennsylvania State University Press, 1996)

Alford, John A., 'Richard Rolle and Related Works', in *Middle English Prose: A Critical Guide to Major Authors and Genres*, edited by A. S. G. Edwards (New Brunswick: New Jersey, Rutgers University Press, 1984), pp. 35–60

Allen, Hope Emily, 'The *Manuel des Pechiez* and the Scholastic Prologue', *Romanic Review*, 8 (1917), 434–62

Areford, David S., 'The Passion Measured: A Late-Medieval Diagram of the Body of Christ', in *The Broken Body: Passion Devotion in Late-Medieval Culture,* ed. by A. A. MacDonald, H. N. B. Ridderbos, and R. M. Schlusemann (Groningen: Forsten, 1998), pp. 211–38

Bast, Robert J., 'Strategies of Communication: Late-Medieval Catechisms and the Passion Tradition', in *The Broken Body: Passion Devotion in Late-Medieval Culture,* ed. by A. A. MacDonald, H. N. B. Ridderbos, and R. M. Schlusemann (Groningen: Forsten, 1998), pp. 133–43

Baswell, Christopher, *Virgil in Medieval England: Figuring the Aeneid from the Twelfth Century to Chaucer* (Cambridge: Cambridge University Press, 1995)

Bawcutt, Priscilla J., *Gavin Douglas: A Critical Study* (Edinburgh: Edinburgh University Press, 1976)

Beadle, Richard, '"Devoute ymaginacioun" and the Dramatic Sense in Love's *Mirror* and the N-Town Plays', in *Nicholas Love at Waseda*, ed. by Shoichi Oguro, Richard Beadle, and Michael G. Sargent (Cambridge: Brewer, 1997), pp. 1–17

Beckwith, Sarah, *Christ's Body: Identity, Culture and Society in Late Medieval Writings* (London: Routledge, 1993)

Bestul, Thomas H., *Texts of the Passion: Latin Devotional Literature and Medieval Society* (Philadelphia: University of Pennsylvania Press, 1996)

Brantley, Jessica, 'The Visual Environment of Carthusian Texts: Decoration and Illustration in Notre Dame 67', in *The Text in the Community: Essays on Medieval Works, Manuscripts, Authors and Readers*, ed. by Jill Mann and Maura Nolan (Notre Dame: University of Notre Dame Press, 2006, pp. 173–216

——, *Reading in the Wilderness: Private Devotion and Public Performance in Late Medieval England* (Chicago: University of Chicago Press, 2007)

Brewer, Derek, ed., *Chaucer: The Critical Heritage*, 2 vols (London: Routledge and Kegan Paul, 1978)

Burrow, J. A., *Medieval Writers and their Work: Middle English Literature and its Background 1100–1500* (Oxford: Oxford University Press, 1982)

——, 'The Languages of Medieval England', *The Oxford History of Literary Translation in English*, gen. ed. by Peter France and Stuart Gillespie, 5 vols (Oxford: Oxford University Press, 2006–08), I: *To 1550*, ed. by Roger Ellis (2008), pp. 7–28

Butterfield, Ardis, *The Familiar Enemy: Chaucer, Language and Nation in the Hundred Years War* (Oxford: Oxford University Press, 2009)

Conway Jr, Charles Abbot, *The 'Vita Christi' of Ludolphus of Saxony and Late Medieval Devotion Centred on the Incarnation: A Descriptive Analysis*, Analecta Cartusiana, 34 (Salzburg: Universität Salzburg, 1976)

Copeland, Rita, 'Rhetoric and Vernacular Translation in the Middle Ages', *Studies in the Age of Chaucer*, 9 (1987), 41–75

——, *Rhetoric, Hermeneutics, and Translation in the Middle Ages: Academic Traditions and Vernacular Texts* (Cambridge: Cambridge University Press, 1991)

Crassons, Kate, 'Performance Anxiety and Watson's Vernacular Theology', in *Literary History and the Religious Turn*, ed. by Bruce Holsinger (= *English Language Notes*, 44.1 (2006)), 95–102

Cré, Marleen, *Vernacular Mysticism in the Charterhouse: A Study of London, British Library, Ms Additional 37790* (Turnhout: Brepols, 2006)

Despres, Denise, *Ghostly Sights: Visual Meditation in Late-Medieval Literature* (Norman: Pilgrim Books, 1989)

Dove, Mary, *The First English Bible: The Text and Context of the Wycliffite Versions* (Cambridge: Cambridge University Press, 2007)

Doyle, A. I., 'Reflections on some Manuscripts of Nicholas Love's *Myrrour of the Blessed Life of Jesus Christ*', in *Essays in Memory of Elizabeth Salter*, ed. by Derek Pearsall (= *Leeds Studies in English*, n.s., 14 (1983)), 82–93

Duffy, Eamon, *The Stripping of the Altars: Traditional Religion in England c. 1400–c. 1580* (New Haven: Yale University Press, 1992)

Edwards, A. S. G., 'The Contents of Notre Dame 67', in *A Mirror to Devout People*', in *The Text in the Community: Essays on Medieval Works, Manuscripts, Authors and Readers*, ed. by Jill Mann and Maura Nolan (Notre Dame: University of Notre Dame Press, 2006), pp. 107–28

Ellis, Roger, 'The Choices of the Translator in the Late Middle English Period', in *The Medieval Mystical Tradition in England: Papers Read at Dartington Hall, July 1982*, ed. by Marion Glasscoe (Exeter: University of Exeter Press, 1982), pp. 18–46

——, ed., *To 1550*, in *The Oxford History of Literary Translation in English*, gen. ed by Peter France and Stuart Gillespie, 5 vols (Oxford: Oxford University Press, 2006–08), I (2008)

Evans, Ruth, 'Historicizing Postcolonial Criticism: Cultural Difference and the Vernacular', in *The Idea of the Vernacular: An Anthology of Middle English Literary Theory, 1280–1520* ed. by Jocelyn Wogan-Browne and others (University Park: Pennsylvania State University Press, 1999), pp. 366–70

Evans, Ruth, Andrew Taylor, Nicholas Watson, and Jocelyn Wogan-Browne, 'The Notion of Vernacular Theory', in *The Idea of the Vernacular: An Anthology of Middle English Literary Theory, 1280–1520*, ed. by Jocelyn Wogan-Browne and others (University Park: Pennsylvania State University Press, 1999), pp. 314–30

Falls, David J., 'The Carthusian Milieu of Nicholas Love's *Mirror of the Blessed Life of Jesus Christ*', in *The Pseudo-Bonaventuran Lives of Christ: Exploring the Middle English Tradition*, ed. by Ian Johnson and Allan Westphall (Turnhout: Brepols, forthcoming)

——, 'Love's *Mirror* before Arundel: Audiences and Early Readers of Nicholas Love's *Mirror of the Blessed Life of Jesus Christ*' (unpublished doctoral thesis, Queen's University, Belfast, 2011)

Geographies of Orthodoxy: Mapping the English Pseudo-Bonaventuran Lives of Christ, c.1350–1550 <http://www.qub.ac.uk/geographies-of-orthodoxy/> [accessed 24 March 2013]

Ghosh, Kantik, 'Nicholas Love', in *A Companion to Middle English Prose*, ed. by A. S. G. Edwards (Cambridge: Brewer, 2004), pp. 53–66

——, *The Wycliffite Heresy: Authority and the Interpretation of Texts* (Cambridge: Cambridge University Press, 2002)

Gillespie, Vincent, 'Chichele's Church: Vernacular Theology in England after Thomas Arundel', in *After Arundel: Religious Writing in Fifteenth-Century England*, ed. by Vincent Gillespie and Kantik Ghosh, Medieval Church Studies, 21 (Turnhout: Brepols, 2011), pp. 3–42

——, 'From the Twelfth Century to *c.* 1450', in *The Cambridge History of Literary Criticism*, ed. by H. B. Nisbet and Claude Rawson, 9 vols (Cambridge: Cambridge University Press, 1989–2012), II: *The Middle Ages*, ed. by Alastair J. Minnis and Ian Johnson (2005), pp. 145–235

——, 'The Haunted Text: Ghostly Reflections in *A Mirror to Devout People*', in *The Text in the Community: Essays on Medieval Works, Manuscripts, Authors and Readers*, ed. by Jill Mann and Maura Nolan (Notre Dame: University of Notre Dame Press, 2006), pp. 129–72

Gillespie, Vincent, and Kantik Ghosh, eds, *After Arundel: Religious Writing in Fifteenth-Century England*, Medieval Church Studies, 21 (Turnhout: Brepols, 2011)

Gleason, Mark J., 'Clearing the Fields: Towards a Reassessment of Chaucer's Use of Trevet in the *Boece*', in *The Medieval Boethius: Studies in the Vernacular Translations of De Consolatione Philosophiae*, ed. by Alastair J. Minnis (Cambridge: Brewer, 1987) pp. 89–105

Hill, Betty, 'Oxford, Jesus College MS 29, Part II: Contents, Technical Matters, Compilation, and its History to c. 1695', *Notes and Queries*, new series, 50 (2003), 268–76

Hodgson, Geraldine, *The Sanity of Mysticism: A Study of Richard Rolle* (London: Faith, 1926; repr. Folcroft: Folcroft Library Editions, 1977)

Hunt, R. W., 'The Introductions to the "Artes" in the Twelfth Century', in *The History of Grammar in the Middle Ages,* ed. by G. Bursill–Hall, Amsterdam Studies in the Theory and History of Linguistic Science, Series III —– Studies in the History of Linguistics, 5 (Amsterdam: Benjamins, 1980), pp. 117–44

Jeauneau, E., 'Deux rédactions des gloses de Guillaume de Conches sur Priscien', *Recherches de théologie ancienne et medievale*, 27 (1960), 212–47

Johnson, Ian, 'The Ascending Soul and the Virtue of Hope: The Spiritual Temper of Chaucer's *Boece* and *Retracciouns*', *English Studies*, 88 (2007), 245–61

——, '*Auctricitas*? Holy Women and their Middle English Texts', in *Prophets Abroad: The Reception of Continental Holy Women in Late-Medieval England*, ed. by Rosalynn Voaden (Cambridge: Brewer, 1996), pp. 177–97

——, 'Hellish Complexity in Henryson's *Orpheus*', in *Scottish Texts: European Contexts*, ed. by Ian Johnson and Nicola Royan (= *Forum for Modern Language Studies*, 38 (2002)), 412–19

——, 'The Late-Medieval Theory and Practice of Translation with Special Reference to Some Middle English Lives of Christ' (unpublished doctoral thesis, University of Bristol, 1990)

——, 'The Non-Dissenting Vernacular and the Middle English Life of Christ: The Case of Love's *Mirror*', in *Lost in Translation?*, ed. by Denis Renevey and Christiania Whitehead, The Medieval Translator/Traduire au Moyen Âge, 12 (Turnhout: Brepols, 2009), pp. 223–35

——, 'Placing Walton's Boethius', in *Boethius in the Middle Ages: Latin and Vernacular Traditions of the 'Consolatio Philosophiae'*, ed. by Lodi Nauta and Maarten J. F. M. Hoenen (Leiden: Brill, 1997), pp. 217–42

——, 'Prologue and Practice: Middle English lives of Christ', in *The Medieval Translator: The Theory and Practice of Translation in the Middle Ages: Papers Read at a Conference Held 20–23 August 1987 at the University of Wales Conference Centre, Gregynog Hall*, ed. by Roger Ellis, with the assistance of Jocelyn Price, Stephen Medcalf, and Peter Meredith (Cambridge: Brewer, 1989), pp. 69–85

——, 'Tales of a True Translator: Medieval Literary Theory, Anecdote and Autobiography in Osbern Bokenham's *Legendys of Hooly Wummen*', in *The Medieval Translator/Traduire au Moyen Âge, IV*, ed. by Roger Ellis and Ruth Evans (Exeter: University of Exeter Press, 1994), pp. 104–24

——, 'Translational Topographies of Language and Imagination in Nicholas Love's *Mirror* and *A Mirror to Devout People*', in *In Principio Fuit Interpres*, ed. by Alessandra Petrina, The Medieval Translator/Traduire au Moyen Âge, 15 (Turnhout: Brepols, 2013), pp. 237–46

——, 'Vernacular Theology/Theological Vernacular: A Game of Two Halves?', in *After Arundel: Religious Writing in Fifteenth-Century England*, ed. by Vincent Gillespie and Kantik Ghosh, Medieval Church Studies, 21 (Turnhout: Brepols, 2011)

——, 'Vernacular Valorizing: Functions and Fashionings of Literary Theory in Middle English Translation of Authority', in *Translation Theory and Practice in the Middle Ages*, ed. by Jeanette Beer (Kalamazoo, Medieval Institute, 1997), pp. 239–54

——, 'Walton's Heavenly *Boece* and the Devout Translation of Transcendence: *O Qui Perpetua* Pietised', in *The Medieval Mystical Tradition in England: Exeter Symposium VIII: Papers Read at Charney Manor, July 2011*, ed. by E. A. Jones (Cambridge: Brewer, 2013), pp. 157–76

——, 'Walton's Sapient Orpheus', in *The Medieval Boethius: Studies in the Vernacular Translations of 'De Consolatione Philosophiae'*, ed. by Alastair J. Minnis (Cambridge: Brewer, 1987), pp. 139–68

——, 'What Nicholas Love Did in his *Proheme* with St Augustine and Why', in *The Pseudo-Bonaventuran Lives of Christ: Exploring the Middle English Tradition*, ed. by Ian Johnson and Allan Westphall (Turnhout: Brepols, forthcoming)

Johnson, Ian, and Allan Westphall, eds, *The Pseudo-Bonaventuran Lives of Christ: Exploring the Middle English Tradition* (Turnhout: Brepols, forthcoming)

Karnes, Michelle, *Imagination, Meditation, and Cognition in the Middle Ages* (Chicago: University of Chicago Press, 2011)

——, 'Nicholas Love and Medieval Meditations on Christ', *Speculum*, 82 (2007), 380–408

Kelly, Stephen, and Ryan Perry, eds, *'Diuerse Imaginaciouns of Cristes Life': Devotional Cultures in England and Beyond, 1300–1560* (Turnhout: Brepols, in preparation)

Lawton, David, 'The Bible', in *The Oxford History of Literary Translation in English*, gen. ed. by Peter France and Stuart Gillespie, 5 vols (Oxford: Oxford University Press, 2006–08), I: *To 1550*, ed. by Roger Ellis (2008), pp. 193–233

Leclerq, Jean, 'Monastic Commentary on Biblical and Ecclesiastical Literature from Late Antiquity to the Twelfth Century', trans. by A. B. Kraebel, *The Mediaeval Journal*, 2 (2012), 27–53

Lutton, Rob, '"Love this Name that is IHC": Vernacular Prayers, Hymns and Lyrics to the Holy Name of Jesus in Pre-Reformation England', in *Vernacularity in England and Wales, c. 1350–1550*, ed. by Elisabeth Salter and Helen Wicker, Utrecht Studies in Medieval Literacy, 17 (Turnhout: Brepols, 2011), pp. 115–41

Luxford, Julian M., ed., *Studies in Carthusian Monasticism in the Late Middle Ages*, Medieval Church Studies, 14 (Turnhout: Brepols, 2008)

MacDonald, A. A., H. N. B. Ridderbos, and R. M. Schlusemann, eds, *The Broken Body: Passion Devotion in Late-Medieval Culture* (Groningen: Forsten, 1998)

Machan, Tim William, *Techniques of Translation: Chaucer's Boece* (Norman: Pilgrim, 1985)

McNamer, Sarah, *Affective Meditation and the Invention of Medieval Compassion* (Philadelphia: University of Pennsylvania Press, 2010)

——, 'The Origins of the *Meditationes vitae Christi*', *Speculum*, 84 (2009), 905–55

Miedema, Nine, 'Following in the Footsteps of Christ: Pilgrimage and Passion Devotion', in *The Broken Body: Passion Devotion in Late-Medieval Culture*, ed. by A. A. MacDonald, H. N. B. Ridderbos, and R. M. Schlusemann (Groningen: Forsten, 1998), pp. 73–92

Minnis, Alastair J., 'Absent Glosses: The Trouble with Middle English Hermeneutics', in *Translations of Authority in Medieval English Literature: Valuing the Vernacular* (Cambridge: Cambridge University Press, 2009), pp. 17–37

——, 'Affection and Imagination in the *Cloud of Unknowing* and Hilton's *Scale of Perfection*', *Traditio*, 39 (1983), 323–66

——, *Fallible Authors: Chaucer's Pardoner and Wife of Bath* (Philadelphia: University of Pennsylvania Press, 2008)

——, '"Glosynge is a glorious thing": Chaucer at Work on the *Boece*', in *The Medieval Boethius: Studies in the Vernacular Translations of 'De Consolatione Philosophiae'*, ed. by Alastair J. Minnis (Cambridge: Brewer, 1987), pp. 106–24

——, *Medieval Theory of Authorship: Scholastic Literary Attitudes in the Later Middle Ages* (London: Scolar, 1984)

——, 'Memory and Imagination', in *The Cambridge History of Literary Criticism*, ed. by H. B. Nisbet and Claude Rawson, 9 vols (Cambridge: Cambridge University Press, 1989–2012), II: *The Middle Ages*, ed. by Alastair J. Minnis and Ian Johnson (2005), pp. 239–74

——, *Translations of Authority in Medieval English Literature: Valuing the Vernacular* (Cambridge: Cambridge University Press, 2009)

Minnis, Alastair J., and Ian Johnson, eds, *The Middle Ages*, in *The Cambridge History of Literary Criticism*, ed. by H. B. Nisbet and Claude Rawson, 9 vols (Cambridge: Cambridge University Press, 1989–2012), II (2005)

Minnis, Alastair J., and A. B. Scott, with the assistance of David Wallace, eds, *Medieval Literary Theory and Criticism c. 1100–c. 1375: The Commentary-Tradition* (Oxford: Clarendon Press, 1988)

Morey, James H., *Book and Verse: A Guide to Middle English Biblical Literature* (Urbana: University of Illinois Press, 2000)

Morrison, Stephen, 'New Sources for the *Ormulum*', *Neophilologus*, 68 (1984), 444–50

——, 'Orm's English Sources', *Archiv*, 221 (1984), 54–64

——, 'A Reminiscence of Wulfstan in the Twelfth Century', *Neuphilologische Mitteilungen*, 96 (1995), 229–34

——, 'Sources for the *Ormulum*', *Neuphilologische Mitteilungen*, 84 (1983), 419–36

Murphy, James J., *Rhetoric in the Middle Ages: A History of Rhetorical Theory from Saint Augustine to the Renaissance* (Berkeley: University of California Press, 1974)

O'Connell, Patrick F., 'Love's *Mirrour* and the *Meditationes vitae Christi*', *Analecta Cartusiana*, 82. 2 (1980), 3–44

Oguro, Shoichi, Richard Beadle, and Michael G. Sargent, eds, *Nicholas Love at Waseda: Proceedings of the International Conference 20–22 July 1995* (Cambridge: Brewer, 1997)

Orme, Nicholas, *English Schools in the Middle Ages* (London: Methuen, 1973)

Parkes, M. B., 'The Influence of the Concepts of *Ordinatio* and *Compilatio* on the Development of the Book' in *Medieval Learning and Literature: Essays presented to R.W. Hunt*, ed. by J. J. G. Alexander and M. T. Gibson (Oxford: Clarendon Press, 1976), pp. 115–41

——, 'Punctuation, or Pause and Effect', in *Medieval Eloquence: Studies in the Theory and Practice of Medieval Rhetoric*, ed. by James J. Murphy (Berkeley: University of California Press, 1978), pp. 127–42

Perry, Ryan, '"Some sprytuall matter of gostly edyfycacion": Readers and Readings of Nicholas Love's *Mirror of the Blessed Life of Jesus Christ*', in *The Pseudo-Bonaventuran Lives of Christ: Exploring the Middle English Tradition*, ed. by Ian Johnson and Allan Westphall (Turnhout: Brepols, forthcoming)

Rice, Nicole R., *Lay Piety and Religious Discipline in Middle English Literature* (Cambridge: Cambridge University Press, 2008)

Rouse, R. H., and M. A. Rouse, *Preachers, Florilegia and Sermons: Studies on the 'Manipulus florum' of Thomas of Ireland*, Texts and Studies, 47 (Toronto: Pontifical Institute of Mediaeval Studies, 1979)

Rudy, Kathryn M., *Virtual Pilgrimages in the Convent: Imagining Jerusalem in the Late Middle Ages*, Disciplina Monastica, 8 (Turnhout: Brepols, 2011)

Salter, Elizabeth, *Nicholas Love's 'Myrrour of the Blessed Lyf of Jesu Christ'*, Analecta Cartusiana, 10 (Salzburg: Institut für englische Sprache und Literatur, Universität Salzburg, 1974))

——, 'The Manuscripts of Nicholas Love's *Myrrour of the Blessed Lyf of Jesu Christ* and Related Texts', in *Middle English Prose: Essays in Bibliographical Problems*, ed. by A. S. G. Edwards and Derek Pearsall (New York: Garland, 1981), pp. 115–28

Sargent, Michael G., 'Bonaventura English: A Survey of the Middle English Prose Translations of Early Franciscan Literature', in *Spätmittelalterliche Geistliche Literatur in der Nationalsprache*, ed. by James Hogg, *Analecta Cartusiana*, 106. 2 (1984), 145–76

——, 'Nicholas Love's *Mirror of the Blessed Life of Jesus Christ* and the Politics of Vernacular Translation in Late Medieval England', in *Lost in Translation?*, ed. by Denis Renevey and Christiania Whitehead, The Medieval Translator/Traduire au Moyen Âge, 12 (Turnhout: Brepols, 2009), pp. 205–21

——, 'Versions of the Life of Christ: Nicholas Love's *Mirror* and Related Works', *Poetica*, 42 (1994), 39–70

Scanlon, Larry, 'Poets Laureate and the Language of Slaves: Petrarch, Chaucer, and Langston Hughes', in *The Vulgar Tongue: Medieval and Postmedieval Vernacularity*, ed. by Nicholas Watson and Fiona Somerset (University Park: Pennsylvania State University Press, 2003), pp. 220–56

Simpson, James, 'Confessing Literature', in *English Language Notes*, 44 (2006), 121–26

——, *Reform and Cultural Revolution: 1350–1547*, in *The Oxford English Literary History*, gen. ed. by Jonathan Bate, 13 vols (Oxford: Oxford University Press, 2001–06), II (2002)

Smalley, Beryl, *The Study of the Bible in the Middle Ages*, 3rd edn (Oxford: Blackwell, 1983)

Sneddon, Clive, 'The "Bible du XIIIᵉ siècle": Its Medieval Public in the Light of its Manuscript Tradition', in *The Bible and Medieval Culture*, ed. by Willem Lourdaux and Daniel Verhelst (Leuven: Leuven University Press, 1979), pp. 127–40

——, 'On the Creation of the Old French Bible', *Nottingham Medieval Studies*, 46 (2002), 24–44

Somerset, Fiona, 'Wycliffite Prose', in *A Companion to Middle English Prose*, ed. by A. S. G. Edwards (Cambridge: Brewer, 2004), pp. 195–214

Tóth, Peter, and David Falvay, 'New Light on the Date and Authorship of the *Meditationes vitae Christi*', in *'Diuerse Imaginaciouns of Cristes Life': Devotional Cultures in England and Beyond, 1300–1560*, ed. by Stephen Kelly and Ryan Perry (Turnhout: Brepols, in preparation)

Verschoren, Marleen, '*De agone christiano*', in *The Oxford Guide to the Historical Reception of Augustine*, ed. by Karla Pollmann and others (Oxford: Oxford University Press, forthcoming)

Waldron, Ronald A., 'Trevisa's Original Prefaces on Translation: A Critical Edition', in *Medieval English Studies Presented to George Kane*, ed. by Edward Donald Kennedy, Ronald A. Waldron, and Joseph S. Wittig (Cambridge: Brewer, 1988), pp. 285–99

Watson, Nicholas, 'Censorship and Cultural Change in Late-Medieval England: Vernacular Theology, the Oxford Translation Debate, and Arundel's Constitutions of 1409', *Speculum*, 70 (1995), 822–64

——, 'Conceptions of the Word: The Mother Tongue and the Incarnation of God', *New Medieval Literatures*, 1 (1997), 85–124

——, 'Cultural Changes', *English Language Notes*, 44 (2006), 127–37

——, 'Theories of Translation', *The Oxford History of Literary Translation in English*, gen. ed. by Peter France and Stuart Gillespie, 5 vols (Oxford: Oxford University Press, 2006–08), I: *To 1550*, ed. by Roger Ellis (2008), pp. 71–91

Watson, Nicholas, and Fiona Somerset, *The Vulgar Tongue: Medieval and Postmedieval Vernacularity* (University Park: Pennsylvania State University Press, 2003)

Wogan-Browne, Jocelyn, Nicholas Watson, Andrew Taylor, and Ruth Evans, eds, *The Idea of the Vernacular: An Anthology of Middle English Literary Theory, 1280–1520* (University Park: Pennsylvania State University Press, 1999)

Worley, Meg, 'Using the *Ormulum* to Redefine Vernacularity', in *The Vulgar Tongue: Medieval and Postmedieval Vernacularity*, ed. by Nicholas Watson and Fiona Somerset (University Park: Pennsylvania State University Press, 2003), pp. 19–30

INDEX

MEDIEVAL CHURCH STUDIES

All volumes in this series are evaluated by an Editorial Board, strictly on academic grounds, based on reports prepared by referees who have been commissioned by virtue of their specialism in the appropriate field. The Board ensures that the screening is done independently and without conflicts of interest. The definitive texts supplied by authors are also subject to review by the Board before being approved for publication. Further, the volumes are copyedited to conform to the publisher's stylebook and to the best international academic standards in the field.

Titles in Series

Megan Cassidy-Welch, *Monastic Spaces and their Meanings: Thirteenth-Century English Cistercian Monasteries* (2001)

Elizabeth Freeman, *Narratives of a New Order: Cistercian Historical Writing in England, 1150–1220* (2002)

The Study of the Bible in the Carolingian Era, ed. by Celia Chazelle and Burton Van Name Edwards (2003)

Text and Controversy from Wyclif to Bale: Essays in Honour of Anne Hudson, ed. by Helen Barr and Ann M. Hutchison (2005)

Lena Roos, *'God Wants It!': The Ideology of Martyrdom in the Hebrew Crusade Chronicles and its Jewish and Christian Background* (2006)

Emilia Jamroziak, *Rievaulx Abbey and its Social Context, 1132–1300: Memory, Locality, and Networks* (2004)

The Voice of Silence: Women's Literacy in a Men's Church, ed. by Thérèse de Hemptinne and María Eugenia Góngora (2004)

Perspectives for an Architecture of Solitude: Essays on Cistercians, Art and Architecture in Honour of Peter Fergusson, ed. by Terryl N. Kinder (2004)

Saints, Scholars, and Politicians: Gender as a Tool in Medieval Studies, ed. by Mathilde van Dijk and Renée Nip (2005)

Manuscripts and Monastic Culture: Reform and Renewal in Twelfth-Century Germany, ed. by Alison I. Beach (2007)

Weaving, Veiling, and Dressing: Textiles and their Metaphors in the Late Middle Ages, ed. by Kathryn M. Rudy and Barbara Baert (2007)

James J. Boyce, *Carmelite Liturgy and Spiritual Identity: The Choir Books of Kraków* (2008)

Studies in Carthusian Monasticism in the Late Middle Ages, ed. by Julian M. Luxford (2009)

Kevin J. Alban, *The Teaching and Impact of the 'Doctrinale' of Thomas Netter of Walden (c. 1374–1430)* (2010)

Gunilla Iversen, *Laus angelica: Poetry in the Medieval Mass*, ed. by Jane Flynn, trans. by William Flynn (2010)

Kriston R. Rennie, *Law and Practice in the Age of Reform: The Legatine Work of Hugh of Die (1073–1106)* (2010)

After Arundel: Religious Writing in Fifteenth-Century England, ed. by Vincent Gillespie and Kantik Ghosh (2011)

Federico Botana, *The Works of Mercy in Italian Medieval Art (c. 1050 – c. 1400)* (2011)

The Regular Canons in the Medieval British Isles, ed. by Janet Burton and Karen Stöber (2011)

Wycliffite Controversies, ed. by Mishtooni Bose and J. Patrick Hornbeck II (2011)

Nickiphoros I. Tsougarakis, *The Latin Religious Orders in Medieval Greece, 1204–1500* (2012)

Nikolaos G. Chrissis, *Crusading in Frankish Greece: A Study of Byzantine-Western Relations and Attitudes, 1204–1282* (2012)

Demetrio S. Yocum, *Petrarch's Humanist Writing and Carthusian Monasticism: The Secret Language of the Self* (2013)

In Preparation

The Pseudo-Bonaventuran Lives of Christ: Exploring the Middle English Tradition, ed. by Ian Johnson and Allan F. Westphall

Alice Chapman, *Sacred Authority and Temporal Power in the Writings of Bernard of Clairvaux*

Religious Controversy in Europe, 1378–1536: Textual Transmission and Networks of Readership, ed. by Michael Van Dussen and Pavel Soukup

Monasteries on the Borders of Medieval Europe: Conflict and Cultural Interaction, ed. by Emilia Jamroziak and Karen Stöber

M. J. Toswell, *The Anglo-Saxon Psalter*

Envisioning the Bishop: Images and the Episcopacy in the Middle Ages, ed. by Sigrid Danielson and Evan A. Gatti